War and Peace

Also by Fulton J. Sheen
from Sophia Institute Press:

Victory over Vice

Archbishop Sheen's Book of Sacraments

Fulton Sheen's Wartime Prayer Book

The Greatest Commandment

God's World and Our Place in It

The Cries of Jesus from the Cross

Lord, Teach Us to Pray

Archbishop Fulton J. Sheen

War and Peace

A Fulton Sheen Anthology

Edited by Al Smith

SOPHIA INSTITUTE PRESS
Manchester, New Hampshire

Sophia Institute Press
Box 5284, Manchester, NH 03108
1-800-888-9344

www.SophiaInstitute.com

Sophia Institute Press® is a registered trademark of Sophia Institute.

paperback ISBN 978-1-64413-688-1

ebook ISBN 978-1-64413-689-8

Library of Congress Control Number: 2022933500

First printing

To Mary, immaculate Mother of God,
gracious Queen of Christ's afflicted ones,
in prayerful petition
that the glorious peace of Christ
may reign in the souls of men

Contents

PHILOSOPHIES AT WAR (1943)

SEVEN PILLARS OF PEACE (1944)

Introduction

When looking back on the life of Archbishop Fulton J. Sheen, there are some that would refer to him as "a man for all seasons." Over his lifetime, he spent himself for souls, transforming lives with the clear teaching of the truths of Christ and His Church through his books, radio addresses, lectures, television series, and many newspaper columns.

Fulton J. Sheen was born in 1895 in El Paso, Illinois. He lived and studied through a time in history in which he witnessed the effects of two world wars and many social, political, and economic conflicts.

While a graduate student and university professor in the United States and Europe, Sheen made friends with a number of the great thinkers and writers of his day such as G. K. Chesterton, Christopher Dawson, J. R. R. Tolkien, and C. S. Lewis.

After his ordination to the priesthood in 1919, Sheen would go on to receive numerous degrees from the Catholic University of America, Louvain University in Belgium, and the Angelicum University in Rome.

From 1926–1950 he was a full-time professor at the Catholic University of America, first in the School of Theology and later in the School of Philosophy. At the beginning of his teaching career, Sheen was regarded with esteem as one of the premier scholars of his time. The publication of his first book in 1925, *God and Intelligence in Modern Philosophy: A Critical Study in the Light of the Philosophy of Saint Thomas*, garnered Sheen extraordinary respect for his scholarship on St. Thomas Aquinas. The book was so well received that Sheen was awarded the Cardinal Mercier International Philosophy Award. Also impressed with the content was G. K. Chesterton, whose admiration is evidenced by his willingness to write the book's introduction.

During his time at the Catholic University of America, Sheen wrote thirty-four books on various topics. He also was the featured speaker on *The Catholic Hour* radio broadcast, having millions of listeners tuning in each week.

Witnessing the increasing threat of Communism in the 1920s, it became sufficiently clear to Sheen that modern atheism was not only an esoteric philosophy preached by learned professors at Harvard and Yale, but it was a new type of Messianism emanating from Moscow, threatening to cover the face of the earth. So in the same year in which Pope Pius XI issued his encyclical on atheistic Communism (1937), Fulton J. Sheen published three books titled: *Communism, Communism and Religion,* and *Liberty under Communism.*

Sheen stressed the need for the use of reason in dealing with Communism. On the subject matter, he was no intellectual featherweight, and he brought his formidable powers of intellect to bear on the problem of Communism, the better to refute it. He absorbed Marx, Lenin, and Stalin to prepare himself for the assaults he would sustain in his deconstruction of their theories. He was a tremendous success. He converted or influenced several Communists and leftists in the heyday of American Communism, including Louis Budenz, Elizabeth T. Bently, Bella Dodd, and Heywood Broun.

Toward the end of the 1930s, talk of war began to surface. When German forces invaded Poland on September 1, 1939, World War II began. Almost immediately, Fulton J. Sheen rose to the occasion of being called to bring sense to a nation that was looking for answers to the questions of war. During his presentations on the radio he encouraged his audience to think of the great spiritual transformation that there would be in America if every Jew, Protestant, and Catholic — according to the light of his conscience — prayed one continuous hour a day, for the president, for Congress, and for victory.

Archbishop Sheen called World War II not only a political struggle, but also a "theological one." He referred to Hitler as an example of the "antichrist." Sheen also said that, "the means of life no longer minister to peace and order because we have perverted and forgotten the true ends of life.... It is not our politics that has soured, nor our economics that have rusted; it is our hearts. We live and act as if God had never made us."

In 1941, the United States officially entered World War II. That same year, Sheen penned the book *A Declaration of Dependence*. In it, Sheen writes,

> The Declaration of Independence, I repeat, is a Declaration of Dependence. We are independent of dictators because we are dependent on God. God is the necessary factor of our salvation. As a result, he is to be the center of our lives. His ways ought to permeate every aspect and area of our lives: education, employment, pleasure, mourning, socializing, etc. All is done in sight of the omnipotent Lord, and all we do should be done reflecting this knowledge. Our every interaction should be filled with the love of our Savior.

Numerous articles, radio reflections, and books would continue to be produced by Sheen throughout the war. Given their importance and the impact they had on society in his day, it seemed appropriate to bring together in this anthology some of Archbishop Sheen's reflections on war and peace taken from five books he wrote from 1941 to 1944.

- *For God and Country* (New York: P. J. Kenedy and Sons, 1941)
- *God and War* (New York: P. J. Kenedy and Sons, 1942)
- *The Divine Verdict* (New York: P. J. Kenedy and Sons, 1943)
- *Philosophies of War* (New York: Charles Scribner's Sons, 1943)
- *Seven Pillars of Peace* (New York: Charles Scribner's Sons, 1944)

The first three books contained in this anthology are a collection of Sheen's *Catholic Hour* radio addresses that were heard by millions of listeners each week. These reflections are a series of short essays that addressed the many concerns of the listeners of his day during the war.

Sheen answers questions about the antichrist, hope, faith, prayer, the power of God, and the divine path to victory. His were some of the most clearly delineated investigations into the underlying causes of the war combined with an entirely sound and hopeful program for winning both the war and the even more important peace. These powerful reflections can be most heartily recommended for their wise counsel, sane and penetrating analysis, and logical conclusions.

In the fourth book of this anthology titled *The Philosophies of War*, Sheen addresses the vexation felt by a great mass of people who were frankly dissatisfied with the ephemeral and superficial commentaries about the war. Like a master surgeon, Sheen applied the sharp scalpel of his crystal-clear logic to lay open the sources of the world's infection.

Sheen writes,

> There are two ways of looking at the war: one as a journalist, the other as a theologian. The journalist tells you what happens; the theologian not only why it happens, but also what matters.... Our approach is from the divine point of view, first of all, because it is the only explanation which fits the facts; secondly because the American people who have been confused by catchwords and slogans are seeking an inspiration for a total surrender of their great potentialities for sacrifice, both for God and country.

In the fifth book of this anthology, titled *Seven Pillars of Peace*, Sheen presents the principles upon which he believes the foundations for a just and lasting peace must be built after the hostilities of war are ended.

Sheen is firm in his conviction that real peace cannot be declared, it must be made. It is with peacemaking and the fundamental conditions on which peace must be based that this book is concerned. In its seven forceful and readable chapters, it challenges the theory of many planners today who posture that military allies are necessarily political allies; it affirms that a common hatred can make nations allies, but only a common love can make them neighbors; it denies the primacy of action over reason, in the sense that the will of the State is that which makes the State right; and it contends that utility does not establish justice, but it is justice which makes utility.

With the same lucid and persuasive reasoning that has made him outstanding both as a writer and as a lecturer, Sheen continues to challenge people of goodwill to unite for the preservation of personal rights, freedom of conscience, human justice, and civilization itself—all of which are in danger in the present conflict. Here, one will recognize the urgency of Sheen's subject matter, and will find pillars of peace and promise in his farsighted principles.

Archbishop Fulton J. Sheen's destiny was encrypted in his name, for in the Gaelic language *Fulton* means *war* and *Sheen* means *peace*. Sheen's lifelong goal was to establish peace, but in that call, he inevitably came up against many obstacles toward that noble ideal. It is as though his very name foretold the kind of life he was to have: an uninterrupted warring against the powers of darkness to promote the peace of Christ's Kingdom.

FOR GOD
AND
COUNTRY

(1941)

1

Antichrist

There is an inconsistency deeply rooted in our national life, which must needs be removed before America can exercise moral leadership among the nations. The inconsistency is between our education and our politics.

On the one hand, secular college and university education teaches in one form or another that there is no such thing as evil or guilt, that there are no absolute standards of right and wrong, that right and wrong depend entirely upon one's point of view.

On the other hand, the very products of this unmoral education are now, in the domain of politics, pointing their fingers at Hitler and Mussolini — not at Stalin, of course — and saying: "They are wicked; they are wrong; they are evil."

Naturally, we are tempted to ask: If right and wrong are relative to a point of view, then from Hitler's point of view he is right and we are wrong, and the only way to settle the dispute is by the methods of the jungle.

Furthermore, if there is no right and wrong, how could Hitler be wrong and how could we be right? If there is no black and white, why call the coal black and the snow white?

Our education denies moral standards while our politics affirms them, but only in particular instances. There is therefore a contradiction between the evil which the modern man would like to condemn in others, and his own denial of evil which his apostasy from God created.

He does not want to give up himself as the final standard of what is right and wrong, and yet sees that the same standard in others produced Hitler, the world war, and chaos.

Like a man who, when his wife awakens him saying she hears a burglar downstairs, insists violently that it is only her imagination, and yet goes downstairs trembling like a leaf fearful of bumping head-on with the marauder; so modern man, who says evil is only a survival of the imagination of medieval theologians, now shakes in fear from the evil he denied but which he knows in his heart to be only too real.

Modern man cannot go on in this inconsistency. He cannot keep his false education which denies guilt and his condemnation of Hitler and Mussolini as guilty. He cannot have it both ways.

But by trying to keep both, he utters such ridiculous judgments as that Hitler is an enemy when he invades the left side of Poland and Stalin is a friend when he invades the right.

Burglary is apparently wrong when you rob a stateroom on the starboard side of a ship, but positively friendly if you steal from the port side.

How shall we describe this abandonment of universal moral principles, except to say that we are stricken with a blindness such as it has been written will come upon all men before the end of time.

Just as the light of faith can be extinguished so that men no longer see the world through the eyes of Christ, so too the light of reason can be snuffed out, so that men no longer see right and wrong.

St. Paul told the Romans they had gone blind: "Because that, when they knew God, they have not glorified him as God, or given thanks; but became vain in their thoughts, and their foolish heart was darkened" (Rom. 1:21).

Something like that has happened to the modern world and with perfect justice might Isaias say to us again: "Woe to you that call evil good, and good evil: that put darkness for light, and light for darkness: that put bitter for sweet, and sweet for bitter" (Isa. 5:20).

Like those who have lost their physical vision, men give names to things which they no longer perceive. To real things we give false names; to false things, we give real names.

Words now refer not to things, but to myths or slogans in a confusion worse confounded than Babel.

In building the Tower of Babel, men used different words to signify the same things and knew not what each other spoke; but today we use the same words but refer to different things.

At that time it was only tongues and ears that were confused; today it is the minds and souls of men.

With Hamlet who said to Polonius when asked: "What readest thou?" a de-Christianized culture can only answer: "Words! Words! Words!" What is large we call small; what is small we call large.[1]

Russia enthrones the cadaver of Lenin and the starving millions dance around the corpse and call it "life."

A word like *democracy* is used to support the anti-democratic, anti-Christian burning of ten thousand churches and chapels.

A word like *civil liberties* is used to defend a violation of "civil liberties"; a word like *freedom* is used to mean absence of law, authority, and restraint.

When a professor teaches gross immorality to students or incites to revolution, we confuse the issue by speaking of "academic freedom."

When a Communist is arrested for sabotage, his fellow travelers call it "persecution."

When the Church pleads for the preservation of the family against artificial restriction of creative married love, the Church is called "reactionary."

The repudiation of intrinsic rights as the endowment of God is labeled by some of our jurists "liberal."

The plea that nations invoke spiritual authority for the settlement of international issues is called "bringing the pope to the White House."

The demand that children be released an hour a week from schools for religious and moral training is opposed not in the name of anti-religion—No!—but in the name of education: "The child has not enough school time now to finish his important studies."

---

[1] William Shakespeare, *Hamlet*, act 2, scene 2.

These same so-called educators who would pull their hair out if a child were given the wrong combination of colors on a toy are the very ones who teach the child there is no such thing as wrong.

What is this blindness which has so possessed us that we deny that evil exists and yet want to go to war to crush it? It is the blindness of the spirit of antichrist.

The spirit of antichrist is upon us, and it is part of our blindness to know it not. The greatest disaster that can happen to a man or a nation is not to do evil; it is to deny that evil exists by calling evil another name like *progress*.

This is the unforgivable sin and the greatest of all sins, for if we deny we are wounded when our body bleeds, what need have we of healing?

We erroneously think that the spirit of antichrist should come with cloven hoofs and a tail, reeking with the smell of sulphur, with smoke belching from his ears and unmistakable green fumes vomiting from his mouth—a spectre so hideous that all men would shrink from him in terror and fright.

The devil would not be wise if he came as the devil, for there is no deceit when evil wears no false face.

If we called vice *vice* and not "self-expression" who would be tempted?

Satan would have no appeal unless he clothed himself as an angel of light; Hell would have no one knocking at its portals unless they were gilded with the gold of Paradise.

Christ comes to men with His Cross: that is why He has so few followers.

Satan comes without a cross, and not until victims are his do they know that the greatest cross in life is not to have the Cross.

Do not evil men disguise their evil; do not the Bolsheviks destroy Christianity in the name of "democracy"; does not Hitler destroy Poland in the name of "justice"; does not Mussolini invade Albania in the name of "protection"; do not the degenerate spread immorality in the name of "art"?

Shall the spirit of antichrist be less wise than his disciples?

Did not our Lord speak of the devil as the "prince of this world" (John 14:30)—certainly, princes are not frightening and particularly when they are princes of this world?

Did not Satan himself in tempting our Lord say as he paraded the nations of the earth before the Savior's eyes: "To me they are delivered, and to whom I will, I give them." (Luke 4:6-7)?

Did not St. John say: "And it was given unto him to make war with the saints, and to overcome them. And power was given him over every tribe, and people, and tongue, and nation. And all that dwell upon the earth adored him, whose names are not written in the book of life of the Lamb, which was slain from the beginning of the world" (Rev. 13:7-8)?

Something is rotten with the world; and that rottenness is so radical and universal that it can be explained not by things, but by a spirit—the spirit of evil.

It is our blindness not to know there is evil because we denied its existence. A man without eyes can be persuaded night is day and day is night.

So too the modern world which has lost both its eyes of faith and its eyes of reason can be made to believe the spirit of antichrist is not here, for having forgotten Christ, who shall persuade it there is an antichrist?

Our blindness is colossal and the root of our evil is our refusal to admit evil and sin. If only we admitted we were blind there would be hope, but Hellish blindness thinks that it can see.

Men think that evil must come in the disguise of a germ, or a bomb, or a raid, or an explosion, or a train wreck, or a bank failure, forgetful that the greatest grief can come to man under the disguise of human ideals.

It is under the masquerade of a progress which denies sin and guilt that antichrist parades the world today, sits in our lecture rooms, writes in our magazines, struts across our stages, promising to redeem man when he has left the Cross and penance behind, but only completing man's enslavement when it is already too late for him to free himself.

There is a radical inconsistency in our way of life; that is, in our education which denies there is evil, and in our politics which says dictators are evil.

If there be no grime, who shall be called grimy? If there is no disease who shall be called sick? If there shall be no decay, who shall be called rotten?

The choice is not between an education which denies guilt and a politics which makes only dictators guilty. Both are false, and both must be scrapped in their present form.

Education which denies evil must be abandoned because it fails to make a distinction between an intellectual error and bad behavior.

If I add ten and ten to make thirty, I err, and an eraser can correct it; but if I tell a falsehood about my neighbor and ruin his reputation, I sin.

Modern education makes no distinction between error and sin; it teaches that what we call evil is only an intellectual error.

That is why it preaches that crime and antisocial behavior are due to mental immaturity. Only the ignorant sin; the intelligentsia can't sin—they know. Hence, educate everyone and evil will disappear.

The fact is, education does not take away evil because the training of the reason is quite distinct from the training of the will; knowing is not doing.

Modern education which trains only the mind takes away error—sometimes, but it does not train the will or take away sin.

Nothing is more destructive of our national life than this fallacy that the educated are sinless because they have an B.A., and that the uneducated are wrong because they never heard of Bertrand Russell.

The truth is rather the contrary, the uneducated in this country have less evil in them than the intelligentsia; they may make errors, but they commit less sin.

And on the Day of Judgment, it will be far better to be ignorant before the face of Almighty God than worldly-wise but sinful.

What is true of education which denies guilt is true of politics which identifies guilt with dictators. This is a very false morality.

First, because those who say that dictatorships are evil do not believe it. If dictatorship were wrong we would condemn it wherever we found it. Not all Americans believe an anti-God, anti-human dictatorship is wrong. If all did, they would not call Russia a "friendly nation."

Second, if the only evil in the world were dictatorships, would we be a moral world if the three were vanquished? Did the world become safe for democracy when the kaiser went to Doorn? Would it be safe tomorrow if Hitler went to Canossa?

Dictators are not the only evils. They are more the creatures of evil than the creatures of godlessness, selfishness, and repudiation of morality, domestic, industrial, and international.

By limiting evil to dictatorships we take eyes off ourselves and thus delay that eradication of evil from our own lives, which would strengthen us more than armaments, to defeat that evil from without.

This denial of evil as evil has hindered our moral development. Evil, when it is recognized as such and repented, leads a man to reach a higher degree of perfection.

Even the angels of Heaven rejoice more at one sinner doing penance than ninety-nine just who need not penance. The recoil of repentance often summons forth energies in the opposite direction.

But if a man denies there is sickness, then how shall he make efforts to restore himself to health? If a man thinks he knows it all, whence shall come his energies to learn? If there be no evil, how shall we repent? How can we defeat evil unless we know it?

The condition of national peace is the scrapping both of false education and false politics, the former of which denies evil and the latter of which limits evil to dictatorships, environment, poor milk, or bad glands.

Evil is real; it is in the human heart; born first in man, then socialized in groups and society.

Like Bartimaeus, the son of Timaeus, who begged on the streets of Jericho, we too are blind. We really have eyes and see not.

We need the touch of a Savior who on His way to the Cross stops in His journey despite the rebuke of a crowd, and opens blind eyes to redemption and salvation.

God grant that we in America may see before it is too late. Today we are fearing the wrong thing. As Sacred Scripture says, we fear where there is no fear (see Ps. 52:6).

We fear the outside when we should fear the inside; we fear external dangers, but not the internal sins which produce collective ills.

We fear man, too, when we should fear God. Man today is afraid of his own kind. Lions do not fear lions; tigers do not fear tigers. They fear only that which is outside their species. But man fears man.

The Capitalist fears the worker, the worker the Capitalist, the poor fear the rich, the rich fear the poor—but no one fears God. If man only knew it, he fears man because he has ceased to fear God; for the man who has lost his roots in God is the terror of his fellow men.

"The fear of the Lord is the beginning of wisdom" (Prov. 1:7) – only the beginning, for in later stages love replaces fear.

But in the beginning, we must fear justice for our injustice; retribution for our sins; consequences for our moral misdeeds. There will never be peace in this world so long as man fears man rather than God.

To fear God is not only to love God, but also to love one's fellow man.

We need a new kind of fear – not just a fear of the invader that strikes our shores, but a fear lest by denying there is evil, we become impotent to strike it; a fear that if we say all we need is bread, bread is all we will get – as if man could live by bread alone; a fear that by denying evil we will lose the ideal of goodness; a fear lest while protecting our boundaries, our inner citadels and our homes will be seized from within.

There are many reasons why we know evil is existent in the world; there are many reasons why we believe in the spirit of antichrist.

Our modern educators, and our press, by the denial of guilt, sin, evil, and penance, sacrifice, and reparation have not convinced us there is no God; they have not convinced us of the futility of the Cross; they have not convinced us there is no evil.

But they have convinced us there is a devil, for the devil is never so triumphant as when he induces his followers to say there is no devil!

2

The Reality of Sin

George Bernard Shaw once said: the "modern man is too busy to think about his sins."

It perhaps would be truer to say the modern man denies that he can sin. In some so-called learned circles sin is explained away biologically as a "fall in the evolutionary process," or as a temporary, atavistic throwback to our animal ancestry "which man can overcome through proper mating."

Others explain it away "physically" by attributing moral aberrations to physical environment, lack of playgrounds, Grade A milk, and bad glands.

Evil is therefore not in the will, but in the bile, not in the soul, but in the organism; is physiological, not moral.

A third attempt to explain sin away is the social; sin is not personal but social. Evil is due not to violations of conscience, but to something external, for example, the Capitalists, in the case of Communists; the dictatorships, in the case of democracy; democracy in the case of dictatorship.

Evil is blamed on a system or on institutions, but never on the person. The distinction between right and wrong thus gives way to "ally" or "enemy."

As the world sins more it thinks less about it, a condition as dangerous for the soul as of indifference to germs in time of pestilence. A sense of drift has been substituted for a sense of sin.

The former acts like an opiate instilling into the soul an insidious acquiescence to evil which is supposed to reside in external circumstances and is therefore beyond the victim's control.

Because the world assumes that evil is wholly external or social, it falsely believes that its remedy lies in the domain of politics and economics, since they deal with the externals or with what a man has rather than what he is.

This very refusal to face the issue that sin is personal, and a moral rather than an economic phenomenon, makes a cure impossible. It puts society in the state of a man who thinks that his jaundice comes from the immigration of the yellow races and that a good alcohol rub or some fine face powder will cure it.

There can be no personal, no social salvation until the sense of sin is restored and evil is recognized not as something external, but also something within each of us.

In other words, the world is not in its present mess because something is out of gear, but rather because something is wrong.

Three disastrous consequences flow from the denial of personal sin and guilt: 1) loss of freedom; 2) national paralysis; 3) neurosis and frustration.

1) Loss of freedom: there is nothing the modern man prizes more than freedom, but does he realize that his denial of sin is the denial of freedom? Does not freedom imply choice? Does not choice imply alternatives of good and evil?

If I do not sin when I choose the wrong alternative, then I am not responsible, but if I am not responsible then I am not free.

Cabbages, horses, adding machines, boots, ships, and sealing wax cannot sin, because they have no freedom, therefore no responsibility. To deny sin is therefore to reduce man to the status of a thing.

Incidentally, this is the basic philosophical reason for Fascism, Nazism, and Communism, for if man is only a thing and not a moral being, free and responsible, then why should he not be absorbed into the collectivity or totality of race as in Germany, class as in Russia, and the nation as in Italy?

We cannot have it both ways: if we are free, then we can do wrong; but if we cannot do wrong, then we are not free.

Our so-called liberal and progressive educators who denied the reality of guilt, did not, as they promised, relieve man from the shackles of "medieval morality"; but they did relieve the person of his responsibility and therefore of his freedom.

Freudian psychologists in democracies who blamed all sin or guilt on the psychical determinism of a subrational or even sexual factor, and the Marxian philosopher in Totalitarian states who blamed sin on to the social determinism of the economic order, did not really explain away sin; but they did explain away freedom.

Men talk most about freedom when they are losing it, as they talk most about health when they are sick.

Real freedom is slipping away from the world today and the era foretold by Dostoevsky is upon us: "The ages will pass, and humanity will proclaim by the lips of their sages that there is no crime, and therefore no sin; there is only hunger.... In the end they will lay their freedom at our feet, and say to us, 'Make us your slaves, but feed us.'"[2]

The denial that we could do wrong is the greatest wrong of all. The devil was wiser than modern man, for the devil tempted Adam and Eve to use their freedom falsely by eating of the fruit of the tree of the knowledge of good and evil.

Satan was never so stupid as to think that freedom meant irresponsibility. But he has so convinced his disciples in the twentieth century! He promised freedom in the beginning by inciting to evil; he takes freedom away now by denying evil. And we in our ignorance call this progress!

2) National paralysis: Once a nation begins to say, "There is no right or wrong, for as Einstein has proven everything is relative; virtue and vice are only questions of a point of view," it, by that very fact, develops a false tolerance. I say, false tolerance because it identifies tolerance with indifference to right and wrong.

"Broadmindedness" then becomes praised as a great virtue, whereas in reality, it is nothing but flat-headedness—an inability to see that mountains are high, valleys are low, virtue is right, vice is wrong.

If there is no evil, then how can we resist it? If there are no broken bones, then why call in a physician?

---

[2] Fyodor Dostoevsky, *The Brothers Karamazov*, trans. Constance Garnett (New York: Macmillan, 1922), 267.

The refusal to recognize wrong as wrong delays or prevents all reactions to wrong. The fact is that if the doctors were as indifferent to disease and as broadminded about germs as the nation is as broadminded about right and wrong, America would have been ravaged long ago.

Some time ago I was invited to be on the committee of a rather well-known group in the United States. Among other reasons, I declined because that same group sponsored a much-publicized attack on religion by a rather well-known scientist.

An appeal was made to my broadmindedness. "After all, you would not be intolerant would you?"

I asked this particular official if he had a child. Admitting he had, I said:

Suppose your child was taken seriously ill. Five doctors were called in and all admitted that it was a dangerous streptococcus infection. But three of them said to you: "We know that there are rather intolerant specialists who say that a streptococcus infection is dangerous, but after all, this is only a point of view. What is healthy and what is unhealthy is purely relative. Personally, we think that you should be broadminded about this germ, and allow us to develop it, for we seem to have a particular good culture in your child."

I then asked him: "What would you say to those doctors?" He said: "I would order them out, for the life of my child is worth more than the life of a germ." But I said:

Aren't you a bit intolerant? In any case, if you consider the life of the soul, more than the body, and the preservation of inalienable rights of God as a gift of God more precious than the feelings of an anti-religious scientist, why is it wrong for me to refuse to be a member of a committee which sponsors lectures destructive of democracy and the country I love? If you are intolerant to a streptococcus germ which destroys a body, why should I not be intolerant about an evil which destroys the nation?

Multiply this indifference to evil, sin, and wrong ten thousand times and there is created a national paralysis, that is, an inability to cope with anti-American activities because we no longer know what is good for America or bad for America.

Why, for example, is America incapable of dealing effectively with Fifth Columnists? Because asserting that freedom means the right to do whatever you please, instead of the right to do whatever you ought, it is unable to draw the line between right and wrong.

If Communism were a germ destroying the pigs on the American farms, our university professors would sit up nights seeking antidotes, but because in the social order we have nothing corresponding to a germ, in virtue of the denial of evil, we have some university professors sitting up nights seeking to find ways to keep them on the ballots to use our freedom in order to destroy it.

Even though they had no moral sense, America would be better off if these same defenders of Communism agreed only to give to Communists in America exactly the same rights they have in Russia.

Can we not see that by denying evil we are rendered impotent to cope with it? What is international appeasement to a great extent but a refusal to recognize the intrinsically evil intentions of men.

Appeasement is based on ignorance of evil. National leaders look to intellectual mistakes to account for moral perversity. Evil having no historic dimensions cannot be recognized.

It was such a national paralysis based on a denial of evil which made France trust Russia and which is making us trust Russia and call it "friendly."

There is no nation on earth that is so intolerant of germs as the United States; there are few nations which are so tolerant of evil and sin.

A pneumonia germ which as a Fifth Columnist gains entry into a body is immediately flanked by an army of surgeons, physicians, and scientists, but a Communist who as a Fifth Columnist penetrates into our labor unions and schools and our army, is flanked by Defenders of Civil Liberties, for if there be no wrong, why is he wrong?

One can lay down the general law that the greater the apathy to righteousness born of God in a nation, the greater is its danger of corruption from within.

3) Neurosis and frustration: The denial of sin is at the base of much of the nervous disorders in the world today. Neurosis to a great extent is due to frustration.

Experiments made on rats prove that by being constantly frustrated in their search for food they went mad. Even pigs, who seem to be most immune from worry, were also driven crazy by similar frustration.

Modern man too is being constantly frustrated by unrealized purposes of expectation and realization of the prospect of a future joy and the unhappiness consequent upon its possession.

This is particularly true of those who, badly educated, are fated to continue in attempts to achieve happiness, which by their very nature, are doomed to end in despair.

Trying to make a Heaven out of earth, to find pie in the sky, or happiness in evil and peace in violation of a moral law is like being condemned to be eternally fitting squares into round holes.

Nothing better illustrates this frustration than the modern attitude toward marriage, that is, between the expectation of romantic love and the reality of the state.

Practically all love songs on the radio center about those who are about to be married, for example, "how happy we will be"; "will you be mine forever." But how often do we hear a love song on the radio about that same couple five years after marriage—if they are still married.

What do we hear instead? Jokes about marriage, most of which are only variations of that old bromide: "That was not a lady, that was my wife."

Why do we joke about marriage, if it be not to repress our deep disillusionment? As an Oriental explained: "Americans are not really happy—they laugh too much."

Not only is this frustration serious, but the escapes from it are worse, for in each instance modern man tries to find the escape in external circumstances; if he is married he thinks he would be happier if he had another wife; if he is a Communist, he thinks he would be happier if he were a Capitalist; if he is a Capitalist he thinks he could be happier if he were a "Fellow Traveller"—but all are destined to bring increased woe because the wrong in the heart cannot be relieved by another wrong in society.

Could we but see it, sin is unreasonableness and unreasonableness is destruction. It is an act against reason to jump from a roof, and if I do jump, I injure myself.

My reason tells me a pencil is to be used for writing; if I use it to open a door, I destroy the pencil. In like manner, reason and revelation both tell me my purpose and my happiness consist in the attainment of the perfect life, truth, and love which is God. If I willfully rebel against the purpose I mutilate myself. And the constant frustration which comes of trying to open doors with pencils or to attain peace without morality intensifies psychoses and often ends in madness.

To escape this inner conflict modern man constantly seeks to fill the void which only God can fill. For that reason he hates repose; he wants to "kill time."

Existence in time cannot be endured; so he seeks to fly from it into a life where he can forget himself. Most of his pleasures are at bottom nothing else than a "pastime" or a substitute for an empty soul. His music with its staccato discontinuity drives him on to a movement which goes nowhere but becomes a narcotic to "dope" his soul.

Nothing is as intolerable as being alone. He cannot stand himself; he almost hates himself and his nothingness and his failures. The virtuous man and woman is to him a reproach so he keeps them off with scorn.

His conscience carries on an unbearable repartee; his whole being becomes eccentric like a planet out of its course, burning itself out; he feels his name is "legion" for there are so many contradictory impulses within him; like a radio tuned in to two stations, he gets nothing but moral static; a veritable civil war rages in his soul and to silence it he loses himself in the crowd; anonymity almost becomes a law of his life.

He is no longer a person, he is one of a herd. When a frustrated man says he has a good conscience, he only means he has a bad memory. The bad conscience is like a dog which is shut up in the cellar because of the bad habit of continually barking, but which will bark more because the master ignored him.

This bad conscience, did man but recognize it, is the way sinners experience the presence of God. As the virtuous feel God in peace, the sinners do so in wrath.

"My conscience hath a thousand several tongues, and every tongue brings in a different tale: And every tale condemns me for a villain."[3]

We may deny sin, but we cannot deny its consequences; they are still with us: a loss of freedom — as men deny responsibility, they surrender freedom; a national paralysis to meet barbarism — because we deny it is evil; a neurosis and a psychosis — induced from trying to find peace in anything short of Him for whom we were made.

But our problem is: What shall we do with our sin? There are three escapes: 1) keep the wound open; 2) cover it over; 3) heal it.

1) Keep the wound open: this is the remedy invoked by hypochondriacs who have an excessive interest in the symptoms of disease. They rush off to psychoanalysts to discover the source of their complex, and ninety-nine times out of a hundred, the psychoanalyst will tell them it has something to do with sex.

The patient likes to hear about sex as the origin of his psychosis, because it takes his mind off guilt. A sublimation is a thousand times easier to get than an absolution. So the wound is kept open because of a false diagnosis.

2) Cover it over: This second escape films over the guilt by rationalizing it, or by inventing false gods or idols. Certain cliches hide bad thinking, such as: "You don't really believe in sin." "Imagine anyone in these days of science believing in God." "You never heard of Bertrand Russell?" This treatment merely films over the ulcerous parts whilst rank corruption mines all within.

The souls which use this remedy are of the same type who run from bill collectors. Someday the collector will catch up with them.

The longer they put off the cure and repress the sense of guilt, the greater becomes their melancholy and despondency and the temptation to suicide.

3) Heal it: but in order to heal it two conditions must be fulfilled.

First, I must recognize the truth of the deliverances of my conscience, that sin is an offense against a Person, for it surrounds me with the same sense of guilt as if I had struck my own mother.

[3] William Shakespeare, *Richard III*, act 5, scene 3.

I feel as if I had made a false declaration of independence like the prodigal son. I feel disloyal to the purpose for which I was made, and this means disloyal to God. I feel like Adam who hid from God after his sin, by which he symbolized the distance a sinner feels from God.

My sin is not disrespectability, it is not fear of the loss of the good opinion of neighbors; it is rather a kind of anticipated death in which I feel the breakdown of the fellowship, not of soul and body, but of soul and God.

Secondly, since sin broke off my relations with the purpose of living and destroyed my freedom by making me the slave of sin, it follows that if ever I am to have peace, I must reestablish relations with that Person, who is God.

I must do it. Why? Because if God forces me to do it, He would destroy my nature. God cannot infringe upon man's freedom, for by so doing He would crush the very freedom that makes love possible.

So God, in order to win us, puts Himself in the attitude of one who is incapable of destroying freedom. He comes to us in a human nature on the Cross. Hands that are pinioned with nails cannot take us prisoner; feet that are dug with steel cannot pursue. True love is always unarmed yet devoted unto sacrifice.

He can only solicit by presenting to us the picture of what the sin did to Him. He seeks to move us by the vision of a sacrifice of which He can say, "Greater love than this no man hath" (John 15:13).

Very often the sight of the suffering which the drunkenness of a husband has brought upon a wife will break him of his habit; so too our Lord hopes that the revelation of what our sins have done to Him will bring us to repentance.

The Crucifixion was not murder; it was deicide—the worst that sin can do. The very sight of His suffering is not only the measure of our guilt, it is at the same time the offer of forgiveness.

Through the Cross our guilt is transformed into sorrow at seeing its consequences—a poignant personal healing sorrow which tortures our soul until we cry out: "O God, be merciful to me a sinner" (Luke 18:13).

From that Cross, Love looked down, for by its nature love descends. Parents love their children more than children love their parents. In fact, children do not know how much their parents suffered for them until they become parents themselves. Love descends from the Cross. We are too dumb to understand that love of the Cross because we are such strangers to sacrifice; we do not know what love is because we have not loved—we have only yearned.

Because we love so little, His love is mysterious to us. We never forgave anyone at such a cost as His; we never loved anyone at such a price as He did. Our own lovelessness has hidden Calvary.

Not until we begin to love goodness will we understand how good God was to die for us. Sin is our fault! What are we going to do about it?

The world will explain it away; our Lord will forgive it. He has conferred that power of forgiveness to His Church unto the consummation of the world: "Whose sins you shall forgive, they are forgiven them" (John 20:23). Thank God, I am a Catholic.

3

The Masses and God

Wherein lies the future of America? The problem is concerned with a choice between two classes: The intelligentsia and the masses.

Our conclusion will be: The future of a better America is in the masses and not in the intelligentsia, for we are witnessing in our national life what might be called the Betrayal of the Intellectuals, or the Treason of the Educated.

Before giving reasons one must define terms. By the *intelligentsia* I mean the intellectuals who have been educated beyond their intelligence; those who deny absolute standards of right and wrong, make truth and error relative to a point of view, and completely ignore the will and its discipline in the training of youth.

Among specimens of the intelligentsia might be mentioned: H. G. Wells, George Bernard Shaw, John Dewey, and the new lawyers who teach ideas are instruments of power.

A few decades ago the influences which made our civilization came from above, that is, from the educated. But today the influences which make civilization are coming not from above, but from below—from the masses. What happened to the rich in the last twelve years is now happening to the intelligentsia.

For a decade, we held up the ideal of wealth as the American ideal; we asked our young to look upon our millionaires as paragons of success and as models in the museum of Americana. But now all that has changed. The rich today are on the defensive. And why? Because they were not loyal to the stewardship of wealth; they thought wealth was something so personal as to be devoid of all social responsibilities.

In like manner, the intelligentsia today are on the defensive because they were not loyal to the stewardship of truth. In the pre-Depression days of wealth, there was such a thing as "economic slumming": The rich went down to the poor, not to relieve themselves of their wealth, not to relieve the poor of their poverty, but to enjoy the shock and thrill of contrast.

In these days, the intelligentsia have gone slumming: university professors go down to the masses not to give the masses truth, for they deny truth; not to relieve them of their ignorance by learned and virtuous leadership, for they say there is no right or wrong; but only to enjoy the shock and thrill of mass movement without intelligent direction. If there be no health, why have doctors? If power is not in truth, ask the masses, why should it not be in violence?

In one well-endowed American university, a professor said there was not a single student in his class who could give a rational justification for democracy; its justification was only its power to assert itself over rival forms.

The intelligentsia in our universities were talking utopian nonsense about progress when the whole of Western civilization was already facing its hour of doom. As a result, students became cynical.

In a novel of Dostoevsky, a young son became more and more opposed to his father who lived in a world of utopian illusions and who believed that the law of evolution would make a better and richer world.

The son realized that the world did not conform to his father's idea of progress and through corrosive cynicism finally ended by believing that nothing in life is worthwhile. A similar attitude is seizing many youths in universities today.

Because the intelligentsia have missed the signs of the time, they have lost their authority. They are paying the penalty for their spiritual frigidity and their moral indifference because they lost the power to fulfill the tasks with which they are confronted.

Something similar happened in the days of the decline of pagan Rome. The intelligentsia had nothing more to offer the world: Their philosophy was only a history of conflicting views of life, and they threw away the precious heritage of reason at the very moment they most loudly shouted they lived by it and, by denying that liberty is inseparable from law, ceased to be sages and dropped to crankiness instead of rising to sainthood.

Our wise men today, like them, are not wise enough. Their prestige for impartiality and objectivity is only a false tolerance of right and wrong; they think a student is not learned unless he has counted something no one else has ever counted before, as one university in the West counted, and I am quoting the title of the Ph.D. thesis — "the microbic content of cotton undershirts" — while another university in the East counted all the datives in Ovid. Understanding became identified with measure, from which they conclude that the immeasurable is the unknowable, and the unknowable is the unreal.

God, the soul, and the supernatural life, are relegated to the domain of myths and fantasies; justice becomes a balance between conflicting opinions; morality a statistical average; and democracy an arithmocracy where a majority makes a thing right, even when a democracy decides to vote itself out of democracy.

Man becomes a spectator of reality, rather than its creator. He observes what goes on outside of him but never learns to connect what goes on inside of him.

Because Jerusalem was not faithful to its vocation, its kingdom was taken away and given to the Gentiles; so too, because the intelligentsia have been traitors to truth, their kingdom is being taken away and given to the masses.

As the betrayal of leadership among the intellectuals of pagan Rome threw the burden upon the mercenaries recruited from beyond the frontiers, so too the slumming of our intelligentsia has shifted the field of influence to the masses. They now hold the key that the educators threw away.

This is no tragedy. The cry of Frederick Ozanam who dedicated his life to them must therefore be renewed in our day: "Passions aux barbares," "Down to the masses," to the broken earthenware of humanity, to the socially disinherited, to those whose wants are too many and whose rights are too few, to those whom Edmund Burke contemptuously called the "great unwashed."

They are the hope of a better America and principally for these reasons: because the masses are capable of far better judgments about world affairs than the intelligentsia.

If I wanted a good moral judgment about the war, I should a thousand times prefer to get it from a garage man, a filling station attendant, a WPA worker, a grocer's clerk, or a delivery boy, than from twenty-three Ph.D. professors I know about in just one American university.

The reason is not difficult to find. The educated know how to rationalize evil; the masses do not. Evil to them is still evil; they have never learned to sugarcoat it with sophism. They never got enough smattering of Einstein to sophomorically pontificate, "everything is relative." If they do wrong, they still call it wrong. Their judgments are better because their moral sense is higher, for virtue does not increase in direct ratio with learning. Knowledge of things is no guarantee of knowledge of self.

And in saying this I am only repeating in poor language the eternally beautiful thought of the Savior: "I confess to thee, O Father, Lord of heaven and earth, because thou hast hidden these things from the wise and prudent, and hast revealed them to little ones" (Luke 10:21).

Having little to defend economically, the masses are not so apt to identify justice with the present order of things. It is easy for the man who is comfortable to fall into the error of believing that any protest against his possessions is revolutionary. But for the masses justice is not the maintenance of the status quo, but an order which gives equal opportunity to all.

Their struggle for the economic necessities has convinced them that the good and just things must be recaptured from day to day: The lawyer must recapture his profession by study; the priest by daily meditation; the government by the solution of new social problems; and even the fortress of life must be defended daily from disease and death.

The masses are the hope of the future for the potentialities of sacrifice, which is essential to the preservation of a nation in time of trouble, are greater in them than in the intelligentsia who too often think they are serving the nation when they are only indulging in sociological adventurism. It is character, not learning, that makes a nation great.

But character is in the will, not in the intellect. Even though the intelligentsia may know more, the will of the masses is greatly superior; and for that reason it is from the quarry of the common man that the stones of a great nation must be cut.

This point must be emphasized for it is too common today to identify moral worth with knowledge — a consequence perhaps of the denial of sins and the attribution of sin to ignorance.

How false this is was strikingly emphasized on the occasion of one of our Lord's visits to Jerusalem when a group of the intelligentsia affronted Him saying, "How doth this man know letters, having never learned?" (John 7:15).

They were of the same group who, when He gave them bread would have made Him king, but who when He said the bread He gave was from Heaven, left Him and walked no more with Him.

Now again they were impressed not by what He did to a man morally, but by His "letters"; by the fact that He was what we would call today a "man of letters."

It is always a revelation of disastrous failure when people are impressed more with what a man knows than with what a man is, or more with the college from which he was graduated than with his virtue.

In answer to their question how He knew so much Jesus answered them, and said: "My doctrine is not mine, but his that sent me" (John 7:16). In other words, His doctrine came from God.

Note that in answering them He referred to His teaching, not to His letters. The intelligentsia are interested only in letters; the intelligent are interested in teaching.

It was as if He said, "Never mind my accent; get hold of my teaching — I am the Voice of God, and if you want to prove it, this is the way: 'If any man will do the will of him; he shall know of the doctrine, whether it be of God, or whether I speak of myself' (John 7:17)."

He placed the grasping of great intellectual truths in goodwill. This goodwill is in the masses, in those who work on our farms, in our industries, our delivery wagons, our stores, or who live on WPA relief. They might make fools of themselves on *Information Please*, by not knowing the color of Henry VIII's beard, but their hearts are right, and their wills are strong.

What greater proof of it is needed than this fact: Communism is supposed to be the philosophy of life for the masses, their hope for an enlightened future, their vindicated justice, and their Paradise on earth.

But despite its raucous appeal to what it calls the proletariat, the masses of America are untouched by Communist propaganda. They were not fooled, but the intelligentsia were. Communism has won more recruits in one single university in New York than it has won among all the farmhands of Illinois and Iowa put together.

The immigrant who works as an iron molder for eighty dollars a month and supports five children is not duped by Communism; but the history professor who receives three hundred dollars a month of the taxpayers' money and supports no children, is fooled, and fooled so badly one thinks of the line of Hamlet: "Let the doors be shut upon him; that he may play the fool nowhere but in his own house"—or should we say "in his own university"?[4]

The worker being up against the economic facts of life sees better than the intelligentsia that Communism would work if it had someone to feed it and clothe it. But since the taxpayer feeds and clothes the professor, he thinks Communism would work.

The intelligentsia, like soldiers who shook their dice, would probably sit at the foot of the Cross of Christ, make an objective record of the execution, but never be impressed. They are either so proud they do not know their misery or, if they do know their misery, they do not know they need a redeemer.

But the masses, like the apostles, are susceptible to the spirit. The Cross offers them something unlike anything which the philosopher and the humanist preacher of "moral uplift" could offer them, and that is a firm foundation of life and thought.

[4] Shakespeare, *Hamlet*, act 3, scene 1.

The intelligentsia who talk of "self-expression" see only nonsense in the Cross; but the masses who feel a cross in the daily routine of their lives know that only in someone crucified like themselves is there hope.

They want not a philosopher to tell them to rely on themselves and their fellow man alone; for they have been doing that all their lives. They look to someone who had to put his trust in God when a fellow man failed.

It is now as it was in the beginning. St. John tells us that when our Lord went up to the feast of the tabernacles, and said, "If any man thirst, let him come to me, and drink" (John 7:37), the masses, learning it, said: "This is the prophet indeed.... This is the Christ" (John 7:40–41).

But the intelligentsia sent out orderlies to apprehend Him. The orderlies, being of the masses, were so impressed by Him they came back empty-handed.

The intelligentsia challenged: "Why have you not brought him?" and they answered, "Never did man speak like this man" (John 7:45–46).

What an amazing reason! They had heard Him utter those tremendous words, challenging the thirst of humanity, and declaring that if men would believe in Him, out of their lives would flow blessings.

So they went back to the intelligentsia and said, in effect: "No, we did not arrest Him, He arrested us."

The intelligentsia thundered: "Are you also seduced?" (John 7:47). And then there came that singularly human retort so common today—they asked the orderlies if they knew anyone in the government or among the intelligentsia who believed in Him. It was a question of false pride and then a contempt for the masses who were so simple as to believe in the Divine, for "this multitude," they sneered, "are accursed" (John 7:49).

Today they would say the masses are crazy; they are not: they are the beloved of God, they are the raw material which the truly intellectual must influence with their truths and sacrifices; they are the ones whom the Savior called blessed; they are ours; He gave them to us.

The intelligentsia do not want them except as instruments of power, but we must want them as children of God and the hope of a better nation.

Your hands may be dirty with work, but your hearts are clean; you may not have the social columns on the occasion of a divorce, but your name is written in Heaven as the husband of one wife or the wife of one husband, or a loyal and devoted friend to another aching heart.

You may keep dogs, but you keep them as companions of your children, not as substitutes for them; you may not have a college degree, but you know more than all the college professors scattered throughout the length and breadth of our land, who have not yet learned why they are here or where they are going.

You may be the tramp on the street, the old woman in the bread lines, the little child in the orphanage, but because you know God made you and act on that belief, you know more than Einstein—a thousand times more, for the man who knows how to get his head into the Heavens is wiser than the scientist who knows only how to get the Heavens into his head.

You know the secret of happiness, for since the world offered you so little, you looked for happiness not on the outside in material circumstances, but on the inside—for "the kingdom of God is within you" (Luke 17:21).

You may commit sin, but you admit it and put the blame on your will, not on bad glands or visceral rumblings; and hence you make your redemption possible. You are not the radicals nor the subversive elements in this country—radicalism and want of patriotism come not from below but from above.

Where among religious groups do you find the greatest degree of theological and social radicalism, if it be not among the affluent suburban churches? It is they who told you Christ was not God; it is they who told you divorce is right, and it is they who, choosing among barbarities, taught you to despise Fascism—but not Communism with it.

It was from among you common people the Savior of the world chose His apostles; it was among you He labored as a carpenter; it was principally from among you the Church recruited her apostles and her saints, and it is among you now that the Church looks for the salt that will renovate the earth when a false wisdom without God finishes its destructive hour.

It is your virtues—the virtues of the common man—the world needs now, not the sophistries of the intelligentsia; it is even your pleasures—the pleasures of the common man—we need to restore us to sanity—not the excitement of intellectual slummers.

The days of the superman are about over; he is dying on the battlefields of Europe. The hour of the common man is dawning, for though the intelligentsia call you ignorant, your ignorance has all the exquisite intuitions of innocence; it is the kind of foolishness which St. Paul says God calls wise (see 1 Cor. 1:25).

For when the self-wise enthroned Jesus on the Cross and then blasphemed and ridiculed, it was one of the masses, a common soldier, who stepped forward and said: "Indeed this was the Son of God" (Matt. 27:54).

That is the kind of vision we need now, for the men and women who see that truth will save the world when the politicians and economists fail.

But what shall the educated do, the truly wise, the intellectuals — not the intelligentsia? They shall serve you.

And may not anyone among them feel it is beneath his dignity, for shall he forget that the Teacher who is the Wisdom of God Itself, came to this earth teaching little children and fishermen?

4

Liberal and Reactionary

The two most abused and thoughtlessly used words in our day are *liberal* and *reactionary*.

These epithets come into prominence whenever wars, revolutions, or depressions disturb an established order. They are born of rapid changes in the tempo of political, economic, or social life.

Now change implies two elements: First, something which changes and, second, something which does not change; in other words, something movable and something immutable.

For example, when meeting a friend whom you have not seen for twenty years, you say, "How you have changed." If this person were not the same person now as twenty years ago, you would not know he had changed. In other words, you cannot recognize change without the changeless.

The reactionary and the liberal have this in common: they never see permanence and change together. They take one to the exclusion of the other. The reactionary seizes upon permanency to the exclusion of change, and the liberal upon change to the exclusion of permanency.

Both are extremists, and because they are extremists both are wrong.

The reactionary wants things to remain as they are; the liberal wants change though he is little concerned with its direction.

The word liberal is derived from *liber*, the ancient god of wine, and hence the term originally and obviously implied intoxication. Shakespeare evidently had that in mind when he wrote in Henry VIII, "When you are a liberal, be sure you are not loose."[5]

The reactionary has rather correctly been defined as a man who has two feet and new shoes, but does not know how to walk, and a liberal as one who has both feet firmly planted in midair.

The reactionary believes that change in the present order is revolution; the liberal believes that change demands the repudiation of sacred and inviolable principles.

The reactionary says: "Johnnie wears a green hat now; Johnnie will wear a green hat in the summer, spring, autumn, and winter; when he is fourteen and when he is forty; he will wear it to breakfast, dinner, and supper." The liberal says: "No, style and conditions have so changed, give Johnnie a new head."

The reactionary wants the clock, but no time; the liberal wants the time, but no clock. The reactionary believes in staying where he is, though he never inquires whether or not he has a right to be there; the liberal, on the contrary, never knows where he is going, he is only sure he is on his way.

The reactionary, instead of working toward an ideal, stagnates; while the liberal instead of working toward an ideal, changes the ideal and calls it progress.

There is a golden mean between the reactionary and the liberal, and the word that seems to fit best is Catholic. It avoids the reactionary position which would make Johnnie always wear a green hat, and the liberal position which would give Johnnie a new head, by letting Johnnie keep his head but giving him a new hat. It admits change without sacrificing the permanent and valuable.

Because a social order needs changing, the Catholic no more advocates the scrapping of the abiding principles of traditional morality than he advocates cutting an arm to fit a sleeve. Just as the cells in a human body change about every seven years and yet man remains identically the same person at seventy that he was at seven, so too, the Church contends, one can reconcile permanence with change without choosing permanence without change, or change without permanence.

[5] Shakespeare, *Henry VIII*, act 2, scene 1.

The Catholic position can best be described in the scene of its foundation. One day our Blessed Lord entered into that ancient city of Caesarea Philippi, where He asked the most important question in the world: "Whom do men say that the Son of man is?" (Matt. 16:13).

When men gave contradictory answers and the apostles gave none, one man, Peter, speaking in the name of all and with divine illumination, answered: "Thou art Christ, the Son of the living God" (Matt. 16:16).

In answer to this, the Divine Savior made Peter, as his name implied, the rock of His Church, and gave him the power of keys: "Thou art Peter: and upon this rock I will build my church, and the gates of hell shall not prevail against it. And I will give to thee the keys of the kingdom of heaven" (Matt. 16:18-19).

In founding His Church our Lord combined two elements: the immutable and the mutable, the permanent and the changing.

The Church would be immutable in her truth—no other doctrine would ever be given her, not even by the angels; not a single iota of her would ever be changed; she would be as immutable as divinity, as intolerant as the multiplication table, as absolute as her Giver.

But that truth would need to be applied to different times and different circumstances. Since it was to last unto the consummation of the world, it would need a different emphasis for the twelfth century than for the first, and a different one for the twentieth than for the sixteenth. There would have to be something mutable in that immutable edifice.

The immutable, changeless character was signified by the rock; the mutable, changing character was signified by the keys. Truth, morality, and justice would be unshakable like the rock enduring to the crack of doom; but the truth, morality, and justice would have to be applied to different social, economic, and political conditions, for the civilization of the fifth century would not be the same as the thirteenth, nor the thirteenth the same as the nineteenth.

Hence, our Lord said, in effect, to Peter: for what is right and good in social and economic order you may open the door, but for what is wrong and false you close the door. Hence, I give you the power of keys: "Whatsoever thou shalt bind upon earth, it shall be bound also in heaven: and whatsoever thou shalt loose on earth, it shall be loosed also in heaven" (Matt. 16:19).

This use of the words *rock* and *key* by our Divine Lord gives the answer to that group of so-called liberal writers who recently proclaimed: "The absoluteness of the Church is inconsistent with the relativity of history."[6] This is just like saying the absoluteness of the multiplication table is inconsistent with the relativity of history, for now, we no longer count pyramids but skyscrapers.

A Catholic is neither a reactionary nor a liberal in the sense of the terms above defined. He is not a reactionary because the Catholic knows that if you leave things alone you will not leave them as they are.

If you leave a cornfield alone, you do not have corn but weeds; if you leave a white fence alone, you soon have a black fence.

So too the Catholic says: if you leave man alone without vigilance and discipline, you have either a rusted man or a rotted man, for man decays more rapidly than he evolves, as modern history so well demonstrates.

Neither will the Catholic be a liberal who wants to make progress by scrapping eternal principles and ideals. The Catholic argues that unless you have a fixed point of departure and a fixed goal, you never know you are making any progress.

How can an artist know he is making progress in painting if every time he looks up from the canvas he finds a different person sitting for his portrait?

The terms *reactionary* and *liberal* are so relative they mean little to thinking men who have either a knowledge of history or a remnant of reason.

For example, the liberal of the last generation invoked liberalism to free economic activity from state control; the liberal of today invokes liberalism to extend state control over the economic order.

The old liberal was a defender of Capitalism; the new liberal is reacting against Capitalism and wants some form of collectivism or state control.

The old liberal wanted liberty of press, speech, and conscience within the framework of democracy; the new liberal, reacting against the old liberalism, wants the liberty without the framework as its safeguard.

The old liberal rebelled against taxation without responsibility; the new liberal wants the taxation as a handout without responsibility.

The old liberal fifty years ago was materialistic in science. His son who calls himself a liberal is today's reactionary for whom science is idealistic.

[6]   *City of Man*, 40.

The French liberals who protested against the authority of king and altar in the name of liberty were reactionaries, for they did not believe in extending that liberty to the proletariat.

Many liberals who wrote they believed in the equality of all men kept slaves. To change it around, every reactionary is protesting against the last liberal.

Sometimes in one man the liberal and the reactionary meet, as they did in the case of Milton.

Milton was a liberal who favored a free press and protested against licensing of books; and then when a handsome salary was offered him he reacted against his liberalism and became an official censor of books.

All that we have in the world is reaction against reactions; revolt against revolts; the reactionary and liberal are on a seesaw, and think they are going places because they are going up and down and see their momentary triumph over their opponent.

In the strict sense of the term, there are no liberals. A liberal is only a reactionary, reacting against the last form of liberalism.

The new liberals are at war against the old liberals; the new rebels in rebellion against the old rebels. The liberal of today will be the reactionary of tomorrow.

This simple analogy will help to make clear how our so-called liberalism is only a reaction against the last liberalism.

A woman buys a new dress for a ball to be held, say on the first of May. This dress is the last word in style; in political language it is *liberal*, *progressive*, far ahead of the reactionaries who bought their dresses last year.

At the ball, jealous and envious eyes are cast upon her, and to her face, the most flattering of compliments. Even the word *daring* is used.

Now it happens that she is invited to another ball, one month later and with the same group of people, and in the same place. Would that woman wear the same gown? She would not. She would rather die first!

Why would she not wear it? Because people had seen it before. She would no longer be liberal. She must have a new gown for the new ball.

In order to be a liberal in June, she has to be a reactionary against her liberal gown of May. That is why I say every liberal is reactionary.

The Church believes it is possible to make a distinction between being fashionable and being well dressed.

Consider, for example, the vestments worn by the priest at the altar. They certainly are not fashionable, for they are really an adaptation of the old Roman toga; but though you never see a chasuble in a fashion magazine, who would deny that the priest at the altar is becomingly and beautifully clothed?

The ideas of the Church are like her vestments; always well dressed but never the slave of passing fashion.

The Church knows after 1900 years' experience that any institution which suits the spirit of any age will be a widow in the next one. The Church, therefore, will never please either the reactionary or the liberal.

She will please only the relatively few who can understand how a house built on an immutable rock with an abiding proprietor, Peter, has a key that admits strangers.

The reactionaries want the rock without the keys; the liberals want the keys without the rock; and we who believe in Christ, who gave both to Peter, want both.

You have been told that the only choice possible is to be a reactionary or a liberal; that you must go either right or left. That would be true if you lived on a two-dimensional plane and this world were all; but you have a soul as well as a body.

You need therefore a three-dimensional universe, one with height where you can stretch not your legs but your hearts.

A mule can travel only in two directions: either right or left. He must be either a reactionary or a liberal. But because you have a soul there is another direction open to you, namely toward God for whom you were made.

Let the unthinking squabble about what a grandson ought to believe, or what a grandfather did believe, but concentrate on what a godson believes because he is born of the Spirit.

If you are honest with yourself you will admit that you are wary of religions, politics, and panaceas that flatter the way you live; you want something that will contradict the way you live and therefore be capable of redeeming you; you are sick of revolutions that only change booty and loot from one man's pocket into another's; you want a revolution that will change your hearts.

Leave it to the comedians to talk about "progress" when humanity is preying upon itself, for what they call progress is only a process—the fashion of the world passing away.

You are weary of the seesaw of reactionaries and liberals; you want a force and a spiritual power that will be hated by both, as our Divine Lord was hated and considered a menace by the reactionary Pharisees and a disturbing factor by the liberal Herodians.

You want today a force that will rescue you from the evil in the world and still let you do good in the world; which unlike the world will not tell you to go right or left, but up: "And I, if I be lifted up from the earth, will draw all things to myself" (John 12:32).

That is what you want: I do not know whether you have found it. Would it interest you to know that I have?

I have found it in the heart of Christendom, in the crystallization of common sense, in the living memory of the centuries, in the Church built upon a rock and governed by the Man with Keys.

I have found it in that which is hated as much as Christ was hated, misunderstood, and maligned as much as He was maligned, but loved as much as He was loved.

I have found it in an institution which millions who are not of its fold recognize as the only moral authority left in the world. I find it in the Church in which is prolonged Christ, whom the reactionaries find too liberal and the liberals too reactionary; something that challenges the world, not pampers it; which speaks a truth that because it is God-made, it cannot be man-remade; which restores me to the Savior's embrace when I sin; which nourishes my soul with the life of Christ when I hunger; which leads me to Calvary when I become undisciplined; which thrusts before me a Cross to inspire service of sacrifice for the poor; which tells me what is right when the world is wrong; and which will minister to my soul when my lease on life is ended. In a word, I am neither a reactionary nor a liberal—*Civis Romanus sum!* I am a Catholic!

5

The Four Columns

America has no need of stressing a danger from without—our press, cinema, radio, and government are of one voice in warning us against dictators.

But it is the duty of those interested in God and morality and peace to emphasize a less popular theme—and a more needed one—the danger from within.

There is no reason why America with its tremendous natural and technical resources should be overcome from the outside; but very frankly, our greatest danger is from the inside.

Our present temper is to assume that our hatred for 66.66 percent of cruel dictators can provide the discipline, order, and authority essential for the preservation of a nation.

It is the purpose of this chapter to challenge that mood and to suggest that a strengthening of our moral fiber must go hand in hand with military preparedness that we be seized from within.

History, Scripture, and nature all come to us freighted with a warning that the graver danger facing individuals and nations is from within rather than from without.

A distinguished historian of London, Professor Toynbee, proves that out of nineteen civilizations in the history of the world no less than sixteen broke down through their own acts before any alien human force succeeded in dealing them a mortal blow.

In sixteen out of nineteen cases all that the foreign enemy did was to give the last blow to a civilization that had already committed suicide; or to change the figure, to devour the carcass after it had already become carrion.

The collapses of these civilizations have not been due to circumstances beyond their control; they were neither the inexorable verdicts of cruel fate, nor the prey of sadistic sport of barbarious warriors, nor the result of catastrophes like floods, fires, and shipwrecks; nor were they the effect of an assassin's blow.

In practically sixteen out of nineteen cases, the historian, as the coroner of civilization, wrote down the verdict of "suicide."

In rebuking the Pharisees who were over-concerned with externals, our Divine Lord said that the things that come into a man from the outside do not defile him, "but the things which proceed out of the mouth, come forth from the heart, and those things defile a man. For from the heart come forth evil thoughts, murders, adulteries, fornications, thefts, false testimonies, blasphemies. These are the things that defile a man" (see Matt. 15, 19-20).

And we might add that since they defile a man they must also defile a nation. Defeat springs less from invasion than from corruption.

Shall we as a whole nation be so self-righteous as to become indignant against applying to ourselves the warning to the Pharisees: "Thou blind Pharisee, first make clean the inside of the cup and of the dish, that the outside may become clean. Woe to you ... you are like to whited sepulchres, which outwardly appear to men beautiful, but within are full of dead men's bones" (Matt. 23:26-27)?

If we turn from God to the nature He made we find the same warning. Collect a flock of pigeons of every shade, color, and marking, then take them to an uninhabited island, and after many years all the pigeons will be one color—a dark slaty blue.

Neglect keeping a garden in order and it will run to weeds; neglect your muscles and they stiffen.

Human life is not always surging upwards by evolution as our pseudo-scientists told us, it is also tumbling downwards by devolution.

Human nature is not only subject to conversion; it may even be subject to reversion and perversion.

Degeneration is a fact of life to which we have been blinded by loose talk about progress; it is now time to face the bias of evil, the possibility of gravitation by which a man gathering momentum as he falls further from God, lands in the Hell of a neglected and ruined life.

The tragedy of life is that this ruin may be so gradual and imperceptible that while concentrating on external dangers the citadel of life is taken from within.

As the poet Meredith put it:

In tragic life, God wot
No villain need be! Passions spin the plot;
We are betrayed by what is false within.[7]

And as the old Greek poet Menander put it so long ago:

Things rot through evils native to themselves
And all that injures issues from within."

And by false within I mean not the Fifth Columnists, because a Fifth Columnist could not operate if there were not already four other columnists. The breakdown of civilization is due more to an inward loss of self-determination than to external blows.

Take for example, the formation of rust on a bar of iron. When the iron begins to disintegrate, there is a dislocation of some of its molecules, which permits the infiltration of an alien force from the outside, namely, the free oxygen in the air. The union of the two produces rust.

The Fifth Columnists correspond to the oxygen in the air; they are the alien social forces. But these Fifth Columnists could never become a part of a civilization unless a decay had already set in within the nation itself.

Iron can be kept from rusting; civilization can be kept from degenerating. But neglect makes rust and decay possible. If we had not abandoned Absolute Truth; if we had not adopted the stupid moral philosophy that freedom means the right to do whatever you please, even the right to destroy freedom, we would have no Fifth Columnists.

[7] George Meredith, *Modern Love*, 43.

That is why I say the Fifth Columnist is possible only because there are already Fourth Columnists and these constitute our danger from within. What are these four columns?

The First Columnists are those educators and publicists who reject a universal norm of morality in favor of a relative morality based either on expediency, pleasure, profit, or selfishness of the individual; in other words, a rejection of the principle that right is right if nobody is right and wrong is wrong if everybody is wrong.

A typical instance of this abandonment of morality based on God and His justice is the tendency in international relations to call Russia a "friendly nation" when the facts prove that Russia has been just as destructive of humanity, as hateful of religion, as oppressive of the masses, and as cruel to hearts as the Nazis—and that is as damning an indictment as could be made of any nation.

We Americans may not say and we must not say before God that we are fighting for freedom of speech, freedom of religion, and freedom from fear, when we choose among the barbarians and dictators and call that nation "friendly" which gave the green light to Hitler to invade the West, and which within its own boundaries as prison walls has extinguished the rights and liberties of one hundred and sixty million people.

The First Column undermines justice, the Second Column undermines charity. The Second Columnists are those who sin against charity and include all those who sin not only by rejecting the solidarity of mankind, because begotten of a common origin and redeemed by our Divine Lord, but also by rebelling against the fraternal spirit and tolerance which should exist between citizens of the same country.

In this Second Column are those in the ranks of capital and labor who through avarice on the one hand and envy and greed on the other turn the nation into a warring camp at the very moment we talk about a war from the outside.

In this Second Column, too, are those individuals who are guilty of anti-Semitism, anti-Catholicism, bigotry, atheism, and immorality, who by their hatreds are not murdering bodies but slaughtering souls with eternal destinies and for which they will one day have to answer before the judgment seat of Almighty God.

The Third Columnists are those lawyers, jurists, and teachers who by divorcing civil authority from dependence on the law of God, make law only an instrument for action, or the social expression of the way beings live, rather than the way they ought to live.

In this Third Column are those so-called educators who complain against the release time from school for religious instruction in the nonsensical plea that it means the union of Church and State.

It is interesting to note that the persons who most oppose religion for the young as being un-American, are often the same ones who draw money from American taxpayers to tie us up with anti-American activities.

Let me say to these Third Columnists that there is no danger in this country of the union of the Church and State, but there is danger of the union of atheism and the State.

If that is what they want, then let them say so, and we will fight back in the name of the Declaration of Independence — Washington, and Lincoln — in a word, in the name of America.

The Fourth Columnists are those who either explicitly or implicitly adhere to the philosophy of "self-expression" and reject the necessity of discipline, authority, and self-sacrifice as the condition of individual and national betterment.

In this Fourth Column are those who think they should get everything for nothing in America and still have the right to complain about the quality; those who refuse to face the responsibility of spending and thus mortgage America's future; those who consider education a social necessity rather than an intellectual privilege; those labor leaders and those Capitalists who shout "Persecution!" as soon as one of their own is convicted of injustice by the government; those parents who are raising a bumper crop of spoiled children because they see too many exhibitions and learn too few inhibitions; those who sue the school and the Board of Education if a teacher scolds for an act of wrongdoing their "darling child" who can do no wrong; and finally those who pamper the rapacious egotism of their children and thus prevent the formation of good habits.

Given amalgamation in iron, you will get rust by the moisture from outside; given these four columns in the inside of a nation, you get the alien Fifth Columnists boring from within.

St. Cyprian centuries ago saw that something had gone wrong with the internal economy of Hellenic civilization; something had crept into the hearts of people which made then so sick on the inside that he wanted to save them.

> You complain that the enemy rises up, as if, though an enemy were wanting, there could be peace for you even among the very togas of peace (*esse pax inter ipsas togas possit*).

> You complain that the enemy rises up, as if, even although external arms and dangers from barbarians were repressed, the weapons of domestic assault from the calumnies and wrongs of powerful citizens, would not be more ferocious and more harshly wielded within.

> You complain of barrenness and famine, as if drought made a greater famine than rapacity, as if the fierceness of want did not increase more terribly from grasping at the increase of the year's produce, and the accumulation of their price.

> You complain that the heaven is shut up from showers, although in the same way the barns are shut up on earth. You complain that now less is produced, as if what had already been produced were given to the indigent.

> You reproach plague and disease, while by plague itself and disease the crimes of individuals are either detected or increased, while mercy is not manifested to the weak, and avarice and rapine are waiting open-mouthed for the dead.[8]

---

[8] St. Cyprian of Carthage, *Ad Demetrianum*, 10, in *Ante-Nicene Fathers*, vol. 5, ed. Alexander Roberts James Donaldson, and A. Cleveland Coxe, trans. Robert Ernest Wallis (Buffalo, NY: Christian Literature, 1886; online NewAdvent version: Kevin Knight), https://www.newadvent.org/fathers/050705.htm.

All can be summed up in a word, we need a little more self-discipline, in the form of less selfishness, less hate, less avarice, more sacrifice, more tolerance, more respect for law and authority, more morality, more God.

This much is certain: we will have discipline in the future, and if we do not enforce it freely upon ourselves, we will have it imposed from without—a cruel, tyrannical discipline.

Want of discipline and morality brought on the slave states of Russia in 1918, Germany in 1933, and the Totalitarian state of Italy in 1922, and the fallen France of 1940. All these people disintegrated from within before they disintegrated from without.

Every Totalitarian state has arisen out of confusion, humiliation, frustration; having no order they were willing to try anything.

Let not America be blind to history, to revelation, and to nature and talk only of the enemy from without and not of the enemy from within, or concentrate on Fifth Columnists and forget the other four. This rebirth of national discipline will not be easy to achieve.

It is unfortunately true that Totalitarian states can more readily appeal to sacrifice than some democracies, for having imbued their people with a diabolical mysticism and having infused them with a false fervor, they are ready to deny themselves for a future glory.

But when democracies lose the spirit of religion they have no fulcrum for self-sacrifice; once the Cross passes out of their vision selfishness enthrones itself. Then the plea for self-sacrifice becomes identified with persecution, Fascism, Communism, or what-have-you.

The preservation of America is conditioned upon discipline and self-sacrifice, but since these are inseparable from religion and morality, the future of America depends on Americans' attitude toward God and the Cross of His Divine Son.

Is not a call to penance and self-sacrifice within the tradition of America? Has not our country before always in times of crisis called upon its citizens not only to pray, but to do penance, to fast, to humiliate themselves before God, and to make themselves worthy instruments of His Justice?

Shall we in America forget that John Adams in 1799 proclaimed that "in circumstances of great urgency and seasons of imminent danger, earnest and particular supplications should be made to Him who is able to defend or to destroy"?[9]

Have we forgotten that when this new and weak nation was swept into the Napoleonic Wars, that President Madison, three times between 1812 and 1815, called for "public homage ... [for] the transgressions which might justly provoke the manifestations of His divine displeasure"?[10]

Have we as Americans forgotten that in the trying days of civil strife President Buchanan set aside January 4, 1861, as the day when all "people [should] assemble ... according to their several forms of worship, to keep it as a solemn fast"?[11]

Have we forgotten that five times during his Presidency, Abraham Lincoln called on the people to "bow in humble submission to [God's] chastisement; to confess and deplore their sins and transgressions, in the full conviction that the fear of the Lord is the beginning of wisdom, and to pray with all fervency and contrition for the pardon of their past offences.... that we may be spared further punishment, though most justly deserved; that.... the Throne of Grace [might] bring down plentiful blessings upon our country"?[12]

Have we forgotten that moving plea of Andrew Jackson for a day of "humbling ourselves before Almighty God"?

Do we remember that Grant in 1871 set aside November 30 as a day for asking Almighty God for "merciful exemption from evils"?[13]

---

[9] John Adams, *The Works of John Adams, vol. 9: Letters and State Papers: 1799–1881* (North Charleston, SC: Createspace, n.d.), 96.

[10] James Madison, Proclamation to Congress, July 9, 1812, in James D. Richardson, *A Compilation of the Messages and Papers of the Presidents: 1789–1902*, vol. 1 (New York: Bureau of National Literature and Art, 1907), 513.

[11] James Buchanan, Address to the People of the United States, December 14, 1860, in James D. Richardson, *A Compilation of the Messages and Papers of the Presidents: 1789–1897*, vol. 10 (Washington, DC: Government Printing Office, 1899), 80.

[12] Abraham Lincoln, Proclamation of a National Fast Day, August 12, 1861, in *Historical Report of the Operations of the Office of Acting Assistant Provost Marshal General, Illinois: Report of the Provost Marshal General*, doc. 11 (Washington, DC: Government Printing Office, 1865), 208–209.

[13] Ulysses S. Grant, Proclamation, October 28, 1871, in James D. Richardson, *A Compilation of the Messages and Papers of the Presidents: 1789–1907*, vol. 7 (New York: Bureau of National Literature and Art, 1908), 138.

Have we forgotten that the last presidential proclamation issued in the United States which admitted the possibility that we ought to ask God for something else than prosperity and which envisaged the possibility that we needed some regeneration was that of President Wilson who proclaimed Thursday, May 30, 1918, as a day of "public humiliation, prayer, and fasting"?[14]

Do we remember that one day when the apostles came to our Lord they confessed their inability to drive out certain devils? Our Lord told them that kind was driven out only by prayers and fasting (see Mark 9:28).

That is the only way the devils of the modern world can be driven out, not only by prayers but by fasting, by sacrifice, by self-discipline.

And if ever our president in keeping with the traditions of America should ask not only for prayers for prosperity, but for humiliation, fasting for our sins, and a renewed spirit of discipline for the sake of America under God, then let us respond, strengthening our moral fibre; for America will never be beaten from without, as long as it is moral from within.

---

[14] Woodrow Wilson, Proclamation, May 11, 1918, in *Supplement to the Messages and Papers of the Presidents: Covering the Second Term of Woodrow Wilson: March 4, 1917 to March 4, 1921* (New York: Bureau of National Literature, 1921), 8495.

6

The Cross and the Double-Cross

The Cross is not incredible to the modern mind, for nothing is more understandable than sacrificial love; rather it is irrelevant.

A person who denies there is such a thing as sickness does not consider the physician a myth; he considers him irrelevant. In like manner, if one denies he is a sinner how can he need redemption?

The sense of guilt, as we have been emphasizing throughout this book, is considered today only as a vestigial remnant of primitive fears, or as a "psychopathic aspect of an adolescent mentality."

If there is guilt in the world, it lies in systems, not in persons—such is the modern mentality.

In the eighteenth century this sort of mind attributed evil to tyrannical governments; in the nineteenth century to tyrannical classes; and in the twentieth century to dictatorships—not all dictatorships of course, only two-thirds of them; for Russia, it is said is a "friendly nation." Yes! Friendly like Judas who blistered the lips of Christ with a kiss.

Since nothing can disturb the modern man's good opinion of himself, the Cross with its redemption is meaningless. But it is not as irrelevant as he thinks.

The purpose of this chapter is to indicate that by denying the Cross of Christ, modern man did not escape a cross—no one can; he got a cross—the double-cross.

What happened to the prodigal son in the Gospel happened to the modern man. In the first scene he threw off the yoke of the Father's house to live his own life; or, in the language of our day, to be "self-expressive" and "free," independent of all restraints.

In the second scene, his wealth is gone, his stomach empty, his heart heavy. But do we find him free and independent?

On the contrary, he becomes a slave to the citizen of a foreign country feeding his swine, whose husks he would have eaten to have filled his belly—no longer his heart—but no man gave him to eat. He who wanted to be free found himself a slave.

Something like that has happened to the modern man. For the last four hundred years he has been striving for total independence and absolute autonomy: first from the Church as a spiritual organism; then from the Bible as the revealed Word of God; then from the authority of Christ; and finally from religion.

By progressive steps he rebelled against his divine destiny. Like the steward who pretended to be the master of the vineyard, he killed his lord's messenger, that he might possess it forever. Like the prodigal he squandered his spiritual capital until he had nothing to eat except the husks of humanism and behaviorism.

He made himself a god, and, in the language of teachers of philosophy in dozens of American universities, he called himself "a creator rather than a creature."

Because man was a god, it followed he could do no wrong. Since he could not sin, he needed no Calvary. The Cross he hated—as George Bernard Shaw, spokesman for the modern man, said: "The Cross in the twilight bars the way."

So modern man forged an educational system without discipline; he fashioned a philosophy which denied truth, and made good and evil only relative to the individual; he labeled every attempt to restore authority as "Fascism"; every restriction on the part of the government against economic selfishness as "Communism"; and every arrest of racketeers and Communist labor leaders as "Nazi persecution."

He formed civil liberty associations to defend every attempt to destroy civil liberty; and, as a sop to sentimentalism, he made a religion without

Hell, a Christ without justice, a Kingdom of God without God, salvation without a crucifix, and a Church where a pulpit and an organ replaced the altar of sacrifice.

In a word, he refused to see the connection between his own selfish autonomy and the chaos which that selfish autonomy produced in others, and which he hated in them.

He was not as logical as Nietzsche who saw that man must either accept the Cross or go mad—and Nietzsche went mad.

Now we are at scene two. As the prodigal found there was no escaping some kind of submission, so the modern man learned that there is no such thing as escaping the Cross. Absolute independence is a myth.

Man is truly free only when he acts within the law and not outside it or against it. I am free to draw a triangle only on condition that I give it three sides and not, in a stroke of progressive broadmindedness, thirty-three.

I am free to fly in a plane only on condition that I submit myself to the laws of gravitation. To want to be free from that law is not to be free to fly, but to be free to fall. The penalty for the violation of law is unfreedom or slavery.

Sin is the opposite of freedom. For that reason our Lord said, "whosoever committeth sin, is the servant of sin" (John 8:34).

If a man gives himself over to drink he loses his freedom; he becomes the servant or the slave of sin.

He began by being free to take a drink or not to take a drink; he ended by being no longer free to do anything but take it.

To be a slave of passion is the opposite of freedom. In seeking to be absolutely independent of God and morality, man lost his freedom.

Freedom, as absolute independence, is impossible. Our liberals who wanted a freedom without authority found that out.

The choice is not: Will we or will we not accept authority? It is rather: Which authority will we accept, the authority of Christ or the authority of public opinion?

Those who rejected Divine Truth did not become free minds; they became slave minds. That is why so many of them cannot make a judgment about anything until they read the Gallup poll or the morning newspaper.

Furthermore, there is no such thing as freedom from discipline. We may only choose between disciplines: a discipline from the inside freely administered by our own sense of righteous self-perfection, or a discipline from the outside inspired by cruel, tyrannical forces.

And that brings us to the point we want to prove: that there is no such thing as living without a cross.

We are free only to choose between crosses. Will it be the Cross of Christ which redeems us from our sins, or will it be the double-cross, the swastika, the hammer and sickle, the fasces?

Why are we a troubled nation today? Why do we live in fear—we who defined freedom as the right to do whatever we pleased; we who have no altars in our churches, no discipline in our schools, and no sacrifices in our lives? We fear because our false freedom and license and apostasy from God has caught up with us, as it did with the prodigal.

We would not accept the yoke of Christ; so now we must tremble at the yoke of Caesar. We willed to be free from God; now we must face the danger of being enslaved to a citizen of a foreign country.

In seeking to live without the Cross, we got a cross—not one of Christ's making or our own, but the devil's!—diabolically cruel, tortured cross made of guns, hammers, sickles, and bombs—the thing that started out to be a cross and then double-crossed itself because it has double-crossed the world.

And that threat throws us into a terrific dilemma. Can we meet that double-cross without the Cross?

Can a democracy of ease and comfort overcome a system built on sacrifice? Can a nation which permits the breakup of the family by divorce, defeat a nation which forcefully bends the family to the nation? Can they, who for seven years tightened their belts, gave up butter for guns, endured every conceivable limitation, be conquered by ease and comfort?

Dr. Alexis Carrel was right in saying that in America,

a good time has been our national cry. The perfect life as viewed by the average youth or adult is a round of ease or entertainment; of motion pictures, radio programs, parties, alcohol, and sexual excesses. This indolent and undisciplined way of life has sapped our individual vigor and imperiled our democratic form of government. Our race pitifully needs new supplies of discipline, morality, and intelligence.[15]

The rise of militarism and the gospel of force in the modern world is a result of the vacuum created by the abandonment of the Cross.

Europe was nourished on Christian virtues; it knew obedience to authority, self-discipline, penance, and the need of redemption. But when it began to starve through the abandonment of the bread of the Father's house, it seized, like the prodigal, on the fodder of militarism and the glorification of the sword.

Like the empty house of the Gospel, the modern world swept itself clean of the Cross of Christ, but only to be possessed by the devils of the double-cross.

As Voltaire said: "If man had no God, he would make himself one!" So too, we might add, if man had no Cross, he would make himself one. And he has.

Apostate from Calvary, the glorification of military virtues in these states is the feeble compensation for a yoke that is sweet and a burden that is light.

As Mussolini said on August 24, 1934, "We are becoming a warlike nation—that is to say, one endowed to a higher degree with virtues of obedience, sacrifice, and dedication to country."

This so-called heroic attitude toward life is being invoked in deadly earnest by millions in Germany and Russia, and by all who espouse their cause in other nations.

In the days when the Cross lived in the hearts of men, war was considered a calamity, a scourge sent by God; but now in the days of the double-cross, it is justified as the noblest of virtues for the sake of the nation as in Italy, the race as in Germany, and the class as in Russia.

They believe what Von Moltke wrote in 1880: "Without War the world would become swamped in materialism."[16] Imagine! To save us from materialism, we must have war!

[15] Alexis Carrel, *Man, the Unknown*.
[16] Helmuth von Moltke to J. K. Bluntschli, December 11, 1880.

He is right in saying that to save us from materialism we must have sacrifice. He is wrong in saying it must come from war. But if there is no Cross to inspire it, whence shall it come but from the double-cross?

We in America are now faced with the threat of that double-cross. To revert to our theme, our choice is not: Will we or will we not have more discipline, more respect for law, more order, more sacrifice; but, where will we get it?

Will we get it from without, or from within? Will it be inspired by Sparta or Calvary? By Valhalla or Gethsemane? By militarism or religion? By the double-cross or the Cross? By Caesar or by God?

That is the choice facing America today. The hour of false freedom is past. No longer can we have education without discipline, family life without sacrifice, individual existence without moral responsibility, economics and politics without subservience to the common good. We are now only free to say whence it shall come.

We will have a sword. Shall it be only the sword that thrusts outward to cut off the ears of our enemies, or the sword that pierces inward to cut out our own selfish pride?

May Heaven grant that, unlike the centurion, we pierce not the heart of Christ before we discover His Divinity and salvation.

Away with those educators and propagandists who, by telling us we need no Cross, make possible having one forged for us abroad. Away with those who, as we gird ourselves for sacrifice based on love of God and Calvary, sneer: "Come down from the cross" (Matt. 27:40).

That cry has been uttered before on Calvary, as His enemies shouted: "He saved others; himself he cannot save" (Mark 15:31).

They were now willing to admit He had saved others; they could well afford to do it for now He apparently could not save Himself.

Of course, He could not save Himself. No man can save himself who saves another.

The rain cannot save itself, if it is to bud the greenery; the sun cannot save itself if it is to light the world; the seed cannot save itself if it is to make the harvest; a mother cannot save herself if she is to save her child; a soldier cannot save himself if he is to save his country.

It was not weakness which made Christ hang on the Cross; it was obedience to the law of sacrifice, of love. For how could He save us if He ever saved Himself?

Peace He craved; but as St. Paul says: "[He made] peace through the blood of his cross" (Col. 1:20). Peace we want; but there is none apart from sacrifice.

Peace is not a passive, but an active virtue. Our Lord never said: "Blessed are the peaceful," but "Blessed are the peacemakers" (Matt. 5:9). The Beatitude rests only on those who make it out of trial, out of suffering, out of cruelty, even out of sin.

God hates peace in those who are destined for war. And we are destined for war—a war against a false freedom which endangered our freedom; a war for the Cross against the double-cross; a war to make America once more what it was intended to be from the beginning—a country dedicated to liberty under God; a war of the *militia Christi*: "Having your loins girt about with truth, and having on the breastplate of justice.... the shield of faith.... the helmet of salvation (Eph. 6:14, 16, 17).

Only those who carry the sword of the Spirit have the right and have the power to say to the enemies of the Cross, "Put up thy sword into the scabbard" (John 18:11).

The great tragedy is that the torch of sacrifice and truth has been snatched from the hands of those who should hold it, and is borne aloft by the enemies of the Cross.

The Pentecostal fires have been stolen from the altar of God and now burn as tongues of fire in those who grind the altars into dust.

The fearlessness born of love of God which once challenged the armies of Caesar is now espoused to Caesar.

We live in an age of saints in reverse, when apostles who are breathed on by the evil spirit outdare those animated by the Holy Spirit of God.

The fires for causes like Communism, Nazism, and Fascism, which burn downwards, are more intense than the fires that burn upwards in the hearts of those who pay only lip service to God.

But this passion by which men deliver themselves over to half-truths and idiocies should make us realize what a force would enter history again if there were but a few saints in every nation who could help the world, because they were not enmeshed in it; who would, like their Master on the Cross, not seek to save the world as it is, but to be saved from it; who would demonstrate to those who still have decent hearts, as we believe we have in America, that it is possible to practice sacrifice without turning the world into a vast slaughterhouse.

There is no escaping the Cross!

That is why the hope, the real hope of the world, is not in those politicians who, indifferent to Divinity, offer Christ and Barabbas to the mob to save their tumbling suffrage.

It is not in those economists who would drive Christ from their shores like the Gerasens, because they feared loss of profit on their swine.

It is not in those educators who, like other Pilates, sneer: "What is truth" (John 18:38)—then crucify it.

The hope of the world is in the crucified in every land in those bearing the Cross of Christ; in the mothers of Poland who, like other Rachels, mourn for their children; in the wives weeping for their husbands stolen into the servitude of war; in the sons and daughters kissing the cold earth of Siberia as the only one of the things God made that they are left to see; in bleeding feet and toil-worn hands; in persecuted Jews, blood-brothers of Christ, of whom God said: "[I will] curse them that curse thee" (Gen. 12:3); in the priests in concentration camps who, like Christ, in other Gethsemanes, find a way to offer their own blood in the chalice of their own body.

The hope of the world is in the Cross of Christ borne down the ages in the hearts of suffering men, women, and children, who, if we only knew it are saving us from the double-cross more than our guns and ships.

We in America are now brought face-to-face with the heritage of a freedom derived from God. The hour has struck when we have to take up a Cross. There is no escaping the Cross.

Who shall give it to us? Shall it be imposed by chastisement, or shall it be freely accepted by penance?

Let us believe in America's power of regeneration. Let us believe we can remake ourselves from within in order that we be not remade from without. Let us believe in the future of America; but let us believe in it only as we believe in Easter—after it has passed through Good Friday.

7

Hope

We live in one of those interludes of history that come upon us once every few hundred years. It is a time between times, the end of one era and the beginning of another which is yet clouded in mist, that twilight zone when darkness seems so real and the light seems so far away.

The whole world seems to be possessed of a sense of impending catastrophe, when liberals doubt their own liberalism, reactionaries fear their own immobility; when defeat, persecution of religion, frustration of hearts, the enthronement of violence, and a gnawing fear turn the prophets of progress into prophets of despair.

As the Jews of old sometimes yearned for the fleshpots of Egypt, so does the modern man look back regretfully at what he thought was a Paradise on earth, when poets sang "glory to man in the highest," when evolution promised to make each of us gods, and philosophers taught man was the measure of all things, when novelists pictured a "Brave New World," when education, politics, and economics no longer needed religion, and when the laws of progress guaranteed us a world without a Cross.

No period in history better reflects the pessimism and despair of our day than that tragic interlude between Good Friday and Easter Sunday, when the Light was put out and the best of men were in darkness wondering if it would ever be light again.

Never did the world seem darker. Economists, who bargained with the Master for the price of a slave, ended in the despair of suicide; politicians like Pilate, who washed their hands with water, still found them red with the blood of deicide; even the apostles who had heard Him say that He would rise again, doubted that there could ever be a victory after such a defeat.

Just as the despairing of our day look back to what they wrongly think was a golden age, so the apostles — after the silhouettes of three crosses were swallowed up in the darkness of Good Friday night — must have looked back to what they thought was their golden age: the Mount of the Transfiguration.

How they must have set in contrast those two mountains, the one where His face did shine as the sun and His garments became white as snow, and the other where His face was as one struck with leprosy and his only garment the purple patches of His own blood.

How different it all would have been, they must have thought, if the Master had only followed Peter's advice and stayed there in His glory instead of coming down from that hill to set His face toward Jerusalem and the Cross!

But now it was too late. They had only the memory of a lost Kingdom which, like Moses, they had seen with the mind's eye but were never destined to enter.

The glory of the Transfiguration was lost; they had now only the defeat of the crucifix.

Then came Sunday morning at an hour when it yet was dark. A woman steals into the garden, a woman who herself had risen from the dead, for the Master had driven out of her seven devils. If there was anyone who might have been expected to have believed in the Resurrection, it was she.

And yet, on Easter Sunday morning she went to the tomb not to await a Resurrection, but to anoint a dead body, uttering all the while the bitter plaint: "They have taken away my Lord; and I know not where they have laid him" (John 20:13).

With her whole heart absorbed in this thought, she turned away and lo! Jesus was standing beside her. But it was not Jesus as she had known

Him. There was something spiritual, something not of earth in the risen and glorified body.

Some accident of dress or appearance through tear-clouded eyes made her fancy that it was the gardener. In the eager hope that he could explain to her the secret of that empty and angel-haunted grave, she exclaims in an agony of appeal, "Sir, if thou hast taken him hence, tell me where thou hast laid him, and I will take him away" (John 20:15).

Jesus spoke to her one word: "Mary" (John 20:16). He was calling His sheep by name, and there was all Heaven in that word.

She looked first to His feet and saw the red scars of the Conqueror of death, and then she uttered but one word, and all earth was in it: "Rabboni" (John 20:16).

The birth of the Savior had been announced to a Virgin, the Resurrection from the dead to a convert prostitute — that all the hopeless world might know that they who slew the foe had lost the day. Before the sun had set on that brilliant Easter day, there burned into the hearts of the apostles and all the world the great lesson: Easter was not within three days of the Transfiguration, it was within three days of Good Friday.

We who believe in the Risen Christ cannot share the pessimism and despair of the modern world which feels that this war is the "end of civilization," "the beginning of chaos," "the return to barbarism," and the "decline of the West."

Why do the very ones who once clapped their hands at seeing the Tower of Babel rise, now wring them in dripping despair as it tumbles on their heads?

Why do they, who once danced to the tune of evolution and progress, now sing the lamentations of disillusion?

It is because they started with a very false premise: namely, there is only matter in the universe but no soul, no divine purpose, no God.

Now if there is nothing in the universe but matter with its various shapes and forms, then once it begins to disintegrate nothing can stop it.

When an apple begins to rot, it rots through and through; when dynamite explodes, it exhausts itself; when a tree begins to decay, the ravage continues until it falls.

Applying that to our civilization, because the materialists have seen cracks in its walls, they say it now must crumble. Prisoners of the material, they are made captive to hopelessness and despair.

This pessimism we cannot share, because we believe there is something else in the universe besides matter, namely the spirit; and the spirit is never so near a victory as when the flesh is most defeated.

The Master was never so close to His greatest victory as when men built Him a Cross, for Easter Sunday was not within three days of the glory of the Transfiguration, it was within three days of the Cross.

There are three reasons for hope, and therefore for not sharing the defeatism of those, who because they have forgotten their God, have lost the hope of resurrection.

The first reason is this: moments of great catastrophe are often the eves of great spiritual renaissance.

It was not when the apostles saw Christ in the transient glory of Transfiguration, but in the ignominy of a tortured man on the Cross, that they were closest to their victory.

Our Divine Lord Himself, speaking of wars, rumors of war, earthquakes, and distress of nations, made the forecast of these calamities the very motive of hope. "But when these things begin to come to pass, look up, and lift up your heads, because your redemption is at hand" (Luke 21:28).

The reason moments of catastrophe may be the eves of spiritual victory is because it is in those moments of defeat that man's pride is most humbled and his soul thus prepared for the help of God. Israel received her greatest prophets in the hour when all hope seemed gone. The prodigal was closest to his greatest joy when his substance had been wasted.

It was only when Peter had labored all the night and taken nothing that he was given the miraculous draught of fishes. And in the spiritual life, "the dark night of the soul," the purification of the senses by mortification, is the prelude to the rapturous joys of the spirit.

I believe we are now in such an age, of which Isaias spoke: "I will give you the treasures of darkness" (Isa. 45:3, RSVCE).

Darkness may be creative, for it is there that God plants His seeds to grow and His bulbs to flower. It is at night that the sheep which are scattered are gathered into the unity of the sheepfold, when the children come home to their mother, and the soul back again to God.

Daylight deceives us, but as we awake at night, we get a new sense of values: darkness seems to tell the awful truth. As the psalmist put it: "Day to day uttereth speech, and night to night sheweth knowledge" (Ps. 18:3).

Night has its wonders as well as day; darkness is not final except to those who are without God.

Applying this to our own time, the beginnings of a new era are often marked by a general barbarization, when the whole historical order is dissolved in a torrent of violence, when Truth in some nations is nailed to a Cross, and in others rejected in a stroke of false broadmindedness.

But since we believe in day as well as in night, and in spirit as well as in matter, we are not without hope in this hour of calamity—for only those who walk in darkness ever see the stars.

We are hopeful not because this is a good world, for presently it is not. Our trust is not in the inherent natural goodness of man, but in the powers of God who can raise him from the dead. Our optimism is based not on "progress," but on its breakdown.

Our modern pagans despair when they become disillusioned about the world. We hope when we begin to be disillusioned about ourselves; and therein is the pathway to repentance and to God, for Easter Sunday was not within three days of the glory of the Transfiguration, it was within three days of the defeat of Good Friday.

The second reason for hope is that in the lifetime of all of us the Church has been more and more emerging into the world from which she was exiled four centuries ago.

Nothing better symbolizes this progressive influence than the manner in which the last three pontiffs have been crowned as successors of St. Peter.

During the days of the last world war, Benedict XV was crowned in the chapel of the Blessed Mother at the rear of the Basilica of St. Peter's. In the year 1922 his successor, Pius XI, moved forward in the Church a few paces and was crowned at the main altar above the very tomb of him who first received the keys of Heaven and earth.

But after his coronation Pius XI did something which no pontiff had done since the year 1870. He walked to the front of St. Peter's, mounted a narrow staircase in the interior of the wall, and then for the first time in half a century, stepped outside of that Church to face the vast throng on the piazza who were awaiting his blessing.

But he did something more than merely step out into that portico; he literally stepped out into the world. The days of defensive warfare were over; from now on there would be a warfare with the breastplate of justice, the shield of faith, the sword of the spirit, and the blessing of Christ.

When the 261st successor of St. Peter was crowned, he moved even still farther. It was not in the rear of the basilica, at the altar of the Blessed Mother, that he was crowned; it was not under the dome of the cathedral and the tomb of St. Peter; it was out on the very portico of the Church itself—more literally still, he was proclaimed a shepherd in the world.

And now as Russia becomes the last hope of nations without faith and is prepared to betray those nations who trusted in her, there will be only one spiritual moral authority left in the world; the only authority which has survived all wars and catastrophes up to this hour and will survive them unto the end.

And as those round about us, who live only on the husks of materialism and mumble their despair, thanks to Christ in His vicar we live in the hope of a better day, even in an hour that is dark and black, for Easter Sunday was not within three days of the glory of the Transfiguration, it was within three days of the ignominy of Good Friday.

The third and final reason for hope is that the strength of material opposition has no relation to the possibilities of spiritual victory.

When there are only material forces in conflict, the stronger force will invariably win. If on one hand I have a force of fifty pounds, and on the other a force of a thousand pounds, I can be absolutely certain that the force of a thousand pounds will prevail.

But when the contending forces are not both material, but one material and the other spiritual, then the strength of the material opposition, however great it be, is no guarantee of its victory.

A man stands beside Niagara Falls; these mighty waters in an instant could sweep him to death and destruction. But there is within that man an immortal soul made to the image and likeness of God, and being spiritual he can conceive and beget an idea of how to harness those waters and make them minister to the service of man. Materially, Niagara should win; actually it loses.

Apply this now to our own times. Let there arise one of the greatest military forces the world has ever seen, let it meet any other material force that is slightly weaker—and barbarism will win; but suppose that that great material force of barbarism is met, not by a foe which attempts to match it in material strength, but by a force that is spiritual, however weak and mean it may seem in the eyes of the world.

The spiritual force will win as the mind of the engineer wins over Niagara. That is why we who believe in Easter and the victory of spirit over matter will not be without hope for America, so long as it trusts in God.

Our hope is grounded not in the magnificent plans for defense, not in increased productiveness of engines of war.

Our hope is grounded in a Risen Christ and a revitalized spirituality, for that lesson of the first Easter must be the lesson of our day: Easter was not within three days of the Transfiguration, it was within three days of Good Friday.

The Church in her liturgy this day begs us to seek the things that are above, to rise in our minds with Christ in His Glory as we await the final resurrection of our bodies.

Taking this truly spiritual outlook of the world, and it is the only one that matters, be not disheartened if the externals and accidentals, the trappings and barnacles of the civilization through which we have lived, go down to defeat.

We should face the hard fact that all civilizations, after a certain length of time, become encrusted with a bad philosophy and a worse morals, such as, in our own nation, the primacy of the profit motive over the human, the triumph of divorce over family life, the abandonment of morality and religion in education, the prostitution of the defense of labor by subversive activities.

The effect of this encrustation is to smother the more vital forces within a nation such as religion, morality, sacrifice, the practice of virtue, and the influence of the Church of Christ.

Inside of every egg is potency for new life; but that inner life cannot be free and independent so long as it is enclosed in a shell. In like manner, the vital Christian forces of this nation and of the world cannot assert themselves so long as they are kept imprisoned by the hard shell of materialism and apostasy from God.

And this war, with all of the horrors, may, under the Providence of God, be the breaking of the shell of modern civilization and the releasing of those spiritual forces which up to this time have been imprisoned by the forces of irreligion.

War is not necessarily the end of a civilization. It may be the beginning of a new and a better world. It can be averted if we discipline ourselves from within and do penance. If we refuse to do that, it may be imposed upon us from without as a chastisement.

But in any case, the shell will be broken and if need be, a war of attrition will be the beginning of our contrition; for Easter Sunday was not within three days of the Transfiguration, it was within three days of Good Friday.

The world does not yet know it, for the spirit of the world fights only for superficial values. But the conflict of our day is not merely between the barbarism of Germany and the rest of the world, but is part of a larger pattern.

This war will eventually emerge into a struggle of two distinct philosophies of life which may cut across national boundaries with the sharpness of a sword. Each of these philosophies of life will have its own tomb: one tomb will be in Moscow, and the other tomb will be in Jerusalem.

One group of minds in the world will rally about a cadaver, the body of Lenin; the other will rally about the empty tomb of One who was sentenced to death, but fated not to die.

Millions of souls in the world who now hate religion because they hate themselves, will prostrate themselves before an immortality long mortalized and rotted.

Millions of others will lift their eyes to the Risen Christ, living in a Church which has survived a hundred crucifixions and a hundred deaths.

And in that conflict between these two forces of evil and good we know not how many swords will be unsheathed or whether they will have to be unsheathed.

We know not whether the conflict will be bloody or unbloody; we know not how far distant in the future lies that battlefield; there is only one thing we do know, and that is, the one thing which will right the world is the one thing which the world today believes to be wrong—the Risen Christ and His Church!

GOD
AND
WAR

✠

(1942)

8

The Things of God in Wartime

In the face of the accumulating disasters in the world today the flight of refugees, the bombing of open cities, the suffering of the innocent, the spectacle of humanity preying upon itself—the modern mind asks the question: Why does God permit this war? The repeated onslaught against goodness and justice are a scandal to men; they cannot understand why God allows these things.

This question is more often asked by unbelievers than by believers. Those who know God, love Him, and trust Him, are less apt to be troubled by evil, war, and a cross, than those whose thinking and loving is geared to the world.

Our Divine Lord told Peter that much when after saying that He must go up to Jerusalem and be put to death and on the third day rise again, Peter took the Savior aside and rebuked Him with some anger: "Lord, be it far from thee, this shall not be unto thee" (Matt. 16:22).

Peter started with exactly the same assumption some do when they consider either war or suffering in relation to God; Peter assumed the Cross was a total loss, incompatible with Divine Power, and disruptive of God's purposes.

But our Lord, turning His back on Peter, said to him whom a moment before He had called the Rock: "Go behind me, Satan, thou art a scandal unto me: because thou savourest the things that are of God, but the things that are of men" (Matt. 16:23).

Notice our Divine Lord set in contrast "things that are of God" and "things that are of men." The "things that are of God" imply a cross as a prelude to glory. The "things that are of men" on the contrary, seek to avoid the cross, to escape the law of sacrifice, or, in the language of the modern psychologists, they seek to be "self-expressive" —which in less euphemistic language means "selfishness." That to our Divine Lord is "scandalous."

In approaching therefore the problem of disaster in any form, there are only two possible points of view: Peter's view, that the Cross is a loss, and the Savior's view, that the Cross leads to salvation.

All who take Peter's point of view look only to the present, which is necessarily self-centered. Many there are who take that point of view today.

All who take the Savior's point of view, however, look not only to the present, but to the past and the future: to the past, because the burden of the world's sin goes to make up our present woe, to the future because by cooperating with God's purposes through sacrifice and prayer we can redeem ourselves from present and momentary defeat and by a cross enter into the blazing triumph of a New Easter and a better world.

When our Lord made the distinction between those who "mind the things of God" and those who "mind the things of men" He implied that it would be the unbelievers rather than the believers in God who would be troubled by a cross, either in the form of a crucifixion, or a persecution and a war.

This is contrary to our modern way of thinking. Today the unbelievers think that the war creates an insoluble difficulty for believers. Our Lord implied just the contrary.

Who is right? Our Lord or the modern mind? Let us try to understand each. The modern mind says that war and evil make God unintelligible. To some extent they are right, for the Christian starts with the simple proposition that God is justice and love.

But once these affirmations are made, the problem of evil is intensified, for if God is just, why is there injustice; if God is love, why is there hate and war? These are legitimate questions and they do throw a difficulty on one who "minds the things of God."

The unbeliever, the materialist, the sceptic, the sophomore who still feeds on the husks of Darwin, Marx, and James never has to answer these questions; for if the world is only a machine, why should it not occasionally get out of order? If there is no purpose in living, then why should life not be meaningless? If we are descended from beasts why not act like beasts?

Since there is no goodness at the root of the universe, no Sun of Justice from which the rays of human rights descend, then there is no reason why these dark and awful cataclysms should not happen.

Given no Providence, why should life not be a mockery, and pessimism our lot? The existence of evil is therefore no mystery to the unbeliever, it is a "natural."

But despite all this, our Lord still suggests that the unbeliever has the greater problem, and He is right. For although the materialist does escape the problem of evil, he runs into an insuperable difficulty which does not exist for the one who "minds the things of God," namely the problem of good.

It is not easy for us to explain why God permits evil, but it is impossible for the unbeliever to explain why good exists; he cannot tell us why a material, soulless, godless, crossless universe should be the center of self-sacrifice, purity, love, faith, a Cross, martyrdom, and a willingness to die rather than offend God.

John Galsworthy expressed this idea in his *Maid in Waiting*. The girl, Dinny, is talking to her mother, Lady Cherwell:

"I suppose there is an eternal Plan," she says, "but we're like gnats for all the care it has for us as individuals."

"Don't encourage such feelings, Dinny," says her mother, "they affect one's character."

"I don't see," replies the daughter, "the connection between beliefs and character. I'm not going to behave any worse because I cease to believe in Providence or an after life.... No; I'm going to behave BETTER; if I'm decent it's because decency is the decent thing; and not because I'm going to get anything by it."

Whereupon the mother asks: "But why is decency the decent thing, Dinny, if there's no God?"[17]

---

[17] John Galsworthy, *Maid in* Waiting (Sydney, Australia: ReadHowYouWant, 2008), 315–316.

That is the ultimate problem. Why out of an unspiritual universe should spiritual lives emerge? If there is no Beauty behind the universe, whence the rose; if there is no Justice behind the universe, then whence comes our war for justice; if there is no distinction between good and evil, then how can our enemies be evil?

The unbeliever is confronted with more baffling difficulties by a war than the believer, for he cannot explain why all those things which should have brought happiness, brought disaster.

If he asks, "Where is your God now?" the believer may retort: "Where are your gods now? Where is your god Progress in the face of two world wars within twenty-one years? Where is your god Science, now that it consecrates its energics to destruction? Where is your god Evolution now that the world is turned backward into one vast slaughterhouse?"

The man of faith can explain this chaos. He knows that science, art, religion, politics, economics, divorced from God their final end, turn against us and destroy us, just as if we diverted gasoline from its rational purpose and used it as a beverage, it would end in our destruction.

In the language of Scripture: "Where are their gods, in whom they trusted?... Let them arise and help you" (Deut. 32:37–38).

Furthermore, the unbeliever cannot explain the growth of evil in the world. The believer can. On what does evil feed? It feeds only on the good. Evil has no capital of its own. It feeds on the capital of God. How could the militant atheism of Communism exist if there were no God? How could the swastika exist if there were no Cross? How could scepticism exist if there were no faith? How could Fascism exist if there were no human rights to deny? On what does persecution thrive except on faith?

You can explain evil only by the absence of good, as you can explain darkness only as the absence of light.

And that is why the unbeliever, in time of crisis and war, mouths slogans and busies himself about many things, but never settles down to the one supreme business of war: To overcome evil by good, and to drive out the devils by the finger of God.

Because I believe in God I can understand why there should be a war. Since God is love, should He not make man in such a way that by want of love pain should arise, just as through want of sun the flower should die? Evil is but a lack of love, and can be conquered only by love.

As the sun's rays pierce the cold not to warm the cold—for the cold is but the negation of heat—but to cause the sluggish air to vibrate, so can love thrill the stagnant evil with its vital force of sacrifice unto new love.

Because I believe in Christ the Son of God, I can better understand war, for why should not men hate God now, as they did when they nailed Him to a tree?

Why should not the Divine Savior who once in His human nature chose Good Friday, choose it now again in all those who are incorporated under His headship?

True, He can never suffer again in the human nature He took from Mary, and which is now at the right hand of the Father; but He can suffer again in other human natures, in His Mystical Body, which is the Church.

Cannot He, who once set His face to Jerusalem, now set it toward Berlin, or Moscow, or Warsaw, or anywhere where Truth is crucified? Do not the Cross and the Passion need to be actualized in each new age?

Is Calvary only an historical event which happened once and will never happen again; or is it a law, which operates whenever evil becomes concentrated in persecution and injustice, that goodness might sacrifice itself as a true soldier, in order that the world perish not?

If He, who valued life more than anyone ever valued life—for He was the source of life—did not think death too great a price to pay to defeat evil, shall there not be those in each generation who, through climbing the same Golgotha, will surrender their lives in Him that the evil of their day that makes war, may be conquered again.

He made us "other Christs"; we believe that, as Christians. Then why shall not His Passion be a single unbroken act in which each of us, through our cross, prove our right to Christhood?

The war, then, need not be for us a reason for denying God, any more than the Cross was a reason for Peter denying Christ.

If the Cross was to a Savior a proof that there was something wrong in man that had to be righted by His sacrificial death, why should not the war be to us a proof that there is something wrong in the world that can be righted only by our sacrificial lives?

Shall we blame God when we give ourselves a headache by violating His physical law by over-drinking? Shall we blame Him when the world generates a war out of its bosom by the violation of His moral law?

Very frankly it means nothing to say that Fascism, Nazism, and Communism, Capitalism, racism, and militarism, caused this war. These things do not exist except in persons, and they exist only in persons who sin.

If therefore it was sin that gave Christ His Cross and sin that gave us the war, should we not take a more humble attitude, and strike our breasts to the extent that we are guilty, saying *mea culpa*—"through my fault"?

Should we not see ourselves as bearing part of the burden of the world's sin, and through penance and the Cross begin the world's redemption?

We are not going to win the war by calling our enemies "devils," for our Divine Lord warned us not to rejoice that the devils were subject to us, but that our names were written in the Kingdom of Heaven (see Luke 10:20).

How shall this be done except by a rededication of ourselves to God, not as individuals but as a mass, a people, a nation?

After this war we want something we did not get in the last war.

We want not victory alone—we had that in 1918; we want not merely the defeat of Germany and its feuhrer—we had that in 1918; we want not a revengeful treaty of peace—we had that in 1918; we want not merely to make the world safe for democracy—we had that in 1918; we want not simply the crushing of barbarism—we had that in 1918.

This time we want something that was left out of victory, left out of Versailles; left out of the so called peace, namely, the restoration to the world of a justice based on the morality of God.

And how shall we get it back? Only by those of us who believe in God, in prayer, in sacrifice, in the Cross and the commandments, creating a public opinion so strong that politicians, economists, generals, and diplomats cannot ignore it.

It gets down to something as simple as this: there can be only one guarantee that the peace following this war will be different, and that is to ground it on God's moral order.

We must influence the world, and the only effective way to do it is to "mind the things of God."

It will do no good to make your demands for moral regeneration felt by wiring your congressmen, nor by holding parades, nor by signing petitions.

We must do it in the way of the French convict, whose innocence was discovered after his death and twenty-three years of penal servitude, and on whose tomb was inscribed: "He has gone to find justice with God." Justice with God, nowhere else.

If we could present to the United States the spectacle of ten or fifteen million Catholics daily uniting their sacrifice for country with the sacrifice of Our Savior on the Cross, America would begin to say of us: "They have gone to seek justice with God."

That is our plan! If enough do it to create a mass opinion, we shall have victory and peace with justice; if not, we shall have another war.

9

Spectators and Actors
in the Drama of the Cross

Why does God permit this war? In this chapter we penetrate a little deeper into the mystery by showing that this question is generally asked by the spectators, not by the actors, in the drama of suffering.

It is the sufferers who manifest the greatest faith; it is the spectators who are the sceptics. No one knows this better than a priest. As we go about administering the consolation of the sacraments which our Divine Lord provided for the suffering and the dying, we are but rarely asked: "Why does God do this to me?"

On the contrary, we find most often a positively joyful submission to the Divine Will, the sufferers saying: "Whatever the good Lord sends me I accept"; or, "Well this suffering gives me an opportunity to do penance for my sins"; or, "This will shorten my Purgatory"; or, "What I suffer is nothing compared to what Jesus suffered on the Cross for me."

But as we priests leave the beds of the faithful who bear the marks of the Cross on their bodies, and go out among those whose lives are comfortable, and who never pray, who are cross because the morning paper has not arrived for breakfast, and who think that a B.A. degree gave them a mind greater than the Almighty—there we are asked: "Why does God allow war and suffering and evil?"

It is generally those who have never had a struggle in life, who never disciplined themselves, who bombard Heaven with their petulant accusations and shout to God their resentful: Why? Why? Why?

On the stage of Calvary a great Actor enacted a role in the world's greatest tragedy, and after bearing the brunt of the world's evil, pronounced with strong voice and clear mind the great last line: "Father, into thy hands I commend my spirit" (Luke 23:46).

But beneath that stage, the spectators queried: "He trusted in God: let him now deliver him if he will have him" (Matt. 27:43).

Why is it that the actors in the drama of tragedy are less puzzled by its cross than the spectators? Three reasons come to mind: because suffering reveals love; because it initiates us into the mystery of life; and because it destroys false values.

An actor in the drama of suffering is better able to understand love than a spectator. What passes for love today is frequently nothing but selfishness. Moderns think of love in terms of having, owning, and possessing, for the pleasure it will give them.

That is not love—that is sin; that is "sex"; that is selfishness.

One of the reasons so many marriages are shipwrecked today is because the parties, thinking of love in terms of the pleasure each receives, feel that if the other no longer gives pleasure, therefore there is no love. As a result there develops in each a loathing for the other, as if the other cheated in not giving all that was desired.

Love of this kind is in the animal part of us, not in the will where love really resides. It is love without responsibility; and love without responsibility is selfishness and hate.

The truth is that we could never understand love if sacrifice were impossible. Because love means not to have but to be had, not to own but to be owned, not to possess but to be possessed; it implies sacrifice, surrender, and otherness.

All love is an act of choice: we choose this thing in preference to that, or this person in preference to that person.

Love is not just an affirmation, but a negation; it implies sacrifice—a surrender of our will, of our selfish interests, for the good of the other. It looks not to the lover's pleasure, but to the happiness of the beloved.

Love is wicked self-centeredness if there is no willingness to make a sacrifice for the one loved.

Our highest joys in life consist in feeling that another's good is purchased by us, and that our labor and our pain is the instrument through which our love is confessed.

All love craves a cross; it measures its love not by the wine it drinks, but by the wine it serves; its greatest jealousy is to be outdone by the cherished rival in the least advantage of self-giving.

And because love is necessarily self-giving and sacrificial, from all eternity God gives Himself in the eternal act of generating His Divine Son, and in time that Divine Son becomes man and gives His life on a Cross for man whom He loves; and the Holy Spirit who proceeds from Father and Son gives Himself in charity to our hearts that we might be adopted sons of God; and finally we give ourselves to Him who as the Perfect Love becomes the secret of our eternal happiness.

The love of God in Christ was revealed by His becoming the Man of Sorrows, for if He did not take a Cross upon Himself as a proof that He loved us unto death, then the mother who suffers for her children, the soldier who dies for his country, would have shown a greater earthly mani-festation of love than the Son of God Himself!

It is from the "Lamb slain from the beginning of the world," and but temporalized on Calvary, that the world derives its inspiration for sacrifice.

Since sacrifice is essential for love, does it not follow that the actors in the drama of suffering are better prepared to understand it?

I say sacrifice, not mere pain or suffering for no one is better because of pain. The difference between pain and sacrifice is love. Suffering without love is pain—sacrifice is suffering with love.

Pain and suffering are from sin and selfishness, but sacrifice is not; it is from love. It is through want of love that pain arises. Suffering brings one to the door of the temple; but love is the key that unlocks the door, and by transmut-ing pain into sacrifice prepares for the happiness of the everlasting dwellings.

Those who have themselves never felt hunger involuntarily through poverty, or voluntarily through fasting, can little understand the legitimate demands of the poor, or the obligation to feed them in charity.

In like manner, those who never have experienced suffering, which can be a condition of love, cannot understand how Christian souls resign themselves to Someone who first loved us.

The actors in the drama of suffering understand it better than the spectators, because suffering initiates us into the great mysteries of life.

The spectators only see half the game; they need announcers to explain the plays. The players know the secrets, where they are going and why.

Consider St. Peter, for example. He slept in the Garden. This may have been excusable, for up to that point he was only a spectator. He was not yet introduced to the full mystery of the Cross. But he understood the mystery when he himself became an actor in the drama of the Cross.

There is an old legend to the effect that Peter followed the advice of some friends and fled from the terrors of persecution then going on in Rome. A short distance outside the city on the Appian Way, he meets the Risen and Glorified Savior bearing the scars of His Passion. Peter asks: "Quo Vadis Domine," "Where art Thou going, O Lord?" And the Savior answers: "I am going back again to Rome to be recrucified."

That was enough for Peter. He saw that his own refusal to love the Savior as the Savior loved him was nailing the Lord again to the Cross.

Back again to Rome he went, and when his hour came to witness to his faith, he, deeming it unworthy to die as the Savior died, asked his executioners to crucify him upside down! And to this day we who venerate his remains in the great Basilica of St. Peter, which stands on the spot where he was crucified—the silent witness of his 261 successors—read with deep affection the letter he left to us:

"But if also you suffer any thing for justice' sake, blessed are ye.... It is better doing well (if such be the will of God) to suffer, than doing ill.... If you partake of the sufferings of Christ, rejoice" (1 Peter 3:14, 17; 4:13).

Suffering revealed to Peter the deep mysteries of eternal life, as it does to millions of others. Like fire, it burns away the dross that the fine gold might be ours.

The log in the forest was once only a spectator of the sun's fire; but brought from the forest into the hearth, it becomes now an actor, and returns fire with fire, and sings as it is consumed.

The only recorded time our Divine Lord ever sang was the night He went out to His death.

So with us our nature is larger than we know, our destiny higher than we know; that is why our higher destinies are best achieved when our lower ends are set at naught.

The silver in the bowels of the earth has a higher destiny than it knows; but only the miners' drill which blasts it from its dark dwelling can assign it to a higher purpose with men.

Plants have a higher destiny than they know; they must therefore be dug up from their roots, and ground between the jaws of death, before they can live in the animal.

Animals have a higher destiny than they know; and only a sacrificial knife can usher them into that higher goal of ministering to the life of man.

Man too has a higher destiny than he knows; but unlike all things below him, he attains it not by self-extinction but by a surrender of the baser part of him, that he may perfect that higher faculty which makes him really a man, a child of God, and an heir of the Kingdom of Heaven.

The tragedy of life is that when the best is before us, we should choose the less—as Adam chose the fruit in preference to the garden, and the prodigal the husks in preference to the bread. The mystery of life comes only to the actors in the drama:

I walked a mile with Pleasure;
She chattered all the way,
But left me none the wiser
For all she had to say.

I walked a mile with Sorrow,
And ne'er a word said she;
But oh, the things I learned from her
When Sorrow walked with me.[18]

Finally, suffering often removes a false sense of values. It makes this problem acute: Are we going forward according to the will of God and

---

[18] Robert Browning Hamilton, "Along the Road."

every law written in our nature, or are we going to stand alone saving our miserable selfish lives, and in the end lose them?

In great moments of tragedy, sorrow, and pain, we are often given sudden intuitive visions of the utter hollowness and emptiness of life apart from God.

Suffering always begets in us a longing for security; that is why, when the staff of the material upon which we lean pierces our hands, we toss it away and look for a new staff upon which to lean.

So long as husks satisfy, we are not likely to yearn for bread; but once they make hungry where most they satisfy, we seek for new food, new hopes, and new securities.

That is why this war, which manifests the utter stupidity of most modern philosophies of life, and which will empty the barns of those who thought only of filling them, will force souls to seek another security, another hope.

Perhaps men will act now as they did when they were children. Many a child, when reprimanded or punished or denied a wish, will turn away from his present discontent, back to something which once gave him pleasure even though it was only a broken toy.

So too, now that the baubles of a godless world have broken, grown children will seek happiness by turning back to something which gave them happiness in their youth in a moment of sorrow—maybe a prayer they learned at their mother's knee.

Coventry Patmore tells us in a poem how a little boy in sorrow found consolation in clasping bluebells and pennies; so may we draw the moral that, in our present sorrow, it might be well for us to clasp the God whom we have so long forgotten.

> My little Son who look'd from thoughtful eyes
> And moved and spoke in quiet grown-up wise,
> Having my law the seventh time disobey'd
> I struck him, and dismiss'd
> With hard words and unkiss'd,
> His Mother, who was patient, being dead.
> Then fearing lest his grief should hinder sleep,
> I visited his bed,

But found him slumbering deep,
With darken'd eyelids, and their lashes yet
From his late sobbing wet.
And I, with moan,
Kissing away his tears, left others of my own;
For, on a table drawn beside his head,
He had put, within his reach,
A box of counters and a red-vein'd stone,
A piece of glass abraded by the beach,
And six or seven shells,
A bottle with bluebells,
And two French copper coins, ranged there with careful art,
To comfort his sad heart.[19]

Perhaps too, in the present sorrow of this war, we as a nation will go back to the God we have forgotten and disobeyed, as He in His goodness consoles us as a Father.

The fundamental difference between the spectator and the actor is that for the spectator, man is an ultimate, for the actor, God is the ultimate; and the spectator is a spectator because he minds the things of man, the actor is an actor because he minds the things of God.

This accounts for these totally different approaches to the problem of pain and suffering: the humanitarian spectator wants to alleviate suffering; he will contribute to hospitals, and he will endow universities—but without ever bothering to inquire whether they teach truth or error.

He believes that a day will come when science will do away with men's ills, and that when education is truly universal there will be no more wars.

His responsibility ends by doing something, whether it be giving an ambulance or securing a job for an indigent foreign revolutionary.

If he fails to alleviate suffering, he never worries, for he feels that he has done all that he could; his responsibilities end with his gift. Where he cannot heal, he ignores; whom he cannot relieve, he passes by.

[19] Conventry Patmore, "The Toys."

But the actor in the drama of Calvary, on the contrary, begins precisely where the humanitarian leaves off.

He does all the things the humanitarian does, but is very careful when he gives money that it will not be used to destroy life in a hospital, even scientifically, nor ever used to spread error and immorality in schools, however disguised under the cloak of academic freedom.

But he goes beyond this. He seeks to take on the sorrow of his neighbor and to fulfill the injunction of Paul: "Bear ye one another's burdens" (Gal. 6:2).

The spectator, seeing Christ carrying His Cross to Calvary, would organize a civil liberties league and present a protest to Pilate signed by four hundred professional signers and then publicize it in the newspapers. But the actor, meeting Christ on the road, would help carry His Cross as Simon did.

The spectator might ask the Savior to lay down His Cross; but the actor will take it up.

The difference between the two is the difference between alleviating and redeeming, between doing all you can, and sharing all you are, for another. The spectator regards trials and sufferings as a problem; the actor regards them as a challenge.

The government is complaining that the people of the United States are too complacent about this war. What is the root of complacency?

It is assuming that we are spectators of the war, rather than actors in it.

If there be national complacency, it is due to a backwash of spiritual complacency.

Peter, James, and John slept in the Garden of Gethsemane, because they were unmindful of the awfulness of the Savior's hour. Worry keeps us awake. Therefore these men did not worry. They were blind to the reality of evil at the gates.

And if we be indifferent to danger, may it not be due to the fact that our secular schools for over two generations have been teaching that there is no difference between good and evil; it all depends on your point of view.

Well, if there be no evil, how shall we be aroused to its existence; if there be no goodness how shall we become fired for its defense; if there be no sin and guilt, whence shall come our moral indignation?

Now that a war is upon us, we must begin to realize that we are not spectators of reality, but actors. As we plunge into the sacrifice, blood, sweat, and toil of war, we must be stirred to a sense of corporate responsibility to our fellow men and the world.

Prayer and adoration must awaken our national conscience, for the whole world is in a mess because of sin—and the sin of all of us, in varying degrees: the sin of forgetting God and His Divine Son.

Since sin is a common debt, let none of us ask to be exempt from that burden. Each holy hour must be made, not for our particular intention, but to pay off some debt of the world's sin and to restore the world once again to the reign of God's moral law and the kingship of His Divine Son.

The ledger of the world reveals a tremendous moral debt. Each time we make an hour we scratch off some of that debt, we draw the world farther away from hate and closer to the mercy of God.

We thus become actors in the drama of restoring the world to sanity, for presently it has gone mad! The whole world is in the state of mortal sin! It needs redemption.

This holy hour is not alone to atone for these sins, it is also to assure the future. It has no political significance; it appeals only to Jews, Protestants, and Catholics who believe they are more than beasts that eat, drink, and die; it will not appeal to weaklings, but only to heroes.

It has no economic or political plans because it seeks not to create a good society; but it does seek to create the creators of a good society.

America is not yet conscious of the necessity of sacrifice and a cross. We are flying from it as Peter did—unable to understand how sacrifice, as conditioned by love, brings life and restores a true sense of values.

And the Lord is meeting America on the roadway of life, asking us the question Peter asked: "Quo Vadis, America"—"Where are you going America?" That's it! Where are we going?

Are we going to the Cross as spectators or as actors? What is your answer? As the majority in America answer so shall be the future of America.

10

The Divine Cost of Stopping This War

In this chapter, we enter into the very heart of the question: "Why does God not stop the war?" The answer is to be found in another question, namely: "What would be the divine cost of stopping this war?" The answer is, God would have to destroy human freedom.

This needs some explanation. Let us begin with this fact: that this is not the only kind of world God could have made. He could have made a world without freedom.

He could have so fashioned us that we would have been good with the same necessity with which the sun rises in the east and sets in the west. We might all have been saintly with the same necessity, with which the lily is white, or fire is hot, or ice is cold.

But God willed not to make a mechanical universe, peopled by automata; rather did He choose to communicate to us something of Himself, namely His Freedom—not in the same degree of perfection, of course, but enough of it to say a no which would give charm to a yes, when we freely chose to say it.

In other words, God chose to make a moral universe, where characters would emerge by the right use of freedom—a universe where there would be patriots because men might be traitors; a universe like a nation, like a battlefield, where there would be heroes because men might be cowards; a universe like the Church, where there would be saints because men might also be devils.

There is no epic for the certainties of life and no lyric without the suspense of sorrow and the sigh of fear; no watchful love hovers over the invulnerable, nor crown of merit rests suspended over those who do not fight.

Take this quality of freedom away from man and there would be no more reason to honor the fortitude of martyrs and soldiers than to honor the flames or the bullets which sent them to their death.

God willed to make a moral universe of praise and blame, but this could be done only by making men captains and masters of their own fate and destiny.

There is one word which sums up God's plan in making the universe, and that is *love*. God made each heart capable of love. But love implies a choice.

A heart that loves must be a heart to give or to keep. Because, therefore, God willed to make us, so we could love Him in this world, He had to make us free; but if He made us free to love, He had to make it possible for us to be free to hate.

The universe thus became populated with free wills, little gods, each armed with a reflection of God's freedom.

That some of these little gods would will wrongly was inevitable, for they had not God's Wisdom; that some of them would be rebellious was inevitable, for, being free, they could make a false declaration of independence and become like little foolish rays of the sun attempting to make themselves independent of the sun.

The fact that we come from God would not necessarily dispense us from the evil effects of such rebellion, any more than because a child is the son of a king he is immune from drowning if he disobeys and goes into the whirlpool.

God gave us the power to rebel that there might be meaning and honor in our allegiance when we freely choose to give it.

God pledged Himself, after giving us that freedom, never to destroy it, regardless of how many petulant souls would shriek against Him: "Why does God not stop the war?"

God could challenge us, overrule us, permit us to be visited by the consequences of our misdeeds—but He would never destroy that great gift of freedom.

Man could, if he so wanted, go on defying God for all time and eternity, subvert His moral law, blast the cosmos, and even break His Heart, but still God would not take away our freedom.

In this sense the decree of Creation to make man free was also the decree of Calvary, for a free man that could break His commandment could also crucify Him.

Not even then would God destroy human freedom; but in His goodness He would make man's misuse of freedom the *felix culpa*, the occasion of offering Himself as a holocaust of love, not to force men back to Him, for His hands and feet were nailed, but to entice them back by a revelation of love greater than which no man hath—that he lay down his life for a friend.

This brings us to the question: "Could God stop the war?"

Most certainly! But if God were ever to be untrue to Himself or to us, what would God have to do? He would have to destroy our freedom! That would be the divine cost of stopping this war.

We say we are fighting for freedom? Then why do we ask God to destroy freedom—and that is precisely what we demand in asking: "Why does God not stop the war?"

We say we are fighting to destroy dictators. Then why do we ask God to become a dictator? We say that dictators are wicked because they would destroy the last vestige of freedom on earth. Then why do we ask for a dictator in Heaven?

Shall we one moment rage against earthly dictators because they trample liberty underfoot, and in the next moment shriek for a dictator in the Heaven who will do the same thing?

Certainly, if we had to choose, it would be far better to live under earthly dictators for a few years than to have a dictator in Heaven who, by one blast of omnipotent power, would take away that quality in us that makes us the paragons of creation.

Fortunately, however, we have no choice in the matter. God will not destroy freedom; He will not be a dictator. And that is why God will not stop the war.

Where then should the blame of war be placed: On God's gift of freedom, or on our abuse of freedom?

Have we not been too proud to admit we might be sinful? When the world goes wrong, we blame it on systems, tyrannies, governments, unsound economics, or bad glands but never on our own will.

Would we know how much the modern world has abused freedom, then cast a glance at the two false theories of liberalism and Totalitarianism?

Liberalism defines freedom as the right to do whatever you please, and that is the way freedom is understood by 90 percent of young Americans educated in nonreligious institutions. If freedom means that, it means anarchy.

Freedom thus becomes a physical power, not a moral power; an absence of law instead of a respect for it; a right without a corresponding duty; a license without responsibility.

Totalitarianism on the other hand defines freedom as a duty to do what you must. If freedom means that, it means tyranny.

Freedom thus becomes a duty without a right, and comes into being only when the individual will identifies itself with the will of the dictator.

Under this system there is no will but the class will or the national will or the race will. The person no longer exists.

Let loose false concepts of freedom like that in the world and you cannot stop war. The first abuse of freedom, which identifies it with absence of law or self-expression, creates war through conflicting egotisms; the second abuse of freedom, which identifies it with the will of the dictator, begets war through force and violence.

That is not the kind of freedom God gave us; that is the way we distorted it.

True freedom does not mean the right to do whatever you please, nor the duty to do whatever you must; but it means the right to do whatever you ought—and oughtness implies law, responsibility, purpose. In other words, freedom is inseparable from the God of Love who made us.

As the pendulum is most free to swing when it has a fixed point of suspension, so we are most free when we are rooted in the law and the Love of the God who made us. And that is what our Divine Lord meant when He said: "The truth shall make you free" (John 8:32).

Our Declaration of Independence affirms that liberty is an "unalienable" right, because a gift of the Creator. In other words, it makes us independent of tyrannies and dictators by making a Declaration of Dependence on God.

The real evil in the human situation, then, lies in man's unwillingness to recognize his finiteness, his creaturehood, or the possibility that there exists something greater than himself.

All pride, vanity, sensuality, cruelty, force, and licentiousness originate in man's denial that freedom is a gift, through which he seeks to give himself the appearance of unconditioned reality.

The sin of man is that he makes himself god, as St. Paul says:

> For the wrath of God is revealed from heaven against all ungodliness and injustice of those men that detain the truth of God in injustice: Because that which is known of God is manifest in them. For God hath manifested it unto them. For the invisible things of him, from the creation of the world, are clearly seen, bring understood by the things that are made; his eternal power also, and divinity: so that they are inexcusable. Because that, when they knew God, they have not glorified him as God, or given thanks; but became vain in their thoughts, and their foolish heart was darkened. (Rom. 1:18–21)

Sin is the abuse of freedom; that is why the modern man, who denied sin, found himself in a world of dictatorship.

Even the idea of Hell is bound up with freedom, because Hell means abuse of responsibility. Deny Hell and you deny responsibility; deny responsibility and you deny freedom.

We began this chapter with the question: "Why does God not stop the war?" Now the question is turned around: "Why do we not stop warring against God?"

This war is not of God's arbitrary making; it is the effect of our abuse of God's gift of freedom. We must therefore not expect God to suspend the operation of His laws to protect us from their consequences.

God will not suspend the law of gravitation to protect the life of a man who violates the "oughtness" of his free life by throwing himself off the Empire State Building. Neither will God suspend the operation of His moral law to immunize man from a war born of the abuse of freedom and the "de-christianization of individual and social life."

We have a war to win for the sake of peace with justice in the world. Apart from the economic, military, and political considerations, necessary for victory, there should be a moral quality underlying them all, namely, humility.

Let us not think of dictators as the creators of the world's woe; but rather as its creatures.

These dictators are like boils, superficial manifestations of an inner rottenness. They would never have come to the surface if there had not been the proper conditions in the world from which they came.

It would therefore be a fatal mistake to think that if we got rid of them, the world would be lovely and rosy. In the last world war we made that very mistake.

We assumed that if we could get rid of the kaiser, the world would once more live in peace and prosperity. Well, we defeated the kaiser: but we have another world war in twenty-one years.

We removed the boil, but we kept the infected bad blood; we rid ourselves of the symbol of the world's wrong, but we did nothing to correct the wrong.

What assurance have we now that if we defeat these wicked dictators, the world will pursue justice and righteousness? Unless we cut down the evil tree that begets this evil fruit, we shall have to go on having more wars.

To change the figure, it will do no good to treat the world for fox-bite if, like the Spartan youth, it is going to carry a fox in its blouse.

This war is really only an episode in the working out of a great truth; it is not the great truth that is an episode of the war. And that truth is that this war is not a sign that men are with God, but a sign that they have been against Him.

What I am trying to say is, God did not start this war and God will not stop it apart from our free cooperation with His law, which is the perfection of our freedom.

Let us stop thinking of our woes and sorrows and wars as having been thrust upon us by systems and dictators, but rather as being the effects of the evil rebellion against God.

When the world is crashing down on our heads it is no time to say that the major frustrations of life are economic or political, or that if there were another system of economics or another system of government all would be well. It is not the systems of the world that have gone crazy, but the hearts.

Economics and politics upset the world because evil and selfishness and godlessness first upset the hearts of economists and dictators.

To assure ourselves that the major ills of our times are not economic, we need but inquire into who are the disillusioned people of the modern world. They are those who possess, who have power, who are selfish and satiated, who need blaring orchestras without melodies to drown their self-consciousness.

There is a thousand times more disenchantment among the intelligentsia than among the proletariat. Something else is wrong, then, besides the economics: our souls have lost God.

From a Christian point of view, there has been a forgetfulness and an outlawry of God's Divine Son from the hearts of men and the society of nations.

As in the days of His physical life, He did not bring a Cross into this world, but found it here, made by the sin and evil of men; so in these days of His mystical presence on earth in His Church, He finds another cross, made from the distortion of His gift of freedom: our wills set against His. No wonder the Cross is a contradiction of one bar with another.

We should enter into a national act of reparation and prayer humbly, as our Lord entered the Garden of Gethsemane. Innocent though He was, He took upon Himself the sins of the world, as if that burden were His own; in the strong language of Scripture was "made sin" (2 Cor. 5:21).

So should we enter this war, not regarding ourselves as innocent victims of others sins for we are all sinners—but as transgressors assuming part of the blame for the sins of the world.

If there is anyone who thinks he is good, let him realize that he lives in an evil world and therefore must redeem it; if, however, we feel ourselves as guilty, because we abused God's freedom, then we have need of making atonement for ourselves.

In either case, we are under God's purposes, humbly submitting ourselves to His Will either to repair the broken fences of our neighbors, or to replant our own wrecked vineyards.

Like unto the Master in the Garden, we will never admit we are under a violence imposed by men, but under the sweet compulsion of furthering the cause of God.

In our hearts, we will feel less that we are suffering from man's injustices than from a free cooperation with God's justice for the redemption of the world.

When evil men came with swords and clubs to apprehend Him in the Garden, He might have said: "This is your hour and power of darkness—your hour of darkness. All you can do with it is to turn out the light, to spread darkness over the world. Evil has its hour."

Evil has its hour now and we are in darkness. No wonder the Savior, when that hour was up, went to His apostles and said: "Couldst thou not watch one hour?" (Mark 14:37). In other words, we must meet the hour of darkness with the hour of watching!

11

Trust in God's Plan

The mere fact that we ask the question: "Why does God permit this war?" is in itself an indication of want of trust in either the wisdom or the goodness of God.

How to explain this want of trust? Generally, it is due to a refusal to admit: first, the possibility that God knows more than I and is better than I; and secondly, that my dignity is not lowered by submitting to His wisdom and His goodness even when they go against me.

Though the great mass of people who ignore God never state their religious perplexities in these simple terms, they are nevertheless the basic reasons why God is exiled from human hearts, from the family, and from our national life.

Pride is at the root of it all: a pride of intellect and pride of will which makes man frame a universe of which a lie, and not God, is the center. Pride has its roots in a false declaration of independence, namely a refusal to recognize that man is not the author of his own existence.

The ultimate manifestation of pride is self-deification: setting oneself up as God. That is why the intellectually proud man will attempt to convince you of his omniscience; he steals the mantle of God's wisdom and drapes it about his own shoulders.

His favorite trick in conversation is to make you think he knows everything.

The result is that today we have information, but not wisdom. Information is uncorrelated bits of knowledge which, like a broken egg, can never be composed into a complete philosophy of life. Wisdom, on the contrary, is a knowledge of truth, human and divine.

Information and quiz programs have indoctrinated us into believing that the man who knows the colors of the three beards mentioned in Hamlet is wise; or who can tell what four novelists of the Victorian era wrote about oysters on the half-shell, is wise; and that if we do not know similar patches of information, we ought to dissolve into an emotional crumble.

True wisdom, on the contrary, correlates information into causes, and equips itself to answer such basic questions as: "What is the purpose of life?" "Why are we here and where are we going?"

A little child who knows the first page of his catechism, which sums up the wisdom of Aristotle and the best thinking of Western culture, knows more than all the university professors who define religion, including an Ohio professor who expresses his thought on this matter as "the projection into the roaring loom of time of a unified complex of psychical values"—whatever that means!

Our Divine Lord implied that much in inveighing against crazy quilt information, when if we may paraphrase His words, He said: "O Heavenly Father, I thank Thee that Thou hast hidden these things from the university professors and the experts and revealed them to the little ones" (see Matt. 11:25).

The salvation of modern man lies not in a pride of what he knows, but in a humility concerning how little he knows. His omniscience must give way to nescience; instead of feeling he knows everything, he must come closer to the truth that he really knows nothing.

His belief that he knows all must surrender to the humiliating truth that someone is wiser than he. For if man knows all, how can God teach him anything?

If there is no law above him, how can he ever do wrong? If the mind is filled with self how to fill it with Divine Wisdom? For not until we become humble can there be trust.

For an illustration of this, turn to the book of Job. "There was a man in the land of Hus, whose name was Job, and that man was simple and upright, and fearing God, and avoiding evil" (Job 1:1).

As the story is unfolded, Job was gradually divested of all the things that clothe the spirit of a man, those things on which a man leans for help and strength.

First he lost his wealth, then he lost his children, seven sons and three daughters; next, his health; then the love and consolation of his wife, who said to him: "Dost thou still continue in thy simplicity? bless God, and die." To which Job answered: "Thou hast spoken like one of the foolish women: if we have received good things at the hands of God, why should we not receive evil?" (Job 2:10).

We now see the naked spirit of the man. There were only two things that were left: God and himself. God, he never denied; himself he could not escape.

But between God and himself there seemed to be no place of meeting, no reconciliation, for here was a man who was suffering—but not because he had done wrong.

Like millions of innocents, through the ages, who have done no wrong and yet suffer, Job at first did not understand the ultimate meaning of the agony that gripped his heart.

His intellect was confronted with a problem too great for his little mind, as from his lips there came a string of whys.

"Why did I not die in the womb, why did I not perish when I came out of the belly? Why received upon the knees? why suckled at the breasts?" (Job 3:11–12). "Have I not dissembled? have I not kept silence? have I not been quiet? and indignation is come upon me" (Job 3:26). "Why is light given to him that is in misery, and life to them that are in bitterness of soul?" (Job 3:20).

Three comforters came to console Job. One of them, Eliphaz, attempted to account for the suffering of Job on the ground that it must be the result of personal sin; his theory was that it is only the wicked who suffer. "Is it a great matter that God should comfort thee? but thy wicked words hinder this" (Job 15:11).

Job protested his innocence, but Eliphaz insisted that Job must be guilty of many crimes, and promised him prosperity if he would repent. "If thou wilt return to the Almighty, thou shalt be built up, and shalt put away iniquity far from thy tabernacle" (Job 22:23).

Another of Job's comforters, Elihu by name, who talked like a university professor who never understood his philosophy well enough to tell it in simple language, began a long speech on the justice and power of God.

Never before in the history of the world was any speech cut short more abruptly, for it was not man but God who broke in on his intellectual droolings, and out of the whirlwind asked: "Who is this that wrappeth up sentences in unskillful words?" (Job 38:2).

How would we feel as we sat alongside the bed of a sick friend, offering him the consolation of our great wisdom, to have God cut short our consolation by driving us into nescience?

Now that God appears on the scene, should we not expect an answer to the questions Job asked?

Certainly if a Broadway dramatist were putting on this play, he would have God step onto the stage and solve all the problems of evil and answer all the questions of Job, or else ring up a cash register and give away a gold mine.

Everything in the universe would click; there would be no loose ends; we would know all when we left the theatre.

But the God of Heaven's way does not do things like the god of Broadway.

When the true God appeared on the stage, what did He do? Here was the Supreme Expert on the Supreme Quiz Program! Information please? And God was there to give it!

But lo and behold! Instead of answering the questions of Job He begins to ask Job questions; instead of giving information, He dispensed wisdom.

And this is how He began:

Gird up thy loins like a man: I will ask thee, and answer thou me.

Where wert thou when I laid the foundations of the earth? tell me if thou hast understanding. Who hath laid the measures thereof, if thou knowest? or who hath stretched the line upon it? Upon what are its bases grounded? or who laid the cornerstone thereof?...

Who shut up the sea with doors, when it broke forth as issuing out of the womb: When I made a cloud the garment thereof, and wrapped it in a mist as in swaddling bands?... Hast thou entered into the depths of the sea, and walked in the lowest parts of the deep?

Have the gates of death been opened to thee, and hast thou seen the darksome doors? Hast thou considered the breadth of the earth? tell me, if thou knowest all things? Where is the way where light dwelleth, and where is the place of darkness.... Didst thou know then that thou shouldst be born? and didst thou know the number of thy days?

Hast thou entered into the storehouses of the snow, or hast thou beheld the treasures of the hail?... Who is the father of rain? or who begot the drops of dew? Out of whose womb came the ice; and the frost from heaven who hath gendered it?...

Shalt thou be able to join together the shining stars the Pleiades, or canst thou stop the turning about of Arcturus? Canst thou bring forth the day star in its time, and make the evening star to rise upon the children of the earth? Dost thou know the order of heaven, and canst thou set down the reason thereof on the earth? Canst thou lift up thy voice to the clouds, that an abundance of waters may cover thee?...

Who hath put wisdom in the heart of man? or who gave the cock understanding?... Will the eagle mount up at thy command, and make her nest in high places?... Shall he that contendeth with God be so easily silenced? surely he that reproveth God, ought to answer him. (Job 38:3–6, 8–9, 16–19, 21–22, 28–29, 31–34, 36; 39:27, 32)

In that whole speech of God, no reference was made to the suffering of Job; no explanation was offered of anything that had transpired.

But God did one thing: He brought Job face-to-face with the universe in which he lived; asked him if he were equal to creating it, to governing it even to the fall of a sparrow, and made him see that he was a small part of a vast and mighty whole.

And when God finished asking Job questions, Job realized that the questions of God were more satisfying than the answers of men; that the true nescience into whose abyss he was driven was really the beginning of wisdom.

Job now saw that he had been asking only one question: How could his individual problem be solved? And God's answer was, that his question was but one of a million others, for he lived among men and things and until he could understand the answers to those million questions, he could never understand the answer to that one.

Job saw too that God's words contained the audacious indictment that he must take his eyes off himself, for he had been too self-absorbed; he must understand the limitations of his own knowledge; he must trust in God because God knows all and wills what is best for all and for each.

Where would trust be if we understood everything? Where would faith be if there were nowhere complexity? Where would love be, if there were no confidence? By driving Job back into nescience God laid the foundation of trust.

And in the light of that unveiling there came to Job a discovery of himself by comparison.

No more did he ask the why of suffering; he saw that he could still accept it and be sure of God; that he could believe in God's righteousness when everything God did seemed to be denying it; that evil fits into the divine good of the world; that even death can be God's servant carrying out God's mysterious ends and purposes, within the limits of the divine permission.

In the agony of war we too must realize that in the divine plan evil may be momentarily victorious, but in the total process it always loses.

Sin may win the booty but it loses the battle, as the devil lost the battle with Job and Job regained more than he lost.

The omnipotence of God does not mean that everything that happens is His Will; it means that nothing that happens can defeat His Will.

Being all-powerful He can allow evil its brief hour for a more ultimate good.

"Suffer both to grow until the harvest and in the time of the harvest I will say to the reapers: Gather up first the cockle, and bind it into bundles to burn, but the wheat gather ye into my barn" (Matt. 13:30).

God would not permit anything to happen that had the power of, and by itself, to separate us from Him.

And in the seeming chaos of war and disorder, God still attaches an eternal value to each individual soul.

"Are not two sparrows sold for a farthing? and not one of them shall fall on the ground without your Father. But the very hairs of your head are all numbered. Fear not therefore: better are you than many sparrows" (Matt. 10:29–31).

If the Kingdom of God not only got over the murder of Christ, but made it the great instrument of redemption, then there is nothing that it cannot get over, and nothing that it cannot turn into an eternal blessing to the glory of His Holy Name.

We do not always understand this plan, because, like Job, we may not understand how our own individual problems fit into it in a general way.

It is easy for us to fall into the error of thinking that the laws of the universe should be suspended or interrupted every time a good man gets in trouble.

If the business of religion was merely to get the religious out of trouble, religion would then cease to be religion; it would become a kind of gigantic insurance policy, which would be the end of religion for the simple reason that it would be faithless.

A mouse that crawls into a grand piano and has its gnawing of the keys disturbed by a great artist entertaining an audience with a Mozart or a Chopin, must in its own puny little brain think that the universe is without a plan.

The spider which weaves its web on the girder of a great steel beam that is lifted into a bridge cannot possibly understand how its own little plan for catching flies must give way to the engineer's greater plans for transportation.

So neither can our minds, given to selfishness and the pursuit of immediate interests, understand how the omnipotent all-wise God of the

Heavens works out all things to that which is best for our salvation, and the triumph of truth and goodness.

Tapestries are woven not from the front, but from the back, and it is only when the last thread is drawn that we see the completed design. As Fr. Tabb has put it:

My life is but a weaving
Between my God and me;
I may not choose the colors
He worketh steadily.

Full oft He chooses sorrow
And I, in foolish pride
Forget He sees the upper
And I, the under side.[20]

We must be patient and trust in God's plan. What makes it difficult is that we are always in a hurry; God is not. Our Divine Lord seems to suggest that the evil things are done in a hurry.

To betraying Judas He said: "That which thou dost, do quickly" (John 13:27); and of an impetuous man, He asked, "And which of you, by taking thought, can add to his stature one cubit?" (Luke 12:25).

Our precipitancy very likely may make us distort the fundamental issues involved. We are very apt to be like James and John on the occasion of our Savior's visit to the Samaritans, who rejected Him because His face was set toward the Cross.

These two brothers, whom our Lord called Boanerges, or Sons of Thunder, were impatient for revenge and asked that God send lightning to burn their villages.

It seemed fitting that the Sons of Thunder should ask for lightning. But our Lord said: "You know not of what spirit you are. The Son of man came not to destroy souls, but to save" (Luke 9:55–56).

---

[20] "The Weaver."

Such is the spirit of the Cross. The spirit that wants to call down fire upon those that are refusing Jesus Christ is the spirit of evil; it lacks the principle of the Cross.

James and John lacked patience; the Divine Savior was willing to suffer the insults of the Samaritans for a moment, in order that He might win their souls later on.

And His patience was rewarded, for one of the very first cities in which the gospel was preached was the city of the Samaritans. And it was from a Samaritan village that there came forth for the first time in the hearing of men the expression, "Savior of the world."

In the parable of the man who sowed a field of wheat and who had it spoiled by the enemy sowing weeds among the wheat, the servants of the householder came to him and said: "Sir, didst thou not sow good seed in thy field? whence then hath it cockle? He said to them: An enemy hath done this. And the servants said to him: Wilt thou that we go and gather it up? And he said: No, lest perhaps gathering up the cockle, you root up the wheat also together with it. Suffer both to grow until the harvest, and in the time of the harvest I will say to the reapers: Gather up first the cockle, and bind it into bundles to burn, but the wheat gather ye into my barn" (Matt. 13:27–30).

Many of us are like the servants, who would want the evil to be rooted up immediately. But the Savior is more patient.

Let both grow until the harvest. Let these two sowings work themselves out to the final manifestation, and then there will be a separation.

The harvest of the sons of the Kingdom will be a harvest of sunlight upon the world. The harvest of the sons of evil will be one of evil, of things which offend and defile, and His reapers will at last gather them up and cast them into the final burning.

What then shall be our attitude? Trust in God while abiding in His will!

Writing to the Thessalonians, St. Paul said: "And the Lord direct your hearts, in the charity of God, and the patience of Christ" (2 Thess. 3:5).

We live in the midst of evil days it is true, but it is not because God is not good; it is because we have not been good.

About one third of the civilized world crucified Him, and another third abandoned Him, and the other third while living good lives as individuals have not had enough influence to affect the political, economic, and moral life in which they lived.

This war, let us be sure about it, is not for "freedom" any more than the last war was for "democracy."

It is a gigantic struggle to decide whether in the next few centuries we shall live by the moral law rooted in God or in the law of force rooted in Satan.

Whether we know it or not, we are fighting for a moral order, not because we willed it in God, but because our enemies, thank God, have forced us into that position.

It may take some time before we realize the greatness of our cause—we may first have to lose much of what we have; but let it not be said that while unconsciously fighting for a morality rooted in God, we consciously abandoned trust in God who alone can save.

Guns and bullets alone will not win this war. We need them—certainly. But we need more a realization that some of our enemies have the devil on their side and man is no match for the devil.

That is why we will either return to God or we will perish. And by returning to God I mean: first, that we ground our law in the authority of God; second, that we make economics a branch of ethics; and third, that we base family life on the moral law.

This cannot be accomplished by legislative enactments, publicity campaigns, or radio appeals. Neither can it be done by retreating from the world's harsh conflicts into individual prayerful isolation.

It can be accomplished only by the prayerful-minded citizens of the United States realizing that they are signed with the social Sign of the Cross, and that when they pray, like our Divine Lord, they take humanity with them—even the humanity of their enemies.

We live in an age where indifference to God and the moral law on the part of economics and politics has led to an invasion of the soul by economics and politics. Such is the meaning of Totalitarianism.

How shall due order be restored except by a vast army of believers in God and His Divine Son creating a new public opinion with social implications of a revolutionary character, whereby we will render to God the things that are God's.

Lose not then your trust in God. Be humble. He has not failed; We have failed: This is the time of probation! Trust in God while abiding in His Will!

In the language of St. Paul: "And the Lord direct your hearts, in the charity of God, and the patience of Christ" (2 Thess. 3:5).

When you go to a mystery play, do you walk out in the first act, because one of the good characters is killed, or because evil is momentarily victorious? Do you judge the play by the first few lines?

If you believe the dramatist has a plot, why not give God credit for a plot?

Perhaps this war so far is only the first scene of the first act, as we witness the bitter fruits of our complacency and the onward march of our enemies.

We may have to sit through a few more acts before we become wise like the prodigal, or before we become humble.

Patience, then! "He that would have a cake out of wheat, must tarry the grinding." What wound ever healed, except by degrees? And our world is wounded.

Give up your faith in everything else if you must, in credit, mass production; wealth; but surrender not your faith in Him who alone can save:

> My soul, sit then a patient looker on,
> Judge not the play before the play is done,
> The plot hath many changes every day.
> Speak a new scene; the last act crowns a play.[21]

---

[21] Francis Quarles, "Respice Finem."

12

Faith in Wartime

In all crises and in particular in time of war we must not worry about getting God on our side; we must worry about getting on God's side.

Before this war began some so-called leaders who lived by Christianity instead of for it, spent their time adjusting Christianity to the way people lived, rather than adjusting the way they lived to Christianity.

When divorce became common they dropped the words of our Lord, "What therefore God hath joined together, let no man put asunder" (Matt. 19:6). When sin abounded, they called sin a myth and Hell an illusion.

The modern mind thus became accustomed to adjust creed to life rather than life to creed. If medicine followed similar tactics and accommodated itself to disease, because it is common, society long ago would have been prostrate.

We must be careful not to transplant that false peacetime mentality to wartimes.

Just as in times of peace some men thought it was the business of God and Christianity to make the world comfortable—whether or not men were doing the will of God—so now, when war comes, these same individuals assume that Christianity exists either to buttress up an order that has outlawed Christ from individual and social life, or else to validate our national slogans.

God, then, is judged to be good, if He does our will; He is judged to be weak and cruel if He refuses to do it.

If religion is to bring any consolation in time of war, we must talk less about whether God is on our side, and more about whether we are on God's side.

When a husband and wife are quarreling, the true problem is not how to fit their selfishness into the Sermon on the Mount, but rather how to fit the Sermon on the Mount into their quarrel.

The clay does not mould the potter, but the potter the clay. In like manner, we are not to attempt to fit Christianity into this war, but to fit this war into Christianity.

Patriotism is a part of religion but religion is not a part of patriotism. Caesar is under God, but God is not under Caesar.

To love God is necessarily to love one's country, but to love one's country is not necessarily to love God.

Goodness is in the will, not in slogans; in persons, not in processes; in souls, not in catchwords.

The idea that God can be used for any purpose, is magic; it is not religion. The modern attempt of some to make Christianity fit this war in its entirety is really the renewal of the Crucifixion, where men attempted to make the Son of God fit something else they had made: the Cross.

As then they patterned the Son of God to a Cross, so now they would pattern Him to a war. To nail the Son of God to our ideologies and ways of thinking is the greatest tragedy of the world. For if God is not above our righteousness, but is identical with it, then why bother with God at all?

If God hates those whom we hate, then who shall forgive them their sins, and how shall we be pardoned our hate? What I am trying to say in a clumsy way, is what Isaias said so clearly in one line: "For my thoughts are not your thoughts: nor your ways my ways, saith the Lord" (Isa. 55:8).

Why, it may be asked, should we be less interested in getting God on our side, and more interested in getting on God's side? Because that is the only way really to insure victory.

But why is identification with God's will the path to victory? Because God's purposes are always preserved from defeat by the very nature of things.

Good is self-conserving; evil is self-defeating. Evil is unstable, because it is contrary to the nature of things.

Excessive eating, excessive drinking, or excessive exercise is contrary to the nature of the body and in the end injures it. Obedience to the laws of hygiene, on the contrary, conserves us in health; rebellion against them begets disease.

How many of us would take the proper care of health if the violation of its laws did not bring a penalty?

There are laws written in the cosmos, across the face of the skies, in the chemicals, plants, and animals, in our bodies and minds, and they are all reflections of the eternal reason of Almighty God.

We are free, of course, to break any of God's laws; but in breaking them we defeat ourselves. We are free to defy the law of gravitation; but in doing so, we do not destroy gravitation, we destroy ourselves.

The prodigal was free to leave the Father's house, but in doing so, he defeated not the Father, but himself.

Judas did not sell the Master for thirty pieces of silver; he sold himself. Judas perished, Christ lives on. Good is self-conserving; evil is self-defeating.

There is no need for God to intervene to frustrate the evil purposes of men who ignore the moral law, for men cannot be in opposition to Him without being in opposition to themselves.

The confusions created by our rejection of God are not determined by our intentions, but by the nature of the reality we negate, namely God. However good my intention may be in holding my hand over fire, my hand will nevertheless be burned.

Nature belongs to God, not to us. That is why it betrays us, but never betrays Him. That is why nature turns against us and punishes us, when we do not use it rationally or as God intended. As Francis Thompson put it:

I tempted all His servitors, but to find
My own betrayal in their constancy,
In faith to Him their fickleness to me,
Their traitorous trueness, and their loyal deceit.[22]

We are punished on earth by the very things we distrust from God's purposes; in this sense: "the wages of sin is death" (Rom. 6:23).

---

[22] Francis Thompson, "The Hound of Heaven."

The Scriptures tell us: "And whosoever shall fall on this stone, shall be broken; but on whomsoever it shall fall, it shall grind him to powder" (Matt. 21:44). In other words, anyone who opposes Christ shall be crushed; it will not be Christ who shall be crushed.

When Nazism and Communism persecute religion they seal their own doom, not the doom of religion. As the Spanish proverb puts it: "He who spits against Heaven spits in his own face."

The universe absolutely will not respond to anti-Christian living. Everything from the stars to the earth on which we live will rebel against a denial of God's law. The divine plan never fails, for "the stone which the builders rejected; the same is become the head of the corner" (Ps. 117:22).

Julian the Apostate found it out when he ran a dagger into his breast, shrieking: "O Galilean, Thou hast conquered."

Since God's purposes are never defeated, it follows that to the extent that our purposes are identical with His, we can never lose. There can be no such thing as fearing their evil if we be on God's side.

Our Lord never once said, "Fear the devil." But He did say, "Fear God" (1 Pet. 2:17). If our enemies are evil, we should fear less being defeated by them, than we should fear defeating ourselves, by forgetfulness of God and His Divine Son.

Evil may be triumphant for a moment, but it is always deprived of the results of its triumphs; it wins the first battle, but it always loses the booty. God's purpose prevails.

Caesar built roads to carry the screaming eagles of militarism throughout the world, but over these same roads Peter and Paul walked to preach the good tidings of the gospel of Christ.

Rome built temples of marble to the pagan gods; the same marble was shaped into tabernacles for the worship of the eucharistic Lord.

Unless our resolves be in accord with God, we can never be assured of victory. But if they are in accordance with the Divine Will, then we shall have His victory; for our Divine Lord said "I have overcome the world" (John 16:33).

His law, His life, and His truth will win therefore, whether we win or lose, because goodness is self-conserving.

If therefore we remain with Him, victory will be ours, though at any one moment it may look like defeat, feel like defeat, and smell like defeat. The Cross looked like defeat too, but it was the condition of His greatest victory.

Wherein lies America's assurance of victory? In the correspondence of our wills to His natural law, to His moral law, to His Christian love for "If God be for us, who is against us?" (Rom. 8:31). As our Divine Lord Himself told us: "Without me you can do nothing" (John 15:5).

If God is eternally the God who is crucified in the tragedies of history, so is He forever and eternally the God who raised Jesus from the dead. That is why faith in Him can triumph over all disaster.

But the condition of that triumph is oneness with Him. Hence this importance of an all-out moral effort, involving a return to the Christian concept of family life, and the acceptance of a system of law grounded on the authority of God and a system of education based on prayer and love of God.

We must remember that in war two factors must be considered: 1) arms; and 2) the courage with which they are used.

The initial success of the Totalitarian armies lies not only in their military equipment, but principally because they used it with a religious enthusiasm — not with the fire of a true faith, but with the fire of a false one. They were fighting for an absolute, a deity, a philosophy of life.

America can match them in arms. But shall we match them in that imponderable factor of morale? Can their faith in the absolute of a false god be matched by our moral relativity, our indifference to God, His moral law, and the redemption of His Divine Son?

Can the flames of their fanaticism be extinguished by the gentle zephyrs of our indifference, which denies there is any distinction between good and evil?

Can their zeal for antichrist be overcome by our indifference to Christ? Can their inspiration for sacrifice born of devotion to their false absolute, be matched by our emphasis on a false freedom which thinks that every appeal for sacrifice is a violation of constitutional rights, or property rights, or the right to organize?

We are united so far because we have a common hate; but where is our common love? Shall we be "united nations" only because we hate the same devil, or because we all love the same God?

This war so far has not provided us with a national slogan, probably because the last war taught us that slogans are dangerous. Twenty years ago we shouted: "Make the world safe for democracy" and all we did was make it unsafe for democracy.

Occasionally a slogan is used today that we are fighting for freedom. But this has not been popular, because the people who think know that freedom from something is meaningless unless we are free for something—and that objective has not been defined.

Freedom is like the atmosphere; it is a condition of happy living, but it is not the purpose of life. We want freedom from slavery but we do not want a freedom so broad as to include the right to destroy it.

Slogans are useful in time of peace, but not in time of war; for a slogan is a myth, a catchword to awaken mass enthusiasm.

Today people want a philosophy of life, a true absolute to knock down the false absolute, and a faith for wartime.

We already have the negative side of that faith; that is, that our enemies have an evil philosophy of life that makes civilization impossible. We have not yet developed a positive philosophy, namely that that evil can be overcome only by good.

No one wants an American victory more than I do; I am just realistic about it, for history attests the truth of David: "Unless the Lord build the house, they labour in vain that build it. Unless the Lord keep the city, he watcheth in vain that keepeth it" (Ps. 126:1).

Victory will come if we arouse ourselves to a sense of duty rooted in God and the moral law. Why is it that the soldiers have a better spirit for wartime than civilians? Because to them duty is primary; to civilians rights are primary.

Think of how many lawyers there are in the United States who are more interested in their fee than in the preservation of justice; think of how many doctors there are who are more concerned about their livelihood than in someone else's life; think of how many teachers there are in the United States who teach because it pays well rather than because it is an opportunity to inculcate God's truth in the hearts of the young; think of how many Capitalists there are who concentrate solely on their profits and their priorities rather than on the common good in wartime; think of how many labor leaders and workers there are in the United States who are more interested in a closed shop, shorter hours, or their particular organization, or in higher wages than they are in serving those who earn one-twentieth as much by risking their lives for America!

But the soldiers, the sailors, the marines, the air corps—all these young men—most of whom earn but a dollar a day, never use the word *right*; they talk about a "job to do." It is not their salary that comes first; they sweat not for reward but for duty. And duty has a moral basis that makes brave men.

Let us of the civilian population imitate the soldiers and talk about duties. Such is the pattern of American life. In brief, if we want a victory over our enemies, let us first get on God's side and then go out and drive the devil out of them that they may be on God's side too!

13

Prayer in Wartime

This war is not a conflict of systems of politics, though a few superficial minds still think it is; it is a titanic struggle to decide whether the moral law of God shall be the basis of individual and social life, or the physical law of the ruthless sword.

The point to be emphasized is that since our conflict is with demonic forces, we can conquer them only by a national surrender to God and His Divine Son. This involves prayer, and prayer is never more necessary than in wartime.

Some of us pray but seldom, because we have kinks in our knees made by a pride that refuses to prostrate itself and acknowledge its dependence on God; others never pray because our ideas of religion are nothing but a jumble of Bible stories, mythologies, and sentiment.

If we believe only in a vague power behind the universe, we will never pray, because we cannot pray to Power any more than we can pray to a stick of dynamite.

Neither can we pray if we confusedly believe in some "Great Architect" behind the universe, for the simple reason that he is behind the universe and not in it and with us.

But if that power ever shared my weakness, and if that wisdom ever shared my struggle, then I could pray. And that is Christ: the Power and the Wisdom of God is Love.

Where there is love, I can pray in spite of power, for impatience can trust love. Where there is love, I can pray in spite of wisdom, for ignorance can trust love. Only when we stand in the presence of Love do we become conscious of sin and the necessity of redeeming grace.

The young man in the Gospel could stand before the face of Incarnate Purity and say: "All these things have I kept from my youth" (Luke 18:21). But he failed in the test of love.

Only when we stand before the self-denying heart of God on the Cross do we begin to realize not only our actual weakness, but our potential happiness. If you could persuade me that God could forgive me without all that the Cross means, you could persuade me that I could forgive myself—then I would never be wrong; then I would never need to pray.

In order to understand the meaning of prayer it may help to make three observations concerning its nature, two of which are negative.

First, the essence of prayer is not petition. The important word here is essence, because petition is a legitimate form of prayer.

We live in a conditional universe and many favors are granted on condition that we pray for them, as our Lord said: "Ask, and you shall receive; that your joy may be full" (John 16:24). There are many favors hanging from the vault of Heaven's blue on silken cords and prayer is the sword that cuts them.

What we are here emphasizing is that we must not pray on the constant assumption that the purpose of prayer is to get something, for if we identify getting with goodness, then when we do not get we may doubt the goodness or the power of God.

When our own will is denied we are too often like the little boy who wanted a gun for Christmas and called his father "bad," because he did not get it.

We meet that same spirit in those who say: "God let me down. I prayed that my brother wouldn't be sent to Hawaii, and he went last week."

These poor souls, if they really knew it, are identifying the goodness of God with His readiness to do whatever they ask. They begin by praying to One whom they admit knows more than they and has more power than they but they end by denying both.

They think of God as being reluctant to do good, which reluctance can be overcome only by petitions that sound like the pounding of fists of angry children, forgetful that God, not us, takes the initiative in giving. He loved us before He made us.

We do not know why God does not answer all our petitions, though He has told us that before we speak, He has already heard us.

St. James, however, suggests selfishness is one reason for unanswered prayer: "You covet, and have not; you kill, and envy, and can not obtain. You contend and war, and you have not, because you ask not. You ask, and receive not; because you ask amiss: that you may consume it on your concupiscences" (James 4:2–3).

Many a man in the United States is living with only one eye or one finger, simply because his parents gave him exactly what he wanted on the Fourth of July.

I am sure that God has never answered and never will answer a bald-headed man's prayer for hair; and a woman could pray from now until the crack of doom, but God would never take the wart off the end of her nose.

Think these reflections through and you will understand why not all prayers are answered. God is omnipotent. He can do all things except one thing: He cannot please everybody.

And what a terrible world this would be if God answered the selfish prayers of everyone we think we could govern the world better than God.

Furthermore, when we pray we forget that in prayer God supplies our needs but not always our wants. Our Lord multiplied the loaves and fishes and gave to every man all that he needed.

Suppose however He multiplied gold bricks. How many among us would have been satisfied? Gold is a want; bread is a need.

Our Divine Lord on another occasion said that: "when you are praying, speak not much, as the heathens. For they think that in their much speaking they may be heard. Be not you therefore like to them, for your Father knoweth what is needful for you, before you ask him" (Matt. 6:7–8).

He knows our needs before we ask and has already arranged to supply them. The problem is, then: Do I want what He knows I need?

Suppose our Dear Lord did come to us as we prayed for something and said: "I will give you anything you want. Choose it!" Would we not rather abandon our will and, counting on His infinite Goodness, ask Him to do the choosing?

At Christmas when someone asks us what we want, do we not say, "You choose," knowing full well that his generosity will be greater than our daring?

Why not begin prayer that way, trusting in Him because He knows what is best? That is why petition is not the essence of prayer: trust, for one thing, underlies it.

St. Paul three times prayed to be relieved of an affliction which was hindering his missionary work, but God did not answer the prayer.

Secondly, prayer is not an insurance policy, a bomb-proof shelter, a bullet-proof vest, a germicide. This observation is for those who think that God should suspend the operation of His natural laws every time they get into trouble.

Did He on Calvary suspend the law that a nail hit on the head by a hammer would pierce His blessed hand?

The very ones who in time of peace think the business of God is to insure prosperity are the very ones who, in time of adversity, think the business of God is to grant immunity from harm.

Some prayers are nothing else but selfish expressions of the self-preservation instinct. Did not our Lord say the sun shines on the just and the wicked? Therefore may we not expect the bombs to fall on the wicked and the just?

If this world were all, if man had not an immortal soul, if the scales of justice were not balanced beyond the grave, if the loss of physical life were a greater evil than sin, then the Goodness of God could be identified with our good health, our fat bank deposits, and our freedom from wounds.

But since this world is the proving ground of character, it must never be assumed that catastrophe is a special sign of sin. Our Divine Savior never spoke of perishing in the physical, but in the spiritual, sense.

When the Pharisee asked: "Rabbi, who hath sinned, this man, or his parents, that he should be born blind?" He answered, "Neither hath this man sinned, nor his parents; but that the works of God should be made manifest in him" (John 9:2-3).

It seems that some Galileans had broken a Roman law. Pilate heard of it and sent out soldiers to punish them. They arrived at the very moment the Galileans were worshipping, slew them then and there, and mingled their blood with their sacrifice.

Now it was likely the Judeans told him this story, for the Judeans hated the Galileans. And our Lord answered and said: "Think you that these Galileans were sinners above all the men of Galilee, because they suffered such things? No, I say to you: but unless you shall do penance, you shall all likewise perish" (Luke 13:2–3).

Our Lord then made reference to another tragedy, when a tower of Siloe fell and killed eighteen people. He asked again: "Think you, that they also were debtors above all the men that dwelt in in Jerusalem? No, I say to you; but except you do penance, you shall all likewise perish" (Luke 13:4–5).

Disaster does not disprove the goodness of God. A man can perish even though no tower fall on him, or a Pilate never slay him. He can die in bed surrounded by friends and flowers, with even soft music pouring into his ears; but he will be damned unless he repents of his sins.

What we seem to forget is that death is not the greatest evil; sin is. Hence, "And fear ye not them that kill the body, and are not able to kill the soul: but rather fear him that can destroy both soul and body in hell" (Matt. 10:28).

The best lives are not always saved in battle; otherwise the heroes who die in battle and whose names we inscribed on our war memorials would all be wicked men. A St. Francis of Assisi in a frontline trench would have no guarantee that God would deflect a bullet to protect him.

But this much we could be sure of: no matter what would happen, nothing could turn him away from God, for as St. Paul says: "And we know that to them that love God, all things work together unto good, to such as, according to his purpose, are called to be saints" (Rom. 8:28).

Please do not misunderstand. It is right and just that we should pray for the safety of our loved ones; but we must not think of prayer always in terms of the suspension of God's natural law, or as a kind of safety device.

A chaplain in the last war said he heard some men praying when he wished they had gone over the top without it, for their prayer was but the mark of a broken will, a selfish desire, and a fear of death, a whimpering of formulas for personal protection in time of crisis.

The man alongside of him who, still unbroken and unbeaten, bore his gun like the Savior bore a scourge against thieves, put the whimpering man to shame.

A prayer for personal safety in time of great crisis when moral issues are at stake, is not what a man ought to be thinking about; it entails putting a greater value on physical life than on duty and justice.

The martyrs of old who were stretched on racks, tortured, and burned, were all men and women of prayer. They prayed for deliverance, like their Savior in the Garden; but they would not take it at the cost of faith or the denial of the Christ whom they bore in their souls. That was too high a price for saving their skins; so they lost their skins and saved their souls.

The answer to prayer, then, is not the escape from death, but the power to face it with trust in God.

This brings us to the third point: what prayer really is — the lifting up of our hearts and minds to God. More simply still, it is communion with God.

Prayer is like tuning in on a radio: it is a means of giving God access to our souls. In order to tune in to a radio program you must set your dial to the proper wavelength. In like manner, in order to tune in to God, you must make your will correspond to His Divine Will.

Once this is done, just as you listen to the radio program to which you are attuned, so now you become obedient to the Divine Will to which your soul is attuned. Once the wavelength of our will is adjusted to the wavelength of God's will, we get what we want.

Then all prayers are answered; the program is just what we wanted. As St. John puts it: "And we know that he heareth us whatsoever we ask: we know that we have the petitions which we request of him" (1 John 5:15).

Prayer, then, is not so much asking God to do our will as asking God to do His will; its purpose is not so much to change God's will as it is to change our will.

We do not go to God with a blueprint of our own desires and ask God to rubber stamp it. Rather, we ask God to give us His blueprint and then we mobilize all our energies with His grace to fulfill it. Instead of Him approving our plans, we approve His.

Instead of going to God saying: "This is what I am going to do. Be with me, O Lord," we approach Him as St. Paul did at the moment of his conversion, and say: "What shall I do, Lord? And the Lord said to me: Arise, and go to Damascus, and there it shall be told thee of all things that thou must do" (Acts 22:10).

In wartime the proper approach is to ask God to use our collective wills and our national arms for His holy purposes, rather than to ask Him to serve our purposes. In prayer we do not ask God to fight on our side; we pray to fight on His side.

We pray not as Americans who happen to be Christians, but as Christians who happen to be Americans. We ask God not to do something for us, but to do something in us, that He may do something through us for the betterment of the world and the restoration of the moral order.

The essence of prayer therefore is a longing at all costs to be caught up in God's purposes.

A little child prayed for a thousand dolls for Christmas. She did not receive them. Her unbelieving father who had taunted both her and her mother for praying, one day cynically asked: "Well, God did not answer your prayers, did He?" To which the child gave the glorious answer: "O yes, He did! He said no!"

That was the child's way of putting what her Savior expressed in the Garden centuries ago. He prayed that the chalice of suffering might pass — "if it be possible" (Matt. 26:39). It was possible! His Father could have done it; twelve legions of angels, He said, could have routed His foes. But it would have been at the cost of not redeeming man.

The Divine purpose mattered more than His personal safety. God said no! His prayer was answered: "Nevertheless not as I will, but as thou wilt" (Matt. 26:39).

And is not that the way we pray every time we say the Our Father — "Thy will be done on earth as it is in Heaven"? Do we mean it?

Does it not imply a continual conversion and purgation of selfish, evil desires, that we may be caught up as an instrument to serve God's purposes and that peace, grounded on His justice, may reign throughout the world?

There is the answer to those who ask: "The Germans pray to God, the English pray to God, the Italians pray to God, the Americans pray to God. On whose side is God?"

Those who ask that question have not the vaguest idea of the meaning of prayer. They assume that God takes sides on the basis of geography, rather than on the basis of goodness. The answer is, that God is on the side of those who do His Will.

If we are with God, no man can be against us. Hence, if the German, the Englishman, the Italian, the American, all prayed as they should, they would all be praying for the same intention: "Thy will be done on earth as it is in Heaven."

Then would be perfect unity on both sides of the battle front. Then we would have peace. "Peace to men of good will" (Luke 2:14)—and short of that there will be no peace.

Pray then, unceasingly, that you may attain in this life, as much as the present condition will allow, a harmony with that perfect life, truth, and love which will constitute the blessedness of Heaven. The more intensely we pray, the fewer will be our words.

In God there is but one word. The more we mean anything, the less expression we can find: "Would that I could utter the thoughts that are within me." Once this Divine Love animates our life, then our conduct will be good. Prayer does not so much help our conduct as our conduct tests our prayers. If we think right, we will live right.

The greatest stupidity ever uttered was, "It makes no difference what you believe, but only how you act." Nonsense! We act on our beliefs; if they are wrong, we live wrong. Prayer then comes before conduct.

Live with the God of love, in prayer, and you will act lovingly toward your neighbor. Think with the Christ on His Cross, and you will be charitable to your neighbor.

Your actions tell whether you ever pray, not your ears. Prayer is not getting something; it is becoming something.

When we become good and glorify His name, then, we will get not only what we need, but what we want. We have His word for it: "Amen, amen I say to you: if you ask the Father any thing in my name, he will give it to you" (John 16:23).

Pray then that we may be victorious by being on God's side. Begin a monologue with God and it will end with a dialogue between you and the God who redeems you.

Bring your sickness to the Divine Light, your wickedness to the sweet ointment of His redemptive Cross, your hungry souls to His Communion rail, your imperfect sacrifices to His immolation on our altars. Pray for one reason—to bring yourselves in communion with a purpose, God's purpose, God's Will.

That's what most of us lack in our lives, a goal, a destiny, a loyalty beyond all fleeting enthusiasms.

If we are unhappy it is because our purpose is at odds with God's purpose which is best for us; we are criss-cross because we ignore the value of the Cross.

You carry a watch, but do not make your own time; you take it from the sky. You make your own journeys, but you do not draw your own map; you take it from creation. In like manner, you live your own life, but you do not make your ultimate goal or perfection. You take it from God. Therefore pray.

14

The Crucifixion

Looking out on the Four Horsemen spreading death, disease, war, and famine over the earth, we are tempted to ask: "Why does God let this happen?"

That is an incomplete sentence from the theological point of view. Finish it and it reads this way: "Why does God let this happen to Himself?

What a different light this casts on the tragedy of war to realize that in some mysterious way Christ is living, suffering, thirsting, starving, and being imprisoned and dying in us, and that this war is His Passion.

This does not mean that the historical Christ, who was born of Mary, suffered under Pontius Pilate, and is now glorified at the right hand of the Father, suffers again in that same human nature; for having died once He can never die again.

But it does mean that the Christ who is the Head of the Body which is the Church, does suffer again.

Just as our Divine Lord took a human nature from the womb of Mary overshadowed by the Holy Spirit, so on the day of Pentecost He took from the womb of humanity a corporate nature, or a Church overshadowed by the same Pentecostal Spirit.

Through that Church He still continues to teach, to govern, and to sanctify.

That is why the Church is infallible, because Christ the Teacher teaches through it; that is why its authority is divine, because He the King governs through it; that is why the sacraments are divine, because He the Priest sanctifies through it.

This union of the Head and the Body is what St. Augustine calls the *Totus Christus*, the Whole Christ, the Church which is the prolongation through space and time of the Incarnation.

The union of Christ and the Church is as intimate, as the vine and the branches which have but one common life: "As the branch cannot bear fruit of itself, unless it abide on the vine, so neither can you, unless you abide in me" (John 15:4).

In the analogy of St. Paul, the unity of Christ with us, and we with one another, is like the unity of hand and foot, head, and body, all with all.

If someone steps on your foot your head complains. St. Paul found out that this applies to the Mystical Body as well, when he was persecuting the Church of Damascus. The Heavens opened and the glorified Christ said: "Saul, Saul, why persecutest thou me?" (Acts 9:4).

In striking the Church which was His Body, Paul was striking Christ; "I am Jesus whom thou persecuteth" (Acts 9:5).

And did not our Lord Himself say that anyone who would do anything to one incorporated to Him would be doing it to Him, for example: "And he that shall receive one such little child in my name, receiveth me" (Matt. 18:5).

Did He not picture Himself as going through the world hungry, thirsty, imprisoned, and sick, and tell us that in serving them in His name we were serving Him: "Come, ye blessed of my Father, possess you the kingdom prepared for you from the foundation of the world. For I was hungry, and you gave me to eat; I was thirsty, and you gave me to drink; I was a stranger, and you took me in: Naked, and you covered me: sick, and you visited me: I was in prison, and you came to me" (Matt. 25:34–37).

Apply this now to the world war. Christ's life in His individual human nature is glorified; Christ's life in His Church and all incorporated to Him by Baptism is not yet glorified. He is growing to His full stature in us as He grew to His full stature in the nature He took from Mary.

The crucifixion on Good Friday is not only something that happened 1,900 years ago, it is something that is happening now as the Cross is erected in our midst today.

From a spiritual point of view there are no national causes; there is only the conflict of those who crucify Christ and those who are crucified with Him. Consider first how Christ is made to suffer today by those who crucify: Pilate and the executioners.

Judas still roams the world in the person of all those who were baptized to Christ and called to be one with Him, but who have fallen away from their high destiny by "selling out."

In the catalogue of Fascism, Nazism, and Communism you will find those who in their youth were signed with the Sign of the Cross, sealed with the seal of salvation, and then like Judas bargained away their Christian heritage for thirty pieces of silver from the coffers of a transitory political power.

Thumb over the lists of other nations and you will discover that those leaders who either welcomed international congresses of militant atheists to their midst, or turned their backs on the rights of religion, were those who, like Judas, were once called to be defenders of those rights and soldiers of Christ.

Those who do most harm to the cause of Christ are not those whose souls were left barren in their naturalism, but those called like Judas to live and move with the Son of God.

The Christ in the Garden of Gethsemane still has His lips blistered by a kiss, and, in His last gracious love to win them back, He still whispers: "Judas, dost thou betray the Son of man with a kiss?" (Luke 22:48).

Pilate too still lives. He lives in all those teachers and jurists who deny an absolute; who feel that right and wrong are only points of view; who flatter themselves on their broadmindedness as they allow the mob to choose between Barrabas and Christ; who have a feeling that possibly Christ is the Son of God, but who would not assert it lest they lose favor with Caesar; who, when they are brought face to face unequivocally with Divine Truth, ask the same question asked by Pilate: "What is truth" and then turn their back on it. Put the Creed therefore in the present tense: "Christ is suffering under Pontius Pilate."

The executioners still walk the earth: brutal, blind forces, which ignore the Divine, take orders from higher-ups, persecute the Christ in His Church and His apostles, profane His eucharistic Presence, nail His Mystical Body to a tree and then, with the calmness of their ancestors beneath Calvary, shake dice, "sit and watch," while before them is being reenacted the tremendous drama of the world.

If there are those who crucify, there are those who are crucified with Christ—those who are hunted because they believe in Him and of whom our Lord foretold: "If the world hate you, know ye, that it hath hated me before you" (John 15:18). "Yea, the hour cometh, that whosoever killeth you, will think that he doth a service to God" (John 16:2).

As our Lord suffered on His Cross He looked forward to all times and all people, and offered not only Himself but all the members of His Body, the Church, to His Heavenly Father.

That oblation we actualize and complete in ourselves; in the language of St. Paul we say "[I] fill up those things that are wanting of the sufferings of Christ, in my flesh, for his body, which is the church" (Col. 1:24).

How can we "fill up" the suffering of Christ? Was His Passion incomplete? Most certainly not.

It means that all our sufferings, pains, and Calvarys were in His thoughts on the Cross and were offered to God the Father for us, but they were "wanting" in the sense that they had not yet been endured in "our flesh."

That the Passion be completed in any soul is necessary that the part assigned to Him be realized and actualized and suffered in his body.

Each of us therefore must finish in his life and in his soul the vision of the dying Christ.

The precise manner in which we concur in the Passion of Christ and give value to our sufferings and communicate with Calvary is, for Catholics, the Holy Sacrifice of the Mass. Because we are in Christ, we are given a chance to cooperate with Him, as we do in the creation. God has called us to share His causality and His freedom.

Man needs a habitation. God, instead of building it Himself, gave man the power to build it with the materials from His bountiful hand.

Man needs food; God does not serve the table—He calls man to share His creative power by sowing the seed and tilling the fields.

And so with redemption. The Son of God has given us the sublime vocation of sharing in the "fellowship of the Cross"; He has called each of us to be a redeemer with a small *i* as He is the Redeemer with a capital *R*. To each of us He says: here is a splinter from the Cross that I have been carrying from the foundation of the world.

It is this consciousness of sharing in Christ's redemption that gives to some men patience and joy in suffering, for in Christ they see that their sacrifices can be taken up into His eternal sacrifice, and can be made creative and redemptive.

We are not to think of God as standing outside the sufferings of the world, apart and aloof, in the untroubled serenity of Heaven. God is not a spectator to the drama of suffering; He has come down as its greatest tragedian and as sin's greatest victim.

If He points to a forest and bids us enter, it is because His feet have already made the pathway through the thickets and the thorns; if He bids us take up a cross daily and follow Him, it is because He has already borne the brunt of it on His shoulders.

God is not outside the tears and the tragedy of life; in every pang that rends the heart of a man, woman, or child, God has His share.

We cannot meet a cross in our respective walks of life but that He already took it at the foot of Pilate's temple and made it the badge of His glory and the symbol of a Christian.

We cannot have feet tired and worn from the service of others but that His own were calloused from going about doing good and nailed to a Cross for having been too good.

We cannot have the sorrow of losing friends or a mother but that He Himself already felt the rent in His own Heart, as He left a friend to a mother on the gibbet of a Cross.

If then He is in us, we shall overcome the world as He did, by the same love.

Our Divine Lord had more enemies than any man who ever lived, and perhaps He had fewer friends, if we are to judge from those who stood by Him in His Passion.

His enemies were our enemies too, for they were the enemies of all that is Christian for all times; and yet when He died He made them His friends through the power of His Love and His friendship and His surrender to death.

"Greater love than this no man hath, that a man lay down his life for his friends" (John 15:13).

As He looked out on the world from that Cross and saw all His enemies who had brought evil into the world, not only for His time but unto the consummation of the world, He saw them not as people to be hated and despised, but as wounded and twisted and mutilated souls not able to heal themselves.

His Divine Love poured out upon them, for the Son of Man came not to destroy sinners but to save them.

If, then, Christ is suffering in us, we have the responsibility of loving those who make us suffer, that we, like Him, may redeem them. Then, if our lot in war is the lot of tragedy and suffering and sacrifice, it will be done gladly because He is in us once more, redeeming a world.

It was this vision that sustained the soldier as he carried his pack, and the true Christian soldier, like Joyce Kilmer, will think of his task in the light of the Passion of Christ:

My shoulders ache beneath my pack,
(Lie easier, Cross, upon His back.)

I march with feet that burn and smart,
(Tread, Holy Feet, upon my heart.)

Men shout at me who may not speak,
(They scourged Thy back and smote Thy cheek.)

I may not lift a hand to clear
My eyes of salty drops that sear.

(Then shall my fickel soul forget
Thy Agony of Bloody Sweat?)

My rifle hand is stiff and numb,
(From Thy pierced palm red rivers come.)

Lord, Thou didst suffer more for me
Than all the hosts of land and sea.

So let me render back again
This millionth of Thy gift! Amen.[23]

Because we are in Christ, we will try to reproduce the sentiments of Christ and His Cross.

To those who make us suffer, who nail us to a cross, we will say: "Father, forgive them, for they know not what they do" (Luke 23:34).

They thought, O Heavenly Father, they were crucifying a man; and they think now they are crucifying a human institution, when in reality they are, like Paul before his conversion, persecuting You.

They do not know their every nail is aimed at Thee, O Christ. They do not know what peace you bring. "Father, forgive them, for they know not what they do" (Luke 23:34).

Two thieves did blaspheme Thee on the Cross, and yet one of them was saved.

Many too are suffering in the world today without solving its mystery in Thee, cursing and blaspheming Thee from their beds and their battlefields.

Give us Thy vision, O Jesus, that we may never despair of converting even those who blaspheme Thee. Grant that some of them, like the thief on the right, may hear Thy Words: "Amen I say to thee, this day thou shalt be with me in paradise" (Luke 23:43).

From Thy Cross, Christ, Thou didst command Thy dear Mother to Thy beloved disciple, and Thy beloved disciple to Thy dear Mother. May we, nailed on our cross like Thee, see that when duty fastens us that we stay to do Thy Will and if need be, make the surrender of loved ones and family. "Woman, behold thy son.... Behold thy mother" (John 19:26-27).

When darkness did so envelop Thy Cross, and the sun hid its light at high noon; when suspended between Heaven and earth, Thou didst feel that both earth and Heaven had rejected Thee—Thou didst never once lose in Thy human nature Thy hold on God, crying: "My God, my God, why hast thou forsaken me?" (Matt. 27:46).

[23] Joyce Kilmer, "Prayer of a Soldier in France."

Give us strength, O Jesus, when we seem abandoned, in darkness and in pain, when all seems lost, and when Heaven never answers our whys, still to cry out in undying force, "My God, my God."

When Thou didst turn to me and say, "I thirst" (John 19:28), Thou meant not a thirst for water but a thirst for love from the hearts Thou hadst made.

May the chalice of Thy Gethsemane, filled with the wine of suffering, be unto my lips as salt; may it make me thirst to spread Thy Name and love before men, so that in the end I may measure my life not by the wine I drank but by the wine I poured forth.

Under Thy Cross men challenged, "If he be the king of Israel, let him now come down from the cross, and we will believe him" (Matt. 27:42). But Thou didst stay until the task was done and in triumph did cry out: "It is consummated" (John 19:30).

O Jesus, grant that, whatever may be my lot in life, whether it be in light or darkness, You will empower me to hold to my faith, to fight the good fight, to run the course, to stay on the cross until the evening comes so that I can say in triumph too: "It is consummated!"

Thou didst give Thy body and blood to earth, Thou wilt soon give Thy body to the tomb, Thy Mother to John, and John to Thy Mother; but Thy Spirit Thou didst keep for the Father.

Grant that I may keep my spirit too amidst the wars and sorrows of this world so that at the end I can give it back to Thee from whence it came.

Let the last word of my life be: "Father, into thy hands I commend my spirit" (Luke 23:46).

15

The Divine Path to Victory

Celebrating Easter in a world that is more like Good Friday, and hearing the chants of peace amidst the explosions of war, makes us wonder what lesson this blessed feast can offer in these tragic days.

The answer is to be found in two scenes in the life of our Blessed Lord, that reveal the divine path to victory.

The first scene takes place in the Garden of Gethsemane when the Savior, in the full majesty of His Person, goes out to meet the devil in the guise of Judas, and the soldiers who came with swords and clubs to apprehend Him.

Reminding them that no one taketh His life away, but He lays it down of Himself, He now surrenders Himself into their hands with these words: "This is your hour, and the power of darkness" (Luke 22:53).

The important word here is *hour*, for apparently evil has its hour and uses it to turn out the lights of the world and deliver it over to the Stygian darkness of despair.

The second scene took place earlier in His public life when the Pharisees sought to get rid of Him by making Him fearful of Herod, whom they said intended to kill Him.

The supreme value of the story is in the answer He gave. In effect He said: "Go and tell that fox, Behold, I cast out devils, and do cures to day and to morrow, and the third day I am consummated. Nevertheless I must walk to day and to morrow, and the day following, for it cannot be that a prophet perish, out of Jerusalem" (Luke 13:32–33).

In other words, go tell that fox who has a mind to kill me, that he is helpless; he cannot kill me until I have done my work, and I have three days' work to do.

This was figurative language: two of these days are for works of wonder convincing men of His Divinity, but the third day will be the day of mystery and perfection. The important word here is *day*.

Setting the two scenes together there emerges this lesson: evil has its hour, but God has His day. And that evil hour is part of God's day, inseparable from it, one with it.

Unless the seed has its "hour" when it falls to the ground and dies, it will never have its "day" when it springs forth into life.

Without that hour of war with evil, there would never be this day of peace; without the Cross there would never be the empty tomb; without Good Friday, there would never be an Easter Sunday; without the crown of thorns there would never be the halo of light.

And there is the answer to our Easter query: "How can we celebrate Easter in a world that is a Good Friday?" By seeing in this war the operation of God's law, that without this hour of suffering and sacrifice we might never come to a day of peace and resurrection of our national life.

Peace is not a passive but an active condition; it is not something given, but something achieved. Our Lord never said, blessed are the peaceful, but blessed are the peacemakers.

Peace must be made, won in battle, as He won it. Good Friday was not a day of appeasement, therefore Easter will not be a day of false peace—God hates peace in those who are destined for war! Evil has its hour but God has His day.

It is highly significant that on the day of triumph He was recognized through some gesture connected with that hour; in no single instance did they perceive His glory except by looking through the windows of Calvary:

Mary Magdalene came to the knowledge of His Glory through the sepulchre where they laid Him in the hour of defeat.

Peter and John perceived the day of triumph through the winding sheets in which He was wrapped in the hour of His ignominious death.

The disciples on the way to Emmaus recognized the Conqueror in the newness of His day, at the breaking of bread—which recalled the deliverance of His body in the hour of darkness.

Thomas, the doubter, saw His Divinity through fingers put in hands and hands thrust in side—the relics of an hour's battle with the power of evil in which the slain had the victory.

So much is the "hour" the part of His "day" that in the triumph of His Resurrection day He keeps the scars received in the hour of defeat.

And He keeps them for all eternity; even on the last day when He will come in glory to judge the living and the dead, He will bear them as pledges of His victory. He is Prince of Peace because He was Captain of Wars and Lord of Hosts.

Soldiers wear medals for bravery but He keeps the scars of the hour in which He fought for peace. The *Via Crucis* is the *via pacis*. The Way of the Cross is the way of peace.

To pass through the hour of evil is in itself no guarantee of a day of peace—we must pass through it with faith in His Resurrection.

The thief on the left passed through evil but it profited him nothing, for his sufferings were not borne in Christ. The thief on the right, on the contrary, passed through his hour in union with Christ, and therefore came to His day: "This day ... Paradise."

As St. Paul says: "A faithful saying: for if we be dead with him, we shall live also with him" (2 Tim. 2:11); but our death must be in Him.

Apply this lesson that only those who pass through Calvary's hour with Him shall ever come to the Day of Victory.

Look out upon Holland, Belgium, France, Germany, Finland, Italy, the Philippines, Greece, Russia, the Balkan States, Mexico, Spain! I speak not of those who suffer, but of those who do so in union with Him.

Like the Christ, these souls are having their hour—the hour of darkness, of famine, of persecution.

Above all the battle flags of the world, beyond the din of national slogans, the scheming of foxes, the debates of politics, and the selfish clashes of economic forces—there is one common bond uniting them all who are in Christ.

They have all been kissed by some Judas, smitten by some soldier, misjudged by some Caiphas, mocked by some Herod, and crucified under some Pilate, in this their hour of darkness; but if the Easter law hold true—and it does—to the extent their sufferings are one with His, there is the guarantee of their resurrection.

Not because of any new shuffling of politicians or any new theory in economics, will they come to greatness, for politics again will fail, economists again will blunder, foxes will be caught in their own traps; but because they have been signed with the Sign of the Cross, sealed with the seal of salvation—because they have borne the cross in Christ—they will rise with Christ!

This war is the sowing of the seed. Evil has its hour, but God will have His day.

Apply the lesson now to our own country. If it be true that those who have already had their "hour" with Christ will have their "day" with Him, then the inverse is true: we shall have our Day of Victory only on condition that we have our hour of darkness with Christ.

We want victory with justice in this war. But Easter teaches us that there can be no true Day of Victory unless we pass through the hour of struggle against evil in union with the Savior. As Our Risen Lord told His disciples on the road to Emmaus, "Ought not Christ to have suffered these things, and so to enter into his glory?" (Luke 24:26).

We have already begun to pass through that hour of sacrifice, not so much because of our own choice, but because our enemies have forced us into it. Like the Savior on Calvary we are already being stripped, not of our garments, as He was, but of our rags of "self-righteousness."

First of all, we are beginning to die to that false notion that there is no evil. Up to a few years ago, we denied there was a devil. Now we are pointing our fingers across the waters saying: "They are wrong; they are devils."

But how can they be wrong, unless there is a right; and how can there be a devil unless there is a God? Our enemies have thus driven us into an hour where we rediscovered God.

We are also being stripped of the false rags of "self-expression." Until a few years ago most all our educators denied the necessity of discipline and restraint.

Now we are dying to that false concept and like Nicodemus beginning to see that unless nations, like men, are reborn they cannot enter into glory.

Finally, we are being stripped of the rags of progress. Up to this time, we believed that progress is in an ever-mounting straight line, or in a spiral ever-ascending; that we became better by the mere fact that we live; that blind cosmic forces of evolution were pushing us on to become supermen.

This war reveals to us just the contrary, namely that no life becomes better unless it dies to its lower self.

This spring is not an ascending progress from last spring, but through the death of an old spring. So must all nations and civilizations die in their hour of darkness, before they may come to the day of their victory.

There will be an hour of humiliation—of that there is no doubt. Our choice as a nation is not between being humbled and not being humbled; it is rather, who shall humble us, our enemies or ourselves.

Would we, as a defeated nation, be more moral and just and Christian than we would be as a victorious, revengeful nation? If the only way that we could be bettered would be by defeat, then we may expect it.

But it is not the only way. Instead of being humbled by enemies, we can humiliate ourselves by recognizing that only by and through God and His redemption can we come to victory.

We have not yet entered into the fullness of that idea, but only the beginning of it. We have yet to complete the lesson and to learn that man of and by himself cannot defeat the devil.

We already know the power of our enemy; we have not yet learned our hidden strength that in Christ we can do all things. "Without me you can do nothing" (John 15:5)!

Our choice is like that which Joshue presented to his people when he said to them: "Choose this day that which pleaseth you, whom you would rather serve, whether the gods which your fathers served in Mesopotamia [or the Lord your God]" (Josh. 24:15).

Our answer must be as that of Joshue. "But as for me and my house we will serve the Lord" (Josh. 24:15).

If an hour comes in our national life when labor will lift up its hands, as Christ lifted His in the carpenter shop, in service to the Father; if capital, like Joseph of Aramithea, will give of its possessions for the service of Christ; if women, like Magdalen, will bring their spices to anoint Him; if educators, like Nicodemus, will come in the dark to find the truth which is His; if the soldiers, like the one at the foot of the Cross, share the wine of their life with Him; if we all begin to see Him wounded in the wounded, hidden in the lost, destitute in the destitute, if we all enter this work of sacrifice as He entered the garden, then we need never fear the outcome—we have already won, only the news has not yet leaked out. We shall have our Day of Victory in Him, because we have already had our hour of darkness.

If there is any figure that adequately describes this lesson, it is that of the eagle. Eagles generally build their nests high in the mountains and most often over great crevices, canyons, and precipices.

When finally the young are hatched, the mother eagle, in virtue of an instinct implanted in her by Almighty God, begins to stir up the nest and scatter the twigs that cradled the infancy of its young. It nudges one of the eaglets to the edge of the nest, where, catching the vision of the yawning depth below, it shrinks back again into the safety of its nest.

But the mother bird, through the infallible urge of its Creator, finally succeeds in pushing the young over the edge of the nest.

Down and down it falls, its feeble wings fluttering in vain to bear it up against what must seem to it catastrophe and death on the rocks below.

But just before the eaglet crashes in the fearful depths, the mother bird swoops under it, catches it in her great wings, bears it aloft into the sky, and then, debarking its living cargo, allows the young one to flutter again and fall—but not to death.

Again the mother bird saves her young from catastrophe, lifts it again unto the sky, and repeats the process until the eaglet at last has learned to fly.

Moses must have seen some such scene as that for he makes use of it to explain God's dealing with the nations. As the eagle stirs the nest of her young, so does God stir up the nations!

Is not the war just like that, if we could but see it aright? Have we not been as the little eaglet, quite satisfied with the little nest we made in the world; were we not so smug, self-satisfied, and complacent that we forgot we had immortal souls, forgot that these souls have wings and were destined by God to carry us to higher realms beyond the earth?

So God, like an eagle, had to stir up our national nests, toss us out of our smug earthliness, let us fall near to disaster before we realized we had need of Him for salvation.

For unless we had that hour of darkness we could never have the day of light; for evil has its hour but God will have His day.

And that is indeed an apt figure of America, for our symbol is not the lion going about seeking whom it may devour, not the fox that would sneak up on its prey to destroy, not the vulture that waits for life to become carrion, but, in the full consciousness of what God destined us to be, our country chose as its symbol the eagle flying upward and upward, unto the sky beyond the "troubled gateways of the stars," across the "margent of the world," up beyond the hid battlements of eternity, up beyond the hour of darkness to the Day of Everlasting Victory in Christ Jesus our Lord!

THE
DIVINE
VERDICT

✠

(1943)

16

Evil Has Its Hour

Perhaps there is no misunderstanding of religion more universal than the one which assumes that evil cannot be reconciled with God.

A war seemingly adds great weight to the difficulty, for in such tragic moments the scoffer asks: "Where is your God now?"

We are never asked to justify God in the days of prosperity, simply because so many think it the supreme business of God to make us prosperous.

As Aeschylus wrote five centuries before Christ: "A state that is prosperous always honors its gods."[24]

As an Italian proverb has it: "In prosperous times no altars smoke."

But in days of adversity, those who retain their faith in God are asked to justify His existence. God, some think, should always be a success in the worldly sense of the term.

The thief on the left, for example, identified the goodness of God with His Power to remove him from the gibbet, that he might be restored to the ways of thievery: "If thou be Christ, save thyself and us" (Luke 23:39).

The bystanders at the Cross mocked in like manner: "He saved others; himself he cannot save. If he be the king of Israel, let him now come down from the cross, and we will believe him. He trusted in God; let him now deliver him if he will have him; for he said: I am the Son of God." (Matt. 27:42–43).

---

[24] From his *Seven Against Thebes*.

This grouping of prosperity with divinity falsely assumes that evil in some way lies outside and beyond the power of God, and that its presence necessarily spells the defeat of God. Nowhere do we find warrant for this view in the Scriptures.

It is interesting to note that one of the very first and one of the last statements our Lord made in His public life was a warning to men that they be not scandalized at His momentary defeat. At the very beginning He said: "Blessed is he that shall not be scandalized in me" (Matt. 11:6). The night He went out into the Garden of Olives He predicted to His apostles saying: "All of you shall be scandalized in me this night" (Matt. 26:31).

Quoting this centuries-old prophecy concerning not only His surrender to evil forces, but also their disloyalty, He said: "I will strike the shepherd, and the sheep of the flock shall be dispersed" (Matt. 26:31).

Scandals are inevitable when God works through the human, and when eternity operates in time!

God in the form of a Babe, is a scandal! God hanging on a Cross in a tattering human form, is a scandal! God present under the form of bread, is a scandal! God absolving from sin in the form of a man, is a scandal! God communicating His infallible truth through a man, is a scandal! God giving to man the power to bind and loose on earth and in Heaven, is a scandal!

But His admonition is: "Blessed is he that shall not be scandalized in me" (Matt. 11:6).

Is God not right in warning us not to be scandalized at His failures? Would God be God if He could use only the good?

The good are His willing instruments, but shall not Divine Power be capable of using unwilling instruments for His purposes? Anyone can make use of the good.

It is not our position here to reconcile the existence of God with evil; for evil is due, as we know, to an abuse of God's gift of freedom. It is the price we have to pay for divorcing freedom from God.

Rather, we seek here to justify the startling thesis that God permits evil from time to time for the sake of a greater good, so that in the language of St. Paul: "Where sin abounded, grace did more abound" (Rom. 5:20).

For some salutary lessons for these darkened hours, let us accompany in our mind's eye the Savior into the Garden of Gethsemane.

Three companions went with Him, Peter, James, and John, whom He strengthened for this ordeal by revealing to them His glory on the Mount of the Transfiguration.

No one in God's Kingdom is ever called to glory and honor, except for the sake of tremendous responsibilities.

Bidding them to watch and pray, He went as far away from them as a man could throw a stone — what a significant way to measure distance — and prayed to His Heavenly Father, pledging to drink the chalice of redemption to its very dregs in ratification of His Divine Will.

Pulling down upon Himself the burden of the world's sin, as if He Himself has been guilty of sin; thrusting into His hand every open deed of evil and every secret deed of shame, as if He Himself has committed them.

He breaks out into a bloody sweat, as the crimson drops like so many words write on the pages of earth the story of its greatest Love and its fondest Hope.

When He had prayed, He came back to His chosen three, and found them wrapped both in their cloaks and in sleep. In return for His Love our Lord had asked but one small thing — that they fall not asleep. He bade them stay awake like sentries of earth and bade them pray like sentries of Heaven.

Everything slept about them. The city with its whitewashed walls sprawling over the hills, was asleep; in all the houses of all the cities of the world, men were sleeping.

Perhaps the only ones awake were a thief in ambush in the dark, or a fond mother at the bedside of her sick child, or a sophomoric youth over a cup of wine in a dimly lighted tavern, asking his fellows: "Does God exist?"

Why did the apostles sleep? Men sleep when they are tired, but they never sleep when they are worried. These men slept, and for only one reason — because they were not conscious of the awfulness of the hour.

They were prepared for external dangers, for Peter was sleeping with his sword. But they were not prepared against themselves.

One can be armed and still be asleep — armed because one fears his enemies, asleep because he is not worried about his sins. Danger is physical; evil is moral.

Are we in America like Peter? Do we think of our times solely in terms of a war? Do we think of the Nazis and the Japs as being our only enemies? If so, as our Lord told Peter, the sword is enough! But suppose they are only symptoms of evil and sin; then will the sword be enough?

When we have defeated them on the field of battle, will we have defeated the godlessness from whose womb they come? Will we in reality be cutting off only the evil fruit, but not uprooting the evil root? Do we realize how evil the times are?

We will search history in vain to find any other ages than our own, when nations made expediency the sole ground of justice, when freedom was derided and denied, when truth was made the slave of a nation, a race, or a class, when some dictators would extinguish religion altogether, when others would poison it.

This war is not against rival political systems or nations, but between contrary philosophies of life.

Man is at war with his brother on the battlefields of the world, because man has first warred with God on the battlefield of the soul. This war involves suffering only because it first involved sin.

We are well armed as Peter was, and if all we had to defeat were the Nazis and the Japs, our task would be easy and victory certain.

But suppose we are fighting a devil? Suppose we are defending ourselves against philosophies of life which, as the Holy Father said of Nazism, Fascism, and Communism, are intrinsically evil. Then let us ask ourselves: Will the sword be enough?

If we think of war only as a physical combat as Peter did, we need to be aroused as he was by the Savior, who reminded him of two other arms: "Watch ye, and pray" (Matt. 26:41). Watch! Be vigilant on the outside. Pray! Pray that you may be armed on the inside with the armor of God.

Taunting Peter's false confidence in the sword alone, our Lord asked: "Could you not watch one hour with me?" (Matt. 26:40). In other words, "Peter, there are twenty three hours a day you may spend with your armaments. But can you not give one hour to invoking divine aid and imploring divine forgiveness"?

But why watch and pray? Because in times of crisis, evil can be more awake than goodness. Evil never sleeps.

Across this hill comes the evil man—Judas is his name. He leads a band of soldiers, Sadducees, and Pharisees, bearing lanterns and torches and weapons.

Judas has already given to them a sign saying: "Whomsoever I shall kiss, that is he; lay hold on him, and lead him away carefully" (Mark 14:44). Then throwing his arms about the neck of Jesus, he blistered His lips with a kiss.

That kiss was at once the first and most horrible sullying of those lips which had pronounced the most Heavenly words ever heard on this mad earth of ours. The betrayal of holy things must always be prefaced by a mark of affection.

The kiss was the first use of the Trojan Horse in the history of Christianity! Oh! How religion must guard itself against those wicked influences which say they are friends of religion.

This was no surprise to the Master. The very day He announced the Eucharist, He made known that Judas would betray Him. A few hours ago, before He gave the Eucharist, He told Judas himself he would betray.

It was thus around His most solemn promise and His most noble gift that the betrayal centered. As St. John put it: "Jesus therefore, knowing all things that should come upon him, went forth, and said to them: Whom seek ye? They answered him: Jesus of Nazareth. Jesus saith to them: I am he" (John 18:4–5).

When He said this the whole cohort of them fell backwards to the ground. Some burst of majesty halted them—some flaming glory which surpasses our puny minds. It was another way of revealing that no man could take His life, but that He could lay it down Himself.

Giving them power to rise, He took no thought of Himself, but of His faithless friends: "If therefore you seek me, let these go their way" (John 18:8).

And Jesus said to the chief priests, and magistrates of the temple, and the ancients, that were come unto him: Are ye come out, as it were against a thief, with swords and clubs? When I was daily with you in the temple, you did not stretch forth your hands against me: but this is your hour, and the power of darkness. (Luke 22:52–53)

"Your hour"—the hour of betrayers, deceivers, and crucifiers. "Your hour"—the hour for evil to put out the Light of the World—for that is all it can do during that hour.

The hour of wolves for scattering the sheep and seizing the Shepherd! The hour of power and might and swords and clubs wherein innocence and truth are beaten to the ground. The hour of concentration camps, Gestapos, OGPUs, the hour of the raping of Poland, the hour of sending a peace envoy with a kiss while preparing an attack!

"Your hour"—not because your weapons are stronger, nor because you come armed to seize me, but because in obedience to the Father's Will, I deliver myself into your hands that evil having done its worst may be overcome by Goodness rising from the dead.

In clear unmistakable language, our Divine Lord here tells us that God permits the evil which the rebellious hearts of men beget to have its brief holiday even at the expense of God Himself.

The ignorant think that a war creates difficulties for belief in God. And here the God-Man says that the evil seed man has planted will bear fruit in our evil hour!

It is not God's goodness we should doubt. It is our own! Evil did not come from God. It came from our sin, our pride, our egotism. Therefore it will have its hour!

Are we not living at such a moment now in the world's history? Do not the times in which we live belong to Satan and the power of darkness, wherein divine law is ignored, sanctuaries polluted, family life trampled under the feet of false freedom, and children raised as if there were no Cross, no Savior, and no Divine Love?

But if evil has its hour, how meet it? Will the sword be enough? Peter thought so!

Profiting by the confusion of the guards Simon Peter came suddenly to himself from sleep, drew a sword and struck Malchus, the servant of the high priest. It must have been a poor blow for it smote only his right ear.

Action is so often used as a substitute for prayer. So many think that the way to conquer an enemy's evil heart is to cut off his ear.

Simon's blundering action was remedied by the last act of Divine surgery wrought by the Savior who heals the wounds that overzealous people make on other's souls.

This untimely action was repudiated by our Lord. Addressing Peter, He said: "Put up again thy sword into its place: for all that take the sword shall perish with the sword" (Matt. 26:52).

Why did our Lord not take up the sword offered in His defense? Certainly not because by using it, He might be courting military defeat; for "Thinkest thou," He said to Peter, "that I cannot ask my Father, and he will give me presently more than twelve legions of angels?" (Matt. 26:53).

And did He not say to Pilate: "If my kingdom were of this world, my servants would certainly strive that I should not be delivered to the Jews: but now my kingdom is not from hence" (John 18:36)?

His motive then in rejecting the sword was not because He would have been no match for His adversaries. He asserts that if He did take to the sword, He would win every victory swordsmanship could achieve. And yet, believing this, He still refuses to use the weapon!

A physical enemy can be conquered with the sword. But moral evil can be overcome only by a cross. Armaments will defeat a foe, but arms alone cannot conquer evil; and that is why He refused the sword in the evil hour!

Apply this to the war. Are we fighting the Nazis or the Japs, or are we fighting evil? If only the former, our guns and tanks will do the job: but if they and other dictators and evil philosophies are the products of our pride and egotism, then our armaments offer no guarantee of victory.

Evil has the devil on its side and no military power on earth can defeat the devil!

How blind are those that say: What good will prayer do? That is what Pater thought as he slept alongside his armaments.

One might just as well ask: What good will courage do? What good will faith in righteousness do? What good will belief in the four freedoms do?

Do we realize that what our Totalitarian enemies are out to destroy is not what we have, but the principles for which we stand—a belief in human freedom and the value of a man against the power of the State? The soldiers who came into the Garden that night did not want Peter, James, or John. They were let go. Caesar wanted only Christ.

Our enemies, who are more numerous than We believe, seek to destroy the last vestiges of Christian civilization, so that they might; in the language of Nietzsche, so transvaluate values that evil from now on might be regarded as good and good be regarded as evil.

This warning, then! Unless we realize the fact that we live in an evil hour and that that hour must be spent watching and praying, we may end by drawing the enemy out of the house of Western civilization, while into that empty house which should have been filled by godliness, seven devils worse than the first will come in and dwell there and the last state of civilization shall be worse than the first.

Not until we realize that sin is the greatest evil in the world, and that wars, revolutions, and sufferings are the effects of sin, will we begin to take the path that leads to peace.

If this tragedy of war will not arouse us to the reality of an evil hour, then how shall we yearn for God's day?

Maybe a Michael is needed again to arouse us to the peril of the hour:

Michael, Michael: Michael of the Morning,
Michael of the Army of the Lord,
Stiffen thou the hand upon the still sword, Michael,
Folded and shut upon the sheathed sword, Michael,
Under the fulness of the white robes falling,
Gird us with the secret of the sword.

When the world cracked because of a sneer in heaven,
Leaving out of all time a scar upon the sky,
Thou didst rise up against the Horror in the highest,
Dragging down the highest that looked down on the Most High:
Rending from the seventh heaven the hell of exaltation
Down the seven heavens till the dark seas burn:
Thou that in thunder threwest down the Dragon
Knowest in what silence the Serpent can return.

He that giveth peace unto us; not as the world giveth:
He that giveth law unto us; not as the scribes:
Shall He be softened for the softening of the cities
Patient in usury; delicate in bribes?
They that come to quiet us, saying the sword is broken,
Break men with famine, fetter them with gold,
Sell them as sheep; and He shall know the selling
For He was more than murdered. He was sold.

Michael, Michael: Michael of the Mustering
Michael of the marching on the mountains of the Lord,
Marshal the world and purge of rot and riot
Rule through the world till all the world be quiet:
Only establish when the World is broken
What is unbroken is the Word.[25]

---

[25] G. K. Chesterton, "To St. Michael in Time of Peace."

17

War as a Judgment of God

Too exclusively and too long has modern man looked on this war in terms of politics and economics, and too little has he thought of it in terms of theology, morality, and the providence of God.

How many ever think of God as the Lord of History and the King of Kings?

Do not a number think of God only as an optional extra to whom appeal may be made at the end of political speeches, but who actually is as irrelevant to world events as poetry is to the problem of unemployment?

It would be nice if the poor knew Shakespeare, and it would be nice if men knew and loved God, but both are often regarded only as stimuli of an impractical character.

Others feel that a belief in God can be sustained in days of prosperity, for it is the business of God to supply "pie in the sky"; but in time of trouble they feel that God's plans are in some way thwarted and His goodness can hardly be justified.

The reason for this is to be found in the liberal Christianity which thinks of God solely as a God of sentimental love — such love as a doting modern mother might have for her erring son who could do no wrong, and even when he did it, must needs be forgiven, for he did not mean it.

Liberal Christianity has too long assumed that it is the sole business of the Church to beat the drums for social reform and to dance to the tunes piped for her by the latest moods and passing mental fashions.

It ignores the fact that the God of Love is also the God of Justice and that His wrath is terrible, and it forgets that the Christ who forgives sinners is also the Christ who will judge all men according to their works—for if God were forgiving without being just why should there ever have been a Cross?

It is the God of Justice who needs to be preached today. Modern man's dictum—"Religion has nothing to give me"—has been too long unanswered. Now let the answer be given: certainly, it can give him nothing; but it can take away something—it can take away his diabolical pride, your self-sufficiency, and thus make room for morality and peace.

Let us discount all political and economic considerations as secondary and look at this war solely from the point of view of Divine Justice.

We commonly speak of this war as a crisis. Our English word *crisis* is taken from a Greek word which means *judgment*; and that is just what this war is—a *Judgment* of God.

History does not, as the liberals believed a few years ago, move in a line of ascending progress. Rather it moves forward through catastrophies.

History is a moment given to man to say yea or nay to his eternal destiny; it is also a sphere wherein society works out the full effects of its allegiance to or its severance from God.

In the life of every human being, there is a *Particular Judgment* and a *General Judgment*.

The *Particular Judgment* comes at the moment of death, for we are individually responsible for the way we used our God-given liberty; the general judgment comes at the end of time, because we work out our salvation in the context of the social order and the brotherhood of Christ, and therefore we must be judged with the entire world.

History too, like individuals, has its particular and general judgments. Particular judgments come at various moments in a nation's history, when it works out the full moral consequences of its decisions and its philosophy of life. The General Judgment will be at the end of time when our Lord shall come to judge all the nations of the world.

We find a reference to both the Particular and the General Judgments in history, in our Blessed Lord's warning to the city of Jerusalem.

Because it had not known the time of its visitation, He said that a particular judgment would come before that very generation would have passed away, when the enemy would beat it flat to the ground. That judgment actually came to pass in the year 70 when Titus destroyed the Holy City.

But our Dear Lord also foretold, in the same passage, the General Judgment of the world in the distant future unknown to the sons of men, when nations which judged Him would then be judged by Him, as He would come in the clouds of Heaven bearing His Cross in triumph.

By speaking of the two together, He seemed to suggest that particular judgments in history are merely rehearsals for the General Judgment when the decisions of free men shall be sealed for all eternity.

We are presently living in a moment of particular judgment on history. In other words, our present world crisis is a Judgment of God on our era and our times.

But what is meant by the Judgment of God? We mean by it a "verdict of history." It is a time when the full consequences of our way of life become evident.

The Judgment of God definitely does not mean that God is *outside* history as a mighty potentate who occasionally, to remind subjects of His power, smites them for His good pleasure. Neither does it mean that this war is a divinely sent visitation or punishment, extrinsic and unrelated to our existence, as a spanking to a child who stole the jam—for a spanking does not *necessarily* follow the stealing.

The Judgment of God means that the Transcendent God is also inside history by His laws, far more intimately than an inventor is in his machine, or an artist in his painting.

God has implanted certain laws in the universe by which things attain their proper perfection. These laws are principally of two kinds: natural laws and moral laws.

What we call the natural laws, such as the laws of astronomy and the laws of physics and the laws of biology, are in reality so many reflections of the eternal reason of God. God made things to act in a certain way. In this sense the oak is a judgment on the acorn; the harvest is the judgment on the seed that was sown.

But God did not make man like the sun which can only rise and set. Having made man free He gave him a higher law than the natural law, namely, the *moral law*. Fire must obey the natural law of its nature, but man merely *ought* to obey the moral law. His freedom gives him the license to rebel.

Now God's purpose in imposing law on things was to lead them necessarily to their perfection; and God's purpose in giving man the moral law was to lead him freely to his perfection.

To the extent that we obey God's will we are happy and at peace; to the extent that we freely disobey it, we hurt ourselves—and this consequence we call judgment.

Judgments are clear in the natural order. For example, a headache is a judgment on my refusal to eat, which is a law of nature; and atrophy of muscles is a judgment on my refusal to exercise.

So too there are judgments in the moral order: "The wages of sin is death" (Rom. 6:23). "What things a man shall sow, those also shall he reap" (Gal. 6:8). "You ... have been called unto liberty: only make not liberty an occasion to the flesh" (Gal. 5:13). "By what things a man sinneth, by the same also he is tormented" (Wisd. 11:17).

Disobedience to these laws entails certain consequences, not because we will those consequences, but because of the very nature of the reality which God *made*.

No one who over-drinks wills the headache, but he gets one; no man who sins wills frustration or loneliness of soul, but he feels it. In breaking a law we always suffer certain consequences which we never intended. God so made the world that certain effects follow certain causes.

When calamity comes upon us, as a consequence of our neglect or defiance of God's will, that is what we call the Judgment of God. The world did not will this war, but it willed a way of life which produced it; and in that sense it is a Judgment of God.

Sin brings adversity and adversity is the expression of God's condemnation of evil, the registering of Divine Judgment.

The frustration resulting from our disobedience to God's law is His Judgment. And in disobeying God's moral law, we do not destroy it—we only destroy ourselves. For example, I am free to break the law of gravitation; but in doing so, I kill myself—and the law still stands.

God therefore does not interfere with the world when it suffers judgment, anymore than He interferes with it when we ruin our health by disobeying the laws of hygiene. He does not need to interfere, because He is already in the universe by His law.

The judgments of God are no more due to God's interference with the laws of nature than thunder is due to His interference.

God did not suddenly decide to applaud at the sight of pyrotechnics in the Heavens. But He so made the universe that where there is lightning there is thunder. It is a certain effect following a certain cause.

Every now and then, we said, there are *particular judgments* in history. Each era of history is a field in which certain seeds are planted. They grow, bloom, bear fruit, and die; and the kind of ideas that are planted determine the lot of that civilization.

The religious revolution was a Judgment of God on Christian people for not living up to the full meaning of the Christian life. There was nothing wrong with Christian dogmas, as the revolutionists assumed; there was only something wrong with Christian morals.

The French Revolution was a judgment on the selfish privileges of a monarchy and the denial of political equality.

Communism was a judgment on Czarist Russia and Capitalism; Nazism a judgment on Versailles; and this war is a judgment on the way the world thought and lived, married and unmarried, bought and sold—a judgment on the world's banks, its schools, its factories, its homes, its legislatures, its international order, its hearts and souls, and above all on its humanist illusion that man could build a peaceful world without God.

This war is to time what Hell is to eternity—the registering of the conflict of the human will against the Divine. It was forged in exactly the same way as the Cross.

As the Cross was made by a horizontal bar of man crossing the vertical bar of God, so the war is the result of the contradiction of the Divine Will by the human.

The whole world stands under doom, because we are all guilty before God. Not all equally guilty, thank God, but guilty in varying degrees.

We have not denied God as does Communism, nor have we set up a false god as does Nazism or Japanese imperialism. But we have ignored God, or treated Him as a benignant power whose sole function it is to bless our plans, to sugarcoat our idealism, and to lend a tone of respectability to a culture that is secularistic and man-centered.

The history of the world for the last few hundred years could be characterized as a progressive repudiation of the moral law and the gradual de-Christianization of society. This war, in other words, is a war within the human brotherhood because there has been a war against the Divine Fatherhood.

For centuries the foundation of our culture has been loosening; now the whole structure is collapsing. The world has completed the grand experiment of living without God! The world poisoned its own wells, and now blames God because the drink is bitter.

As Hell is not sin, but the effect of sin, so this war is not sin — it is the wages of sin. We cannot war against God without warring against ourselves.

What is the purpose of divine judgments in history? They are guarantees of the permanence of the laws of God. Would men so universally respect the laws of health, if the violation of those laws did not entail such painful consequences?

Where would moral development be if fire burned today and froze tomorrow, if refusal to sleep strengthened us today and weakened us tomorrow, and if the moral law of God had consequences in the morning but not in the afternoon?

Judgment, or the consequence of our decisions, affirms that the world is informed by God's presence and is under His guidance. It is a reminder that God's moral law will never be destroyed, as the sun will never cease to rise in the east. He made the world that way.

In disobeying His Will, we destroy ourselves. In stabbing Him, it is our own heart we slay. By catastrophies must we sadly learn that the moral law is right and will prevail.

The judgment at the end of the world will be a guarantee of the eternal distinction between right and wrong. That is why there is a Heaven and a Hell; namely, because right is everlastingly right and wrong is everlastingly wrong.

The various judgments within history, such as this war, are guarantees of that distinction for the time in which we live. In plain simple language, the world that has blurred the distinction between right and wrong must be brought to the realization that "it cannot get away with it." It is a sign that we are on the wrong track.

Fire burns, therefore let us not stick our hands in it; godlessness causes war, therefore let us be godly.

All nations and all peoples must learn, in sorrow and tears and blood and sweat, that wrong attitudes toward the natural law and the moral law are simultaneously and necessarily a wrong attitude toward God, and therefore bring inevitable doom, which is the Judgment of God.

Up to this point we have spoken of the Judgment of God on the world. Now a word about that judgment in relation to our own beloved country. We have said that the terrible and awful consequences which follow a violation of God's law are reminders and guarantees that God's moral law is right.

As a nation we have never set up as a standard any other philosophy of life than the moral law. But we did permit the distinction between right and wrong to be blurred, particularly in education, where unprogressive teachers declared that the difference between right and wrong was only a question of a point of view.

It took a war to make education abandon that false notion, for no one now would say that the only difference between our cause and our enemy's was simply a matter of a point of view. In that sense, at least, this war is a Judgment of God on that false way of thinking.

The war has thus driven us back to a moral law outside ourselves, and, in fact, outside the world. For if the moral order for which we are fighting was of our *own* making, then why should not the Nazis say they had a right to fight for a moral law of their own making, that the only way to decide between the two would be by force and war.

If morality is national, there is no criterion except might. But suppose that the moral law for which we fight is not our own, but a derivative of the eternal reason of God. Then we fight not to decide which is the stronger, but rather to defend what is right.

This war is a judgment! A crisis! An effect of the repudiation of the moral law! And we are seeking to make the moral law prevail over the law of expediency and force.

We are fighting not for freedom from something, but freedom for something; namely, the right to develop personalities which are made to the image and likeness of God.

We are fighting not for the right of religious worship, for religion is not a right anymore than patriotism is a right. They are both duties. Patriotism is a duty to country; religion is a duty to God.

We are fighting not for any particular form of government, but for the right of all peoples to choose their own governments, which will exercise power with responsibility because that power comes from God alone.

We are fighting not for democracy, but for something deeper, namely, for the moral and religious foundations which make democracy possible.

We are fighting not because the Nazis and the Japs are devils, for how could there be devils unless there were fallen angels, and how could there be fallen angels unless there was a God against whom they freely rebelled?

Rather are we fighting to preserve a moral law of righteousness and justice, which we never realized was all-important until we saw its tragic and chaotic effects, but which now, with God's help, we will uphold, and in the name of which, with God's help, we will conquer.

A war could be the condition of world regeneration. Once before in history, on the Hill of the Skull, three crosses with outspread beams, like giants with outstretched arms, silhouetted themselves against a sweet spring sky.

On the central Cross, hewn from a tree sown by a bountiful Creator, there now hung, by the perversity of man, Him who made the flowers to bloom and the trees to grow. He had called men to holiness, and so He had fallen into the hands of unholy men and demons.

When finally He, unlike all other men, went out to meet death—for death did not come to Him, He bowed His head and died. His loud cry was so powerful that it rang around the earth and made the dead come from their graves.

A centurion who stood nearby—a typical sergeant in the great Roman Army, who thought little of God and then only the gods Mars and Jupiter—ran a lance into the heart of the dead King. And as he did so, he exclaimed: "Indeed this was the Son of God" (Matt. 27:54). He had found faith in the very moment he was using this lance.

And may God grant that we in America, who thought of God so little in the days of false peace, may perchance find faith in these days of war, as did the centurion—and cry out in the joy of regeneration: "Have Thy way O Lord, it is best for me."

18

Judgment of Nations

War, it was said above, is a Judgment of God, not in the sense that God acts *outside* history, but *inside* history, not as a smiting of creatures in an arbitrary fashion, but as a catastrophic effect following the breaking of His moral law.

These catastrophies are the guarantees that God's Will will prevail. God asserts His Sovereignty by the judgments which follow the disobedience of His laws; without such judgments, there is no sovereignty—even in our earthly courts. The world stands under doom because it pronounced antagonism to the gospel of love.

History affords us many interesting examples of the Judgment of God. Here we shall mention two instances of how forgetfulness of God brought on the ruin of nations, namely Jerusalem and Rome, and then show how two great Americans expressed the same vision of Judgment in our national life.

First the fall of Jerusalem. The Great Patriot who loved the Holy City as His own, stood on a hill opposite, and looking down upon it wept at the consequences which He knew would inevitably follow from a refusal to submit to the truth of which their consciences had already been convinced.

Amidst the shedding of tears, He lamented: "Jerusalem ... how often would I have gathered together thy children, as the hen doth gather her chickens under her wings, and thou wouldst not?" (Matt. 23:37).

That is the heart of sin! "Would I ... thou wouldst not." The human will set up against Divine Will.

"Would I have gathered." One man? A carpenter? No man can gather a civilization. Only the Son of God can gather a whole people.

"Behold, your house shall be left to you, desolate" (Matt. 23:38).

> For the days shall come upon thee: and thy enemies shall cast a trench about thee, and compass thee round, and straiten thee on every side, and beat thee flat to the ground, and thy children who are in thee: and they shall not leave in thee a stone upon a stone: because thou hast not known the time of thy visitation. (Luke 19:43–44)

And it came to pass as foretold. That generation did not pass away until the calamity happened. Vespasian, going to Rome to become emperor, gave the order to his son Titus, on Easter Day in the year 70 to lay waste Jerusalem. The Temple was destroyed, not a stone left upon a stone.

History was the stage on which Jerusalem worked out the full effects of its severance from the laws of God. The city had not known the time of its visitation. "Unless the Lord build the house, they labour in vain that build it" (Ps. 126:1).

The second example of how forgetfulness of God brought on the ruin of nations is the fall of Rome. During the winter of AD 57–58, St. Paul addressed a letter to the Romans, from the city of Corinth, telling them of a judgment that awaited them because of their sins:

> And thinkest thou this, O man, that judgest them who do such things, and dost the same, that thou shalt escape the judgment of God?... Knowest thou not, that the benignity of God leadeth thee to penance? But according to thy hardness and impenitent heart, thou treasurest up to thyself wrath, against the day of wrath, and revelation of the just judgment of God. (Rom. 2:3–5)

St. Peter writing from Rome about the very year of his death, sounded the same warning: "Whose judgment now of a long time lingereth not, and their perdition slumbereth not.... shall perish in their corruption, receiving the reward of their injustice" (2 Pet. 2:3, 12–13).

These two men foretold the judgment of Rome, because it had forgotten God. Years later, in the year 370, at the mouth of the Danube, of a great Visigoth family, was born Alaric. None could have foreseen either his importance in history or the fact that he would unconsciously inspire one of the greatest heroic works ever written, namely, *The City of God*, by St. Augustine.

Alaric himself was probably a Christian, but Baptism had not destroyed in him a warlike lust. On three occasions he made visits to Rome, the third time being on the fourth of August, 410. With horses darting like hawks, and moving battering rams like mountains, he forced the Salarian gate, allowing his soldiers, who were the scum of Europe, to put the metropolis of the earth to sack and to humble the giant of the nations of the world.

On the seventh of August, followed by a long train of carts laden with spoils, he set forth from Rome proceeding to the conquest of Africa. But before setting sail for Sicily, he was overcome by sudden death.

His soldiers, in accordance with an old Goth custom, turned aside the River Busento from its course, that they might bury in its bed the body of Alaric the Daring, who had thrice violated the Eternal City.

The fall of that city was terrible. It terrified the whole empire. The superb palaces of the patricians were invaded, plundered, and set on fire by the drunken barbarians. Virgins, Christian and pagan, were violated, except those who fled into Church.

Not for eight hundred years, since the taking of Rome by the Gauls in 387 BC, had the capital of the empire been invaded and outraged by barbaric hordes. Her surprise then was greater than her terror, and her shame greater than her surprise.

St. Jerome, writing on the Scriptures in the cave of Bethlehem, heard the news and wrote: "At the news my speech failed me, and sobs choked the words that I was dictating. She had been captured ... the City by whom the whole world had once been taken captive."[26]

---

[26] Quoted in Arnold Toynbee, *A Study of History, vol. 5: The Disintegrations of Civilizations* (New York: Oxford University Press, 1939), 223.

At the close of that century, the Holy Father, Gregory the Great, standing at the tombs of the apostles Peter and Paul, preached this sermon affirming the truth of the words of these apostles already quoted:

> Today, there is on every side death, on every side grief, on every side desolation, on every side we are smitten, on every side our cup is being filled with draughts of bitterness ... (on the other hand) these saints at whose tombs we are now standing lived in a world that was flourishing, yet they trampled upon its material prosperity with their spiritual contempt. In that world life was long, well-being was continuous, there was material wealth, there was a high birth-rate, there was the tranquillity of lasting peace; and yet when that world was still so flourishing in itself, it had already withered in the hearts of these saints.[27]

In other words, almost four centuries before Rome fell, Peter and Paul said it would, because it had forgotten God. Now Gregory, representative of the Church which has survived the fall of all civilization, says that these men of the Church knew it would fall—and they saw it when Rome was strong and mistress of the world. In their eyes the city had written its own sentence of death with its own godless hands.

In our own American history, too, we find a recognition of the Divine Judgment. When Thomas Jefferson wrote the Declaration of Independence he penned these lines: "All men are created equal." He made no exception: "*All men.*" But he kept slaves! And he knew it!

To his credit, it must be said that he introduced a law into the Virginia legislature in 1778, prohibiting the slave trade, though slavery continued in the state.

Recognizing, however, the inconsistency and knowing that the blood of some men was in his own time being spilled by other men because they were denied equality, he expressed his fear in these words: "I tremble for my country when I reflect that God is just: that his justice cannot

---

[27] Quoted in Arnold Toynbee, *A Study of History, vol. 4: The Breakdowns of Civilizations* (New York: Oxford University Press, 1939), 60–61.

sleep forever."[28] It was a language almost identical to that which Peter used against Rome.

And well might Jefferson be concerned, for any nation which spills blood, either its own or another's, will have its own poured forth in reparation. "All that take the sword shall perish with the sword" (Matt. 26:52).

We know well when the injustice was righted and the judgment came, for one man was great enough to see in the Civil War, a manifestation of the justice of God: Abraham Lincoln. He said,

> It is the duty of nations as well as of men, to own their dependence upon the overruling power of God; to confess their sins and transgressions in humble sorrow, yet with assured hope that genuine repentance will lead to mercy and pardon; and to recognize the sublime truth, announced in the Holy Scriptures and proven by all history, that those nations only are blessed.
>
> And insomuch as we know that by his divine law nations, like individuals, are subjected to punishments and chastisements in this world, may we not justly fear that the awful calamity of civil war which now desolates the land may be but a punishment inflicted upon us for our presumptuous sins, to the needful end of our national reformation as a whole people?
>
> We have been recipients of the choicest bounties of Heaven. We have been preserved, these many years, in peace and prosperity. We have grown in numbers, wealth, and power as no other nation has ever grown; but we have forgotten God.
>
> We have forgotten the gracious hand that preserved us in peace, and multiplied and enriched and strengthened us; and we have vainly imagined, in the deceitfulness of our hearts, that all these blessings were produced by some superior wisdom and virtue of our own. Intoxicated with unbroken success, we have become too

---

[28] Thomas Jefferson, *Notes on the State of Virginia* (Philadelphia, PA: H. C. Carey and L. Lea, 1825), 222.

self-sufficient to feel the necessity of redeeming and preserving grace, too proud to pray to the God that made us:

It behooves us, then, to humble ourselves before the offended Power, to confess our national sins, and to pray for clemency and forgiveness.[29]

Thus spoke Abraham Lincoln.

This is one of the greatest documents ever written by the pen of any American. To Jefferson goes the credit of writing our Declaration of Independence. To Lincoln goes the credit of writing our Declaration of Dependence. Jefferson declared we were independent from tyrants; Lincoln added, we are dependent on God. The ethical complement to our Bill of Rights, he told us, is our Bill of Duties.

If Lincoln could come back today, would he not remind us in the midst of this awful war that we are under the Judgment of God, and that prayer and reparation for our national sins may well be the essential condition of victory?

"It does behoove us," as he said, "to humble ourselves before the offended Power." And why? Because we will have greater burdens in peace than we will have in war. We will need God's assistance to make effective in deed the words of our Atlantic Charter!

We are on record in the Atlantic Charter as guaranteeing the freedom and integrity of small nations. The Atlantic Charter is a kind of political counterpart to the Sermon on the Mount, for it is a defense of the weak and the poor.

The day our Blessed Lord preached that Sermon on the Mount, He prepared His own Crucifixion; but little do those who isolate the Beatitudes from the Cross understand that one is inseparable from the other.

He knew that the weak could not be defended except by bearing the slings and arrows of the strong, and that to speak for the poor was to invite a cross from the rich.

[29] Abraham Lincoln, Proclamation of a National Fast Day, March 30, 1863, as quoted in *Life and Works of Abraham Lincoln*, vol. 6, *State Papers: 1861–1865*, ed. Marion Mills Miller (New York: Current Literature, 1907), 156–157.

How then shall our Atlantic Charter, which defends the integrity of small nations, become effective except by bearing the opprobrium of the strong? How shall we liberate the oppressed, except by being smitten with the sword of the oppressor?

The day we wrote that Atlantic Charter we wrote in ink something that can be fulfilled only in blood. The Atlantic Charter can come into being only as the Sermon on the Mount—by enduring a Golgotha for a few hours from the powerful Caesars of the earth!

Lincoln saw that when he wrote his proclamation for freedom of the Negro—and we must see it too as we proclaim the freedom of the children and nations of the world.

No human power is strong enough to overcome the temptation to compromise with the strong? Whence shall come our energy to resist except from Him who went from the mount of His defense of the poor, to the mount of a Cross where the Beatitudes became the flesh and blood of the civilized world?

The word *God* was left out of the Atlantic Charter, but our president did not leave it out of his declaration of war, for he ended it with these words: "So help us God."

And all Americans who are one with him in this war trust that when the Day of Victory dawns, we will begin to talk of peace with the same words: "So help us God!"

19

Freedom in Danger

To avoid the Judgment of God by catastrophe we must relearn the meaning of freedom and justice. Justice will be the subject of the next chapter. Here we contend that freedom is in danger.

A proof that we are in danger of losing freedom, is because everyone is talking about it. If you suddenly came into a country where everyone was talking about the health of the lungs, you would immediately conclude that a disastrous microbe was rampant.

In the last war everyone spoke about "making the world safe for democracy," and yet the world became so unsafe for democracy, that within twenty-one years democracy had to stumble into another war to preserve itself.

Now, we ought to be worried about freedom, simply because everyone is talking about it! Slaves talk most about freedom; the oppressed, most about justice; the hungry, most about food.

We are all agreed that the external threat to our freedom and the freedom of the world comes from the Totalitarian states. There is no need to develop this thesis. They are Satan's vice-regents of tyranny, the antichrist's advance agents of adversity.

But our point is that the gravest threat to freedom comes from within; not from *within America alone*, but from within the hearts and souls of men throughout the world.

While the world is attempting to preserve freedom in the political order, it is surrendering it in those deeper realms upon which the political reposes.

Picture a group of men on a rooftop proclaiming in song and story the glories of an architecture, while below, saboteurs have already knocked out half the foundations of the house, and you have the picture of modern freedom.

Politicians in the upper stories are glorifying freedom, while false philosophy, false education, and so-called liberal Christianity have knocked away its supports.

The philosophical foundation is being undermined by the modern tendency to give the primacy to *will* over *reason*. In reality, however, the *reason* determines the targets or the goal of life; the *will* shoots the arrows.

The Christian mind, continuing the best tradition of the ancient world, contended that first there must be the truth of *reason*; then there is the action of the will—first the *target*, then the *arrows*. The modern world turns it around; first there is the *action*, then the *rationalization* of the action.

The difference between the two is well expressed by St. John and Goethe. St. John wrote: "In the beginning was the Word.... And the Word was made flesh" (John 1:1, 14). In other words, first the idea, then the deed; first the dogma, then the morals; first the program, then the fulfillment.

Goethe reversed it because he reflected the world-spirit in which he lived: "In the beginning was the deed." First you do whatever you please, then you use reason to justify what you have done; first you seize Poland, then you appeal to law; first you bomb Pearl Harbor, then you give reasons for declaring war; first you use power, then you find a law to support it.

Now, modern philosophy and modern law, by making the will primary, have made reason its servant. But will without reason is will to power. Reason then has no other function than to justify its violence.

If we live without the goals and purposes of life, which reason gives us, and if we define freedom as the right to do whatever we please, then how can we decide between conflicting wills except by force and violence?

We are thus destroying freedom in our souls by bad thinking while we mouth it most loudly with our lips. We are in graver danger than we know.

Freedom is also denied in education today. This may sound bizarre to some educators who have been shouting catchwords about *freedom* for decades. But I submit they are talking about *license*—not *freedom*.

They are concerned with freedom *from* something; not freedom for something; they are interested only in freedom without law and discipline, rather than freedom within the law.

And the proof? Do not many educators today assume that evil and sin are due to ignorance, and that if we educate, we will remove evil? Do not others assume that evil is due to bad environment, bad teeth, or bad glands, and that an increase of material wealth will obliterate evil?

Can they not see that these assumptions destroy freedom; for if evil is the result of ignorance, and not the result of a perverse use of freedom, then Hitler is an ignoramus, but he is not a villain.

Can they not see that education without a proper philosophy of life can be made the servant of evil, as well as good? Have they not the vision to see that if evil and sin are to be attributed solely to external circumstances, then man is not free to do wrong? Then wrong is in our environment, but not in us.

Is it not inconsistent to praise a free man for choosing what is right, and at the same time, when he does wrong, deny that he is free?

The fact is that sin and its possibility in this world are the evidence of freedom—a freedom not used rightly for God's purpose, but freedom abused for man's selfish ends.

Deny sin and you deny freedom. Deny that man can do evil, and you deny that man can in this world freely do good! That kind of education is destroying freedom in our schools, while our soldiers are fighting for it on the battlefronts of the world.

Modern religion has also denied freedom. Do not misunderstand! It preaches freedom. But here we are searching hearts, not lips. Modern religion denies freedom because it denies Hell. In a recent survey of ministers it was discovered that 73 percent did not believe in Hell.

If there is no Hell, why should there be a Heaven? If there is no wrong, and hence no sin for which men might be punished, why should there be a Heaven where they should be rewarded for their virtues? If there are statues erected to our heroes, why should there not be prisons for our traitors!

Whom do they think God is—a kind of grandmother who laughs off the wrongdoing of His children, as if there were no scales of justice, and He were not the God of Righteousness?

This sugary, pale ersatz of Christianity has not only set at naught the very words of the Christ whom they preach—the Christ who on more than a dozen occasions said there was a Hell. Hell is the eternal guarantee of human freedom. If God were to destroy Hell, at that moment He would destroy human freedom.

So long as there is a Hell, we know that He so respects human freedom, that He will not by force or power destroy even that free will which rises up against Him with an everlasting "I will not serve."

These are the reasons why we ought to fear for freedom in the modern world. We should fear for it externally, because of the chains the dictators would forge on the anvil of war. We should fear for it internally because of the chains that are tightening within the modern heart—chains forged by a philosophy which destroys freedom by denying reason, by an education which destroys it by denying sin, and by a religion which destroys it by denying Hell.

Satan is thus destroying our freedom at the very moment he has let us believe that we are most free. He has succeeded in destroying our freedom by the very same temptations in which he failed in tempting Christ.

Our Lord based His Kingdom on love and therefore on freedom, for love is the essence of freedom, as force is its very negation.

Satan tried to tempt our Lord from His gospel of love by offering three substitutes. In the first temptation, instead of winning souls through love, Satan suggested Christ buy them with bread, inasmuch as men are hungry.

In the second temptation, instead of winning souls through freedom and love, Satan suggested Christ win them by manifesting great power over nature, such as throwing Himself from a temple tower unhurt.

In the third temptation, Satan suggested winning souls through politics. He unfurled before the mind's eye of the Savior all the kingdoms and empires and nations of the world, and in a frightening boast said: "All these will I give thee, if falling down thou wilt adore me" (Matt. 4:9).

Our Lord refused to surrender freedom. If souls would not love Him without the bribery of bread, without the exhibitionism of power, and without selling Himself to Caesar, He would still not force them. Freedom would endure through an eternal Heaven and an eternal Hell.

Satan is now back again in the world, and how he is succeeding in destroying freedom!

Souls are today selling themselves out for that bread which they call security; for the power which is now called science and progress; while others, in over a fifth of the world's surface, have bartered their freedom for a political system under the control of a dictator.

Dostoevsky, that great Russian writer of the last century, was right when in a great flash of genius he warned that the denial of sin and Hell in education and religion would end in a world Socialism where men would surrender freedom for a false security.

Making the new antichrist speak to Christ, he says: "Dost thou know that the ages will pass, and humanity will proclaim by the lips of their sages that there is no crime, and therefore no sin; there is only hunger?"[30]

Finally with license, freedom and science without God. The antichrist tells Christ in the words of Dostoevsky that license will end in class conflict, hatred, and a surrender to an omnipotent State in a vain attempt to correct these very evils:

> Freedom, free thought and science, will lead them into such straits and will bring them face-to-face with such marvels and insoluble mysteries, that some of them, the fierce and rebellious, will destroy themselves, others, rebellious but weak, will destroy one another, while the rest, weak and unhappy, will crawl fawning to our feet and whine to us: "Yes, you were right, you alone possess His mystery, and we come back to you, save us from ourselves!"[31]

Finally, in place of free men, the antichrist pictures the new Socialistic State in which he and his followers will organize everything after convincing people there is no sin—there is only hunger.

[30] Dostoevsky, *The Brothers Karamazov*, 267.
[31] Dosteovsky, *The Brothers Karamazov*, 272.

They will tremble impotently before our wrath, their minds will grow fearful, they will be quick to shed tears like women and children, but they will be just as ready at a sign from us to pass to laughter and rejoicing, to happy mirth and childish song.

Yes, we shall set them to work, but in their leisure hours we shall make their life like a child's game, with children's songs and innocent dance. Oh, we shall allow them even sin, they are weak and helpless, and they will love us like children because we allow them to sin.

We shall tell them that every sin will be expiated, if it is done with our permission, that we allow them to sin because we love them, and the punishment for these sins we take upon ourselves. And we shall take it upon ourselves, and they will adore us as their saviours who have taken on themselves their sins before God. And they will have no secrets from us.

We shall allow or forbid them to live with their wives and mistresses, to have or not to have children—according to whether they have been obedient or disobedient—and they will submit to us gladly and cheerfully.

The most painful secrets of their conscience, all, all they will bring to us, and we shall have an answer for all. And they will be glad to believe our answer, for it will save them from the great anxiety and terrible agony they endure at present in making a free decision for themselves.[32]

And antichrist continues:

What I say to Thee will come to pass, and our dominion will be built up. I repeat, to-morrow Thou shalt see that obedient flock who at a sign from me will hasten to heap up the hot cinders about the pile on which I shall burn Thee for coming to hinder us. For if anyone has ever deserved our fires, it is Thou. To-morrow I shall burn Thee. Dixi.[33]

[32] Dostoevsky, *The Brothers Karamazov*, 273.
[33] Dostoevsky, *The Brothers Karamazov*, 274.

Where shall we go for a defender against this slavery of antichrist? Only to Him who resisted and overcame him on the mount of temptation and on the Mount of Calvary.

On Calvary it was not only the ancient world, but our own world of today which challenged: "Come down and we will believe." They were willing to admit that they would believe if He would only show His Power by stepping down from His gibbet!

Poor fools! Did they not see that they were asking Him to force them to believe, which would have been the end of freedom? They were free to believe that He was the Son of God, as the thief said, so long as He did not come down to smite them!

They had freedom so long as He left their faith in their own hands and not in His. His refusal to come down was the battle flag of freedom. The nails which pierced Him were the stars of the flag of freedom; the bruises of His body battered by free men, were the stripes of that flag. His blood was its red; His flesh its blue and its white.

So long as our Lord hangs on His Cross, man is free! The moment He comes down in power, man is His slave, and He is man's dictator. But come down He will not! Freedom will never be destroyed. Not even in Hell will He dictate, for even man has the eternal choice of his rebellious will.

So He did not come down! Because it is human to come down! If He came down He would have made Nazism, Fascism, and Communism before their time. The coming down is the death of love. If He came down, He never would have saved us! It is divine to hang there!

Unfurl and wave to the four winds of the world, "O battle flag of freedom." There will always be freedom when men are not forced to love; but there will always be love when we are not forced to be free!

20

Moral Basis of Peace

All our talk about spheres of influence, global strategy, Balkan Federa-
tions, international courts, Beveridge plans, freedom and democracy, will
collapse like a house of cards unless based on the moral order of justice.
As Pius XI said:

"To create the atmosphere of lasting peace, neither peace treaties
nor the most solemn pacts, nor international meetings or conferences,
nor even the most disinterested efforts of any statesmen, will be enough,
unless in the first place are recognized the sacred rights of natural and
divine law."[34]

In other words a strong sword can put an end to the war, but it cannot
beget peace; for peace does not come from the womb of arrested hostilities,
but from justice rooted in God.

Families who are quarreling over a back fence may stop fighting when
one of them runs out of bricks, but peace will not follow unless a change
takes place in their hearts.

Perhaps then this talk may not be so impractical after all. Maybe the
world is in this mess simply because our world is controlled by men who
are too impractical.

---

[34] Pius XI, Encyclical Letter on the Sacred Heart *Caritate Christi* Compulsi
(May 3, 1932), no. 26.

When a machine is half out of order any tinkerer can fix it, but when it is completely broken down it calls for the attention of the expert. Practical men are always trying to build a Bethlehem of peace and glory and angel songs with the modern counterparts of gold, frankincense, and myrrh—namely, money, chemistry, and death-dealing armaments, but they never think of the Babe.

These practical planners who think that all the conditions of peace are within the domain of politics, economics, and finance are going to end like a man who might add two and two together and get the surprise of his life. They assume that the international order is a great machine which will run perfectly if it is efficiently planned and oiled from the international vats of good will.

But the tragic fact is the international order is more like a living organism composed of human beings with their own wills and springs of actions, and hence the functioning of the organism depends on the thoughts they think, the law they obey, and the justice they serve.

In order to bring home the importance of a moral basis for peace, we ask these questions: Why should any of the treaties or pacts signed at the close of this world war be kept? What guarantee have we that they will be honored more from 1943 to 1963 than they were in that twilight of honor from 1918 to 1939?

What right have these journalists and educators who have been sniping at the moral law for decades, to expect that the honor born of morality—which they impugn—will be the unbreakable code of international affairs?

What promises can we trust, in what agreement can we confide, what treaty is not a scrap of paper, if pragmatic education, now called *realist*, assures us that the absolute distinction between right and wrong is not grounded in eternal justice, but is a relic of primitive taboos and a hangover from medieval blindness?

No one ever seems to discuss this question: but it is so elementary that until we answer it there is no reason for making any treaties.

One reason given for the keeping of treaties is based on custom, but what makes the custom? And is it not more customary to break treaties today than to keep them? As Shakespeare might say: "a custom honored more in the breach than in the observance."[35]

Another reason given is that treaties bind because nations freely enter into them. But what is to prevent nations from freely walking out on treaties, as Russia and Germany did in the case of Poland, and Japan did in the case of China, and Italy did in the case of Ethiopia?

A third reason, which is the pragmatist or positivist theory of law, and which is most common today even among our own jurists, is that a treaty is binding because it is advantageous or expedient to have it so.

But suppose it ceases to be advantageous, or suppose it becomes more expedient to abandon it—Alas! Hitlerism! Pragmatism is the philosophy which holds that the true is the useful, and certainly nothing could be more useful today than to be something more than a pragmatist.

As Longfellow once said: "Morality without religion is only a kind of dead reckoning—an endeavor to find our place on a cloudy sea by measuring the distance we have run, but without any observation of the heavenly bodies."[36]

When one gets down to rock bottom, there are only two possible reasons for keeping treaties; either because of force, or because of moral obligation. If force, then might makes right; then the Nazis are right in Holland and Belgium, and the Japs are right in the Philippines; then if the Nazis and Japs conquered us, which God forbid, the treaties they would make would be just because imposed by force.

The theory of force sees right when we can apply the force, but in itself force can never make right. Force works on brutes, it does not work on men.

Power without morality is power without responsibility. As Lord Acton said: "Power corrupts, and absolute power corrupts absolutely."

And shall we who live in the tradition of the Declaration of Independence forget that the pursuit of happiness is not down the road of the

---

[35] Shakespeare, *Hamlet*, act 1, scene 4.

[36] Henry Wadsworth Longfellow, *Kavanagh: A Tale*, 13, as quoted in *The Complete Prose Works of Henry Wadsworth Longfellow with His Later Poems*, ed. Octavius B. Frothingham (Boston: Houghton Mifflin, 1883), 1262.

pursuit of power. As Thomas Jefferson said: "[I have never] been able to conceive how any rational being could propose happiness to himself from the exercise of power over others."[37]

Beware of power. It is more dangerous now than ever, for power is today passing again from the many to the few. It used to dwell in the masses; now it is enthroned in dictators.

Like other Pilates they still say to Innocence and Truth and Justice: "Knowest thou not that I have power to crucify thee?" (John 19:10). Shall we who boast we are defending the Christian cause, forget that against all who would make power the seed of justice, the Master said: "Thou shouldst not have any power against me, unless it were given thee from above" (John 19:11)?

Outside power-force there is only one reason for keeping treaties, namely, because a treaty imposes a moral obligation rather than a physical one. A treaty is a sacred thing because the God of Justice is its witness.

That is why certain things are eternally right and others eternally wrong. And in its general outlines, there is no difference between Christian morality and pagan morality, for God is the source of both.

Christianity did not impose a set of moral sentiments on the world of which the world never heard before; and the pagans would never have accepted the supernatural standards of morality if they had not already found a response in the natural standards of morality already written on the tablets of their hearts.

That is why there runs through history a record of sacredness of treaties based on the moral order. The Jews made their treaties "in the name of the Lord God of Israel." Almost all the nations of antiquity surrounded their treaties with religious symbols and rites.

Horace, expressing the best of the Roman tradition, warned: "What profit vain laws without moral support."

---

[37] Thomas Jefferson to M. D. Destutt Tracy, Monticello, January 26, 1811, as quoted in *Memoirs, Correspondence, and Private Papers of Thomas Jefferson*, vol. 3, ed. Thomas Jefferson Randolph (London: HenryColburn and Richard Bentley, 1829), 166.

Lincoln, in his first inaugural address, expressed the American tradition by reminding himself that his oath was registered in Heaven: "You can have no oath registered in heaven to destroy the government; while I shall have the most solemn one to preserve, protect and defend it."

And Benjamin Franklin, in November, 1728, expressed the idea that a word ought to be kept, not because it is prudent policy, but because we are children of God and under His moral law: "That I may have a constant regard to honor and probity, that I may possess a perfect innocence and a good conscience, and at length become truly virtuous and magnanimous — Help me, good God: Help me, O Father!"[38]

And all the treaties of Christian Europe from the very beginning were written in the spirit of an obligation rooted in morality, for they all began: "In the name of the Holy and Undivided Trinity." So they continued until the Treaty of Versailles, which began "In the name of the High Contracting Parties." Men had become "wise."

In the meantime they learned that man came from a monkey, that progress was due to evolution, that evil was due to bad glands, that morality was convention, and that God, in the language of a professor from Ohio, was "a projection into the roaring loom of time of a unified complex of psychical values."

And we wonder why we should have a second world war in twenty-one years?

Are we blind? Can we not see that if law is divorced from morality and religion, then treaties cease to be obligatory and begin to be mere arrangements, binding only so long as they are advantageous? Rob international justice of its roots in morality and treaties are hypothetical, not categorical; convenient tools, not honorable obligations, while law becomes an attorney's cloak woven from the flimsy fabric of legalistic phraseology artfully placed on the shoulders of arbitrary power.

No wonder we had 4,568 treaties signed before the League of Nations from 1920 to 1939 and 211 signed the eleven months before the war.

---

[38] Benjamin Franklin, *Memoirs of the Life and Writings of Benjamin Franklin*, ed. William Temple Franklin (London: Henry Colburn, 1818), 192.

Cowper described the result:

And hast thou sworn on every slight pretence
Till perjuries are common as bad pence;
While thousands careless of the damning sin
Kiss the book outside, who ne'er look within?[39]

What difference does morality make in the international society? The same difference it makes in domestic society. When Catholics enter into a marriage pact, they know it is binding; they stake their eternal salvation on its timeless character; and they acknowledge that they should live up to its terms even when it goes against them. "Till death do them part" means "till death do them part."

But our modern pagans who have left religion behind do not scruple to make a marriage a pact terminable at the fancy of either party. Now international treaties grounded on morality are like marriages between Catholics, in the sense that honor is inseparable from morality; but international treaties without a basis in the moral law make orphan nations as divorces make orphan children.

A recent decision of the United States Supreme Court required one state to honor divorces of its own citizens obtained in another state with a six weeks divorce law, even though the divorcees went to the latter state merely to escape the greater severity of its own laws. I wonder if the advocates of such a system would agree that the treaties we make with Germany and Japan should be breakable at the end of six months on the ground of mutual incompatibility!

We cannot build up a stable, international society and pass peace on to the next generation until we lay to heart the basic conditions of peace: "Seek ye first the kingdom of God and his justice, and all these things shall be added unto you" (Luke 12:31).

Two impractical corollaries follow from the impractical principle:

First, the new League of Nations, or whatever it is called, should not be open to everyone, but should have membership in it conditioned upon

---

[39] William Cowper, "Expostulation."

the acceptance of certain basic moral principles of justice. It should be more like a club than a streetcar; that is, it should have certain standards of admission.

The subscription rate of the last league was too low. Because anyone could walk in, anyone could walk out. Hence a nation or a state that will not accept a common ethos or set of moral principles, as superior to the sovereignty of any nation and existing before any nation began, and binding even when its application goes against itself, should not be permitted to sit in that august body, any more than a foreigner may sit in the councils of the United States.

Hence if a big nation makes a condition that it will not enter the League unless it can swallow up half a dozen small nations then let that power, whether it be Japan, Germany, Italy, Great Britain, Russia, or the United States, be quarantined until it recovers its ethical health. No court of justice can survive if the thief agrees to its decision only on condition that he can keep his loot.

Another corollary from the impractical principle that peace is inseparable from Divine Justice has to do with domestic society.

The loss of repentance in the spiritual order is paralleled by a loss of discipline in the social order. The very moment the liberal theologians denied Hell, which is one aspect of Divine Justice, educators denied discipline. Since there was no Divine Justice which had to be restored by repentance, so neither was there a social justice which had to be righted by appropriate penalties.

It was exactly the same mentality that produced Hitlerism in the international society and which produced hoodlumism and violent juvenile delinquency in domestic society.

Once Hitler found that he could seize the territory of other nations and trample on human lives with impunity because there was no vindictive justice, so in our large cities, individuals felt they could play fast and loose with property and human lives.

FBI Chief, Mr. J. Edgar Hoover, reported to the House Appropriations Committee that prostitution by girls under twenty-one had increased 64.8 percent over last year; that sex crimes by girls had increased 104.7 percent;

that assault by males under twenty-one had increased 17 percent and rape 10.1 percent—that in spite of the fact that many young men are in military service. "Practically all these are civilian arrests."

Commenting upon it, he said: "If, during these trying periods we forget the moral needs of the next generation, we have not fulfilled the trust placed in us."

We found out that the only way to stop international brigandage was by going to war to restore justice; and we have yet to learn that lesson in civil society.

Pupils who know they can insult their teachers and escape punishment; youths who know they can injure others without themselves feeling pain; delinquents who know they can destroy property and then on trial, as in one instance, be given candy by a sentimental judge, or else have their evil called "a fall in evolution" by a fuzzy social worker, will go on and on disrupting the social order as Hitler did, until they feel a few hard blows of justice. There is nothing either in our social system or in our educational system that cannot be cured by discipline and the restoration of justice.

Thus the denial of Divine Justice with Hell as the penalty for its repudiation inevitably implies the denial of human justice with discipline as the penalty for its violation. A reprimand or a fine is no cure for a man arrested for violence to his fellow man. There is only one language such men can understand, as there is only one language even Christians can understand when we break God's law—there is a Hell!

Is there hope for the restoration of a moral order based on justice? There is! Mr. Churchill last week told England that the nation's education must return to religion and morality—or perish. Mr. Roosevelt too said: "We are especially conscious of the Divine Power.... It is seemly that we should, at a time like this, pray to Almighty God for His blessing on our country and for the establishment of a just and permanent peace among all the nations of the world."[40]

---

[40] Franklin D. Roosevelt, *The Public Papers and Addresses of Franklin D. Roosevelt*, vol. 9, ed. Samuel Irving Rosenman (New York: Random House, 1939), 328.

There is hope too in the new America that is being forged on the anvil of war with the hammers of a Divine Justice. Most of the young men in our armed service are getting a sounder education than if they stayed in school, for they are now learning that the difference between right and wrong is so hard and so absolute that it takes death sometimes to make the right prevail. Their thinking has broken with our gilded past.

Some marines at Guadalcanal, looking at a few moronic, pathological youths bedecked in those glorified diapers called "zoot suits," said: "Maybe we ought to go back and clean up America."

Another wounded boy just back from the Pacific said: "Before I went to war, I believed that justice was what I wanted; now I have learned to live and to fight for others."

And one need hardly recall the words of the soldier at Bataan: "There are no atheists in foxholes."

These boys are learning justice the hard way, and they will love America even more when they come back.

For a parallel look to the American Legion of the last war, which more than any other organization in the United States — outside of the Catholic Church — consistently and fearlessly opposed the growth of Communism in our midst, which opposition within the past few days found its echo in the statement of the attorney general of the United States: "It may not be good for Russia to get rid of the Communists, but it will be good for America."

These boys of ours in like manner will know the wrong things and the right things when they come back, for they are now finding them out in the mud of Africa, on the rolling seas of the Atlantic and the Pacific, in the jungles of New Guinea and the swamps of the Solomons.

When we go out to work, we know we will come back; when they go on the field, in the air, or on the sea, they have a rendezvous with uncertainty and they seem to care less because they have one supreme interest — the taking of the "objective." And all morality is grounded on an objective, on an end, a goal — on God.

We will have an invasion when this war is over — not from a foreign enemy, but an invasion of great men, twice-born Americans. And unless we get down on our knees and transform our hearts by prayer as they have by sacrifice, we will not even understand the language they speak. Their values will be different; their outlook on life will be different. They will be the new America!

And those who do return will never be able to blot out of their memory the thousands of little white crosses they left behind marking a spot where foreign earth is piled high on hearts that loved American soil.

Those crosses will be symbols of the justice for which they fought, vertically pointing up to God from whom justice is derived, and horizontally pointing outward to America to whom that justice will be applied. Each little white cross will be as a miniature Calvary and cameo Golgotha, and as a splinter from a great Cross whence comes "Greater love than this no man hath" (John 15:13).

And when finally the taps sound on the first night when the guns of the world go to sleep, we will join with them in beloved memory to those little white crosses and we shall pledge with them, that America shall have a rebirth of justice under God, thanks to our martyred dead who have given to the earth some of the noblest red blood this earth of ours has drunk since Calvary drank the Blood of Christ.

21

Jew and Christian

The two greatest vocations ever given to any peoples by God were given to Jews and Christians. The vocation of the Jew was the "giving of the law, and the service of God, and the promises" (Rom. 9:4).

Beyond all the ties of flesh and blood, and transcendent to membership in the same ethico-historical community, was the great supra-historical mission to be a chosen people selected by God, to be the vehicle of His revelation to men.

The vocation of the Christian was to establish the brotherhood of men under the Fatherhood of God in the unity of the Spirit: "One body and one Spirit.... One Lord, one faith, one baptism" (Eph. 4:4–5).

Not because of a common ethic, nor because they shared a vague admiration for a great humanitarian, but because of fellowship founded on the merits of Jesus Christ, the Christians have the supra-historical mission of proclaiming a fraternity of all men under the kingship of Christ.

We must not allow individual defections from this unity to blur the picture. Whether individual Jews ignore the God of their fathers, or whether individual Christians live as if Christ had never died for their sins, does not alter the fact that there is in each instance a communal vocation, a divine mission entrusted to a people and to a kingdom.

The relation between the Jew and the Christian, from the Christian point of view, is the relation of father to son, of roots to branches.

In the magnificently strong language of Pius XI, who—commenting upon the words of the Canon of the Mass, "sacrificium Patri archae nostri Abrahae," the sacrifice of our father Abraham—said: "Notice that Abraham is called our patriarch, our ancestor. Anti-Semitism is incompatible with the thought and the supreme reality expressed in this text. It is a movement in which we Christians can have no part whatsoever.... Anti-Semitism is unacceptable. Spiritually we are Semites."[41]

The Jew was given the vocation to be the chosen people announcing the law of God. The Christian was given the vocation of establishing the brotherhood of men in the Fatherhood of God, through the merits of Jesus Christ. That brings us to this question: Have the Jews and Christians been faithful to their vocations?

First the Jews. There is a vast number who still are a devout, God-fearing, and God-loving people, but the spiritual condition of many Jews throughout the world today is sad—I say spiritual condition, for that is even more serious than their political condition. Very distinguished rabbis have told me that only one out of ten Jews attends a synagogue, either liberal or orthodox.

Some of their most distinguished fellows have repudiated all connection between Judaism and God.

Ludwig Lewisohn, well known in the Zionist movement, says "the Jew need believe nothing [to be a Jew]";[42] and Albert Einstein proclaims disbelief in a personal God, paying homage to a "cosmic religion" rather than to the God of Abraham, Isaac, and Jacob. Louis D. Brandeis confessed that he "had never gone to a synagogue."

To all who have the interests of God and immortal souls at heart, this condition is regrettable. It once awakened in the heart of St. Paul a great regret: "I lie not, my conscience bearing me witness in the Holy Ghost: That I have great sadness, and continual sorrow in my heart. For I wished

[41] Pius XI, Allocution to Directors of the Belgian Catholic Radio Agency (September 1938), as quoted in Jacques Maritain, *Anti-Semitism* (London: Centenary Press, 1939), 27.
[42] Ludwig Lewisohn, *Israel* (New York: Boni and Liveright, 1925), 87.

myself to be an anathema from Christ, for my brethren, who are my kins-men according to the flesh" (Rom. 9:1–3).

On the other hand, how many Christians are living up to their vocation?

A survey made by a professor of Northwestern University into the belief of seven hundred ministers in and around Chicago representing twenty denominations revealed that 43 percent disbelieved in the inspiration of Sacred Scripture, though four hundred years ago that was their basic article of faith; 51 percent disbelieved in the necessity of Baptism.

And among the theological students who are today in the pulpit, the results were more staggering still: 69 percent disbelieved in the resurrection of the body; 52 percent denied that Christ would come again to judge the living and the dead; 61 percent denied the redemption of Christ on the Cross; and 37 percent denied the Divinity of Christ.

Suppose the same proportion of Americans disbelieved in the first ten amendments to the Constitution of the United States. What would be the condition of democracy!

How many so-called Christians in the United States can recall the third commandment, and how many join with their fellow man in the worship of God?

This mass defection of Christians from Christ is tragic and it grieves the heart of all good Protestants who, with Catholics, confess Christ to be the Son of the Living God.

The fact is that both Jews and Christians are failing in their vocation: the Jews are failing in their vocation to be the people chosen to propagate God's law, and the Christians are failing in their vocation to preserve the brotherhood of men under the headship of Christ.

This may not seem disastrous to a man without faith—but that is be-cause the man without faith can see disaster only when it happens, never before it happens.

In order to bring home the awful consequences of this vocation failure among Jews and Christians, look to its social effects in the contemporary world. Before our very eyes there is being fulfilled the terrible warning: "The kingdom of God shall be taken from you" (Matt. 21:43). And so it has! By the Nazis and by the Communists.

Hitler, in so many words, says to the Jews:

You have had a vocation: the vocation to announce and to preserve the knowledge of the law of God, and to await as a chosen
people the fulfillment of the promise given to you by God. But you
have either forgotten it, or abandoned it.

So I shall take the empty shell of your past, created by your own
apostasy, and I shall further empty it of its divine content: I shall
prostitute and further secularize and profane it.

I shall substitute the idea of the German race in place of the race
of God, and the German mission in place of the divine mission.
This shall be the Messiahism of the twentieth century.

Communism says to the Christians:

You spiritual heirs of the Jews, who thought you also had an
additional vocation—the vocation to preserve the brotherhood of
men under the Fatherhood of God and under the headship of His
Son Jesus Christ—you have repudiated your Christ, your need of
redemption, your oneness in the Spirit. You have failed this supposed vocation and it has failed you.

But we shall take it up, empty it of its Christian content, des-
ecrate it, pervert it, harden it, and substitute the comradeship of
violence for the brotherhood of love, and unite society on the basis
of class hatred instead of the universal love of man in Christ. And
this shall be the new brotherhood of the twentieth century.

Just as the French Revolution once prostituted the altar of Notre Dame
by enthroning on it a courtesan as the Goddess of Reason, so now these
new pseudo-religions and false mysticisms empty the people of God of
God, and the brotherhood of Christ of Christ, and give to the world its
anti-Semitic and anti-Christian Nazism and Communism.

As we supplied the Japanese with steel which they converted into bullets
to turn against us, so too have Nazism and Communism melted down the
steel of two great vocations and made them instruments of persecution, of
slavery, and of world disorder.

The chaos of the world is due in great measure to our failure to live up to the full responsibilities of our vocation. Neither of us has been all he was destined to be; we have failed in what God wanted us to be. "These things you ought to have done, and not to leave those undone" (Matt. 23:23).

A vocation to bear witness to God and a vocation to bear witness to Christ, like fine gold, have been melted down and an alloy substituted to make a base counterfeit. The very ideas that were meant to be channels for the salvation of souls have become sewers for the pollution of the world.

But they would not have so overflowed modern history if we, Jews and Christians, had been faithful unto the mission given us by God.

Nazism and Communism in a certain sense are a punishment on the Jews for failing to be faithful Jews and on the Christians for failing to be faithful Christians.

Both of them have forgotten the rock from which they were hewn, the fountain of living waters from which they sprang; and both have provided the instruments of the world's apostasy.

For that reason Nazism and Communism are in their essence not the resurrection of primitive barbarisms; they are worse — they are perversions of the spirit due to abandonment of faith in God.

Jews and Christians alike are being persecuted by the very ideas they either rejected or forgot. Never before in the history of the world has there been such a persecution of Jews and Christians.

There is as much anti-Semitism as there is anti-Christianity, and there is as much hatred of the Christians as there is hatred of the Jews. This should be to us a sign that we have entered into an apocalyptic period of history.

Drinking, as we are, from a common chalice of misery, means that we have a common destiny.

In this new era of the world into which we are entering, there will be no persecution of one without the other. We are and will continue to be persecuted together, because the new spirit of the world is not nonreligious, or indifferent to religion, or secularist, or humanist — it is anti-God. That means that all those who have any relation with God in their collective capacity will be persecuted.

To Nazism and to Communism the Jews and Christians alike are demons. If the world hates the Jews and hates the Christians, it is because by vocation they are both "outsiders" to the spirit of anti-God, regardless of how many faithless Jews or faithless Christians join their ranks.

There is a natural "divine discontent" in anyone who has a mission from God. Whether he be faithful to that mission or not, does not alter the fact. The anti-God world hates us because we have been God-summoned, and that is sufficient to inspire a persecution.

The Jews and Christians both possess a revolutionary character; they are in the world but not of it. Since God gave them a work to do, they are both alien, a ferment, a leaven forever disturbing the slumber of an anti-religious world.

That anti-God world will be touched neither by the finger of Abraham nor the finger of Christ, neither by the historical mission of Israel in time, nor by the healing mission of the Cross for eternity. It will, as the new City of Man, make war against the City of God until the consummation of the world.

It has stolen our thunder and now we must shrink in fear from its bolts.

In the name of God therefore let the Jews stop talking about anti-Semitic persecutions and the Christians stop talking about anti-Christian persecutions, as if a tree could be cut down without affecting both root and branch.

Opposition to the persecution of the Jews is and ought to be a Christian cause, as it is in Paris where the Catholic auxiliary bishop wears the five-pointed star of David on his sleeve. Opposition to the persecution of the Christians is and ought to be a Jewish cause as it is with some Dutch Jews who make their defense synonymous with Christianity.

The solution to the problem of the persecution of Jews and Christians is therefore not along lines of good fellowship, so-called tolerance meetings, or social unities which never mention religion.

Rather does the solution lie in these great vocations snatching back from Nazism and Communism the ideas of a chosen people and the brotherhood of man, and infusing them once again with the Spirit of God, unto the regeneration of a world already reeling on the abyss of great disaster.

Let the Jews go back into their glorious history and relearn the words: "Salvation is of the Jews" (John 4:22). What more glorious mission could one have than to be God's instrument of salvation?

Re-read your Jeremias! Renew a sense of your vocation: "But this shall be the covenant that I will make with the house of Israel, after those days, saith the Lord ... I will write it in their heart: and I will be their God, and they shall be my people" (Jer. 31:33).

Open your Scriptures, ye Christians, and read the injunctions to walk worthy of your vocation to "press towards the mark, to the prize of the supernal vocation of God in Christ Jesus" (Phil. 3:14). "For if we be dead with him, we shall live also with him. If we suffer, we shall also reign with him" (2 Tim. 2:11–12).

Take back from Nazism the idea of the elect of God; steal back from Communism the idea of the brotherhood of man; revitalize them with the natural law and divine revelation and build a new and a decent world where a Jew and a Christian can live together in a world of God's righteousness and peace.

We are being driven together by the anti-God forces of the world. Hence the Jew will look in vain for peace in a secularized Messiahism or a Kingdom of God in some distant future here below. And the Christian will find only chaos in a humanism that attempts to make men brothers without a common Father.

Flimsy, indeed, is the unity of Jews and Christians which is based only on the hatred of a common enemy. Strong will it be the day we ground it on prayers to a common God.

This imaginative parable will illustrate our meaning. Picture the Nazis desecrating a Christian Church, turning it into a kind of temporary Hall of Nazi Justice. Hitler walks in and sits down before a large crucifix above the main altar. All the Jews in the neighborhood are dragged in by the soldiers to hear their death sentence. After a mock trial they proceed to march out of the Christian Church, under the eyes of the soldiers of the double-cross, as Hitler cries out: "Death to every Jew."

Before they reach the door, the figure of Christ on the Cross loosens His hands and feet from the gibbet and walks in a blaze of glory behind the last Jew, as He turns and says to Hitler: "In that case, you will want Me too!"

Someday we will learn that Christ is the Savior of all men.

22

The Power of God

The supreme instance of all history that the voice of the people is not necessarily the voice of God, was the moment when a mob passed beneath a Cross, flinging at the helpless figure there upon it the blistering sneer of the ages: "He trusted in God; let him now deliver him" (Matt. 27:43).

That taunt had a strong point: For how could He give life, who Himself could not master death? What added to its force was the apparent non-interference of God, which even He on the Cross acknowledged in that dereliction: "My God, my God, why hast thou forsaken me?" (Matt. 27:46).

Two days later, early in the morning, a converted prostitute is found walking in a cemetery—she whose heart has been captured by Him without, as other men had done, laying it waste. It was one of those calm dawns, suggesting the sleep of innocents and the gentle stir of angels' wings.

She was in search of a tomb and a dead body which she hoped she might anoint with spices. Arriving, she found a great stone rolled back from the rock-hewn grave, which on Good Friday had been guarded by Pilate's soldiers and the seal of which no man might break without penalty of death.

The idea of the Resurrection did not seem to enter her mind—she who herself had risen from a tomb sealed by the seven devils of sin. Finding the tomb empty she broke again into a fountain of tears.

No one who weeps ever looks upwards. With her eyes cast down as the brightness of the early sunrise swept over the dew-covered grass, she vaguely perceived someone near her, who asked: "Woman, why weepest thou?" (John 20:15).

Mary, thinking it might have been the gardener, said: "Because they have taken away my Lord; and I know not where they have laid him.... Sir, if thou hast taken him hence, tell me where thou hast laid him, and I will take him away" (John 20:13, 15).

The figure before her spoke only one word, one name, and in a tone so sweet and ineffably tender that it could be the only unforgettable voice of the world; and that one word was: Mary.

No one could ever say "Mary" to her as He said it. In that moment she knew Him. Dropping into the Aramaic of her mother's speech she answered but one word: "Rabboni!" "Master!" And she fell at His feet—she was always there, anointing them at a supper, standing before them at a Cross, and now kneeling before Him in the glory of an Easter morn.

A few minutes before she was asking: "Who shall roll us back the stone?" (Mark 16:3). Now an angel clad in white is saying: "Behold the place where they laid him" (Mark 16:6).

The Cross had asked the questions; the Resurrection had answered them. The Cross had asked the question: How far can power go in the world? The Resurrection answered: power ends in its own destruction, for those who slew the foe lost the day.

The Cross had asked: Why does God permit evil and sin to nail Innocence and Justice to a tree? The Resurrection answered: that sin, having done its worst, might exhaust itself and thus be overcome by love that is stronger than either sin or death.

Thus there emerges the Easter lesson that the power of evil and the chaos of any one moment can be defied and conquered, for the basis of our hope is not in any form of human power, but in the Power of God who has given to the evil of this earth its one mortal wound—an open tomb, a gaping sepulchre, an empty grave.

If the story of Christ ended with that cry of abandonment on the Cross, then what hope have we that bruised Goodness and crucified Justice will ever rise triumphant over the massed wickedness of men?

If He who died to give us the glorious liberty of the children of God could not break the chains of death, then what hope is there that the enslaved peoples of Europe will ever rise from the slavery of their graves to a freedom where a man can call a soul his own?

If the human power of Caesars could nail Supreme Innocence to a tree and then mingle His dust with the split rocks of a Jerusalem hillside, then what hope have we, who are far from that innocence, that we will ever master those modern Pilates who, in their vain boasts, say again: "Knowest thou not that I have power to crucify thee?" (John 19:10).

If there be no Power of God that can raise to the newness of life Him who said, "I am the light of the world" (John 8:12), then, in brokenhearted misery must we say to our soldiers: "Out, out brief candles, there shall be no light again."

If there be no Power of God which can rescue from the ravenous wolves of death Him who said, "I am the good shepherd" (John 10:11), then let all the innocent victims of the wolves of Nazism, Fascism, and Communism throughout the world shed their tears in vain as the cold bleak earth takes the measure of their unmade graves.

If there be no Power of God to bring back to life the Physician of our souls, the Redeemer of our sins, the Teacher of our minds, then the pathos of man's mortality is deepened and the riddle of human existence darkened forever, as the prison doors of death are everlastingly shut by the Jailer whose name is Black Despair.

You say the Resurrection contradicts science and human experience; I say to you that the rotting in the grave of Supreme Truth would contradict it a thousand times more.

I can accept a universe where Goodness is crucified by power, but I cannot accept one where there is no higher power to raise it to justification. I can accept a world where the Church is buried in a grave, but I cannot accept a world where she stays there. I can accept a world where evil has its hour, where a Poland is crucified between two thieves, where Jews and Christians are exiled, where the Cross is double-crossed by a swastika, where forty thousand churches are closed in a land where religion is called the "opium of the people," but I cannot accept a world wherein Goodness does not have its Easter Day to sing triumphant on the wings of victory.

Thus there emerges the Easter lesson that the power of evil and the chaos of any one moment can be defied and conquered, for the basis of our hope is not in any construct of human power, but in the Power of God who has given to the evil of this earth its one mortal wound—an open tomb, a gaping sepulchre, an empty grave.

Apply this Easter lesson to the dark hour in which we live. Whence shall come our hope of victory? Shall it be in the power of arms alone? Shall it be in the power of the common man alone?

Our hope for victory in this war must not be in the power of arms alone, for the enemy has the devil on his side, and guns, planes, tanks, and shells are no match for boasts.

As Isaias warned: "Woe to them that go down to Egypt for help, trusting in horses, and putting their confidence in chariots, because they are many: and in horsemen, because they are very strong: and have not trusted in the Holy One of Israel, and have not sought after the Lord" (Isa. 31:1).

Let the enemy come as so many armored and panoplied Goliaths thinking that steel must always be met by steel alone, and we shall, like other Davids, go out to meet them unto victory clothed in the Power of Him who gave to the evil of this earth its one mortal wound—an open tomb, a gaping sepulchre, an empty grave.

Nor, on the other hand, should our hope for a more democratic life in the world be in the common man unpurified by faith; for once in power, he will cease to be the common man unpurified by faith; for once in power, he will cease to be the common man of the proletariat and will become the uncommon man or the bureaucrat. The common man who trusts in flesh alone can be counted on to abuse his power just as much as the class he overthrew.

Rather we must trust in the common man made uncommon by the Power of Him who dared to say to the first of all Totalitarian Caesars of Christian history: "Thou shouldst not have any power ... unless it were given thee from above" (John 19:11).

And for all of us who have the fullness of faith, be not cast down because the persecutors of religion, having laid the Church, like her Founder, in the tomb, utter the boast: "Behold the place where we laid her." Remember the law of progress of the Church is the reverse of the law of progress of the world.

We are most progressive when we are most hated. Since we belong to no civilization, we do not die with any civilization. If the world loved the Church, the Church would be no salvation to the world. If she were not hated, she would be weak.

It is only because the fires of her truth are blinding evil eyes and convicting them of sin and judgment, that they vainly try to put them out. The Church is nearest victory when she is most defeated.

And though the world is tearing up all the photographs and blueprints of a society and a family based on the moral law of God, be not disheartened. The Church has kept the negatives.

And someday they will be used again for our trust is not in human power, but in Him for whom the tolls of execution are always sounding, though the execution never takes place.

Francis Thompson compared the Church to the lily, depicting first her defeat, then her resurrection, in these magnificent lines:

O Lily of the King! low lies thy silver wing,
And long has been the hour of thine unqueening;
And thy scent of Paradise on the night-wind spills its sighs,
Nor any take the secrets of its meaning.
O Lily of the King! I speak a heavy thing,
O patience, most sorrowful of daughters!
Lo, the hour is at hand for the troubling of the land,
And red shall be the breaking of the waters.

Sit fast upon thy stalk, when the blast shall with thee talk,
With the mercies of the King for thine awning;
And the just understand that thine hour is at hand,
Thine hour at hand with power in the dawning.
When the nations lie in blood, and their kings a broken brood,

Look up, O most sorrowful of daughters!
Lift up thy head and hark what sounds are in the dark,
For His feet are coming to thee on the waters![43]

We are living in a period of history like unto that of the Roman Empire when Julian the Apostate sat upon the throne of the Caesars. The persecution of Christ which he initiated was not like the earlier persecutions, which were prompted by the release of a barbaric instinct, but rather was due to the perversion and the loss of faith in Christ. Like his successors in the modern world, Julian persecuted because he had lost his faith—and since his conscience would not let him alone, he would not let the Church alone.

There is a story to the effect that he made a tour of the Roman Empire to investigate the success of his persecutions. He came to the ancient city of Antioch where, disguising himself, he entered into the inns, taverns, and public markets to better learn the fruits of his hate.

On one occasion, watching thousands of people crowd into a temple dedicated to Mithra, he was recognized by an old Christian friend whose name was Agathon. Pointing to the crowd and to the apparent success of the pagan cult, he sneered this question to his friend: "Agathon, whatever happened to that carpenter of Galilee—does he have any jobs these days?" Agathon answered: "He is building a coffin now for the Roman Empire, and for you."

Six months later Julian thrust a dagger into his own heart. Throwing it toward the Heavens against which he had rebelled, as his own unredemptive blood fell back upon him, he uttered his last and most famous line: "O Galilean, Thou hast conquered!"

He always does!

---

[43] Francis Thompson, "Lilium Regis."

PHILOSOPHIES

AT WAR

✠

(1943)

23

War and Revolution

There are two ways of looking at the war: one as a journalist, the other as a theologian. The journalist tells you what happens; the theologian not only why it happens, but also what matters. If we look at this war through the eyes of a journalist or a commentator, it will be only a succession of events without any remote causes in the past, or any great purpose in the future. But if we look at the war through the eyes of God, then the war is not meaningless, though we may not presently understand its details. It may very well be a purposeful purging of the world's evil that the world may have a rebirth of freedom under His holy law, for:

> Every human path leads on to God;
> He holds a myriad finer threads than gold,
> And strong as holy wishes, drawing us
> With delicate tension upward to Himself.[44]

Our approach is from the divine point of view, first of all, because it is the only explanation which fits the facts; secondly because the American people who have been confused by catchwords and slogans are seeking an inspiration for a total surrender of their great potentialities for sacrifice, both for God and country.

[44] Edmund C. Stedman, "The Protest of Faith."

The great mass of the American people are frankly dissatisfied with the ephemeral and superficial commentaries on what is happening. Being endowed with intelligence, they want to know why it is happening. We all know what we are fighting against; we want to know what we are fighting for. We all know what we are in a war; we want to know what we must do to make a lasting peace. We know whom we hate; but we want to know what we ought to love. We know we are fighting against a barbarism that is intrinsically wicked; we want to know what we have to do to make the resurrection of the wickedness impossible.

It is necessary to clear away three false conceptions of the war by reminding ourselves what that this war is not.

This war is not merely a political and an economic struggle, but rather a theological one. It is not political and economic, because politics and economics are concerned only with the means of living. And it is not just the means of living that have gone wrong, but the ends of living. Never before in the history of world have there been so many abundant means of life. Never before was there so much power, and never before have men so prepared to use that power for the destruction of human life. Never before was there so much material wealth; never before has there been so much poverty. Never before have there been so many means to draw people together through rapid communications and the radio; never before have they been so pulled apart by hate and strife and war.

The means of life no longer minister to peace and order because we have perverted and forgotten the true ends of life. Dynamite can be used as a means to build the foundations of a hospital, or it can be used as a means to destroy the entire hospital. The purpose or the intention for which it is used will determine how the means are used. Now the basic reason why our economics and politics have failed as a means to peace is that both have forgotten the end and purpose of life. We have been living as if civilization, culture, and peace were by products of economic activity, instead of the other way round, so that economics and politics are subordinated to the moral and the spiritual. Politics and economics alone are as incapable of curing our ills as an alcohol rub is in capable of curing cancer; and if we assume they will, then this world war will end in Socialism, and Socialism is only an obligatory enforced organization of the means of living to prevent utter ruin. It is not our politics that has soured, nor our economics that have rusted; it is our hearts. We live and act as if God had never made us. That is why this war is not political and economic in its fundamental aspects; it is theological.

This war has not been caused by evil dictators. It is too commonly assumed that our milk or international peace has curdled, because a few wicked dictators poured vinegar into it. Hence if we could rid the world of these evil men, we would return to a world of comparative prosperity where we would have to worry only occasionally about a fellow citizen watering our milk. What a delusion! These dictators are not the creators of the world's evil; they are its creatures; they are only boils on the surface of the world's skin; they come to the surface because there is bad blood beneath. It will do no good to puncture the boils, if we leave the source of the infection. Have we forgotten that from 1914–1918 our cry was "rid the world of the kaiser and we will have peace." Well, we got rid of the kaiser but we had no peace. On the contrary, we prepared for another war in the space of twenty-one years. Now we are shouting, "rid the world of Hitler and we will have peace." We will not! We must rid the world of Hitler, but we will not have peace unless we supply the moral and spiritual forces, the lack of which produced Hitler. There are a thousand Hitlers hidden under the barbarism of the present day. It is indeed significant that the era between 1918 and 1939 was called only an "Armistice," and such it was, an interlude between wars. Peace does not follow the extermination of dictators, because dictators are only the effects of wrong philosophies of life; they are not the causes. They come into environments already prepared for them, like certain forms of fungi come into wet wood. Nazism is the disease of culture in its most virulent form, and could not have come to power in Germany, unless the rest of the world were already sick. Were we honest we would admit that we are all citizens of an apostate world, a world that has abandoned God. For this apostasy, we are all in part responsible, but no more than we Christians who were meant to be the salt of the earth to prevent its corruption. No! It is not the bad dictators who made the world bad; it is bad thinking. It is, therefore, in the realm of ideas that we will have to restore the world!

This war is not like any other war. When hostilities cease, we will not go back again to our former way of life. This war is not an interruption of the normal; it is rather the disintegration of the abnormal. We are definitely at the end of an era of history. The old wells have run dry; the staff of unlimited progress on which we leaned, has pierced our hands; the quicksands of our belief in the unqualified goodness of human nature have swallowed the superstructure of our materialistic world. We are now face-to-face with a fact which some reactionaries still ignore, namely, that society can become inhuman while preserving all the technical and material advantages of a so-called advanced civilization. We will not get back again to the same kind of a world we had before this war, and he who would want to do so, would want the kind of world that produced Hitler. The world is pulling up its tents; humanity is on the march. The old world is dead!

That brings us to what the war is. They are really two great events in the modern world: the war and the revolution.

A war involves nations, alliances, men, armies, defense plants, guns, and tanks; a revolution involves ideas. A war moves on a horizontal plane of land, territory, and men; a revolution moves on the vertical plane of ideology, doctrine, dogmas, creeds, and philosophies of life. This distinction is very important, for it explains how nations can be on the same side of a war and on different sides of a revolution. Russia, for example, is on our side of the war, but Russia is not yet on our side of the revolution; please God some day it may be. The distinction also explains the war between Germany and Russia. Their conflict is not one of ideologies, for Communism and Nazism are both destructive of human freedom. As president Roosevelt said on February 10, 1940: "The Soviet Union, as a matter of practical fact known to you and to all the world, is a dictatorship as absolute as any other dictatorship in the world."

The war is only an episode in the revolution—something incidental. It is the military phase by which the revolution is working itself out. The revolution is far more important and will long outlast the war, for this world war is but a conflict of ideologies. It is not so much a struggle between alliances of men, as it is between dogmas and creeds. The battles fought on land and sea and in the air are merely episodes of a greater struggle, which is being waged in the realm of ideas. A far more important question than "Who will win the war?" is the question: "Who will win the revolution?" In other words, what kind of ideologies or philosophies of life will dominate the world, when this war is finished?

A revolution we said involved ideologies, dogmas, and creeds. How many philosophies of life are involved in this revolution? It is quite generally and falsely assumed that there are only two: democracy and Totalitarianism, or the Christian and the anti-Christian. Would to God it were that simple! There are actually three great philosophies of life or ideologies involved:

First, the Totalitarian which is anti-Christian, anti-Semitic, and anti-human.

Secondly, the secularist world view which is humanistic and democratic, but which attempts to preserve these values on a nonreligious and non-moral foundation by identifying morality with self-interest instead of morality with the will of God.

Thirdly, the Christian world view which grounds the human and the democratic values of the Western world on a moral and religious basis. This Christian view includes not only Christians but also Jews, who historically are the roots of the Christian tradition, and who religiously are one with the Christian in the adoration of God and the acceptance of the moral law as the eternal reason of God.

In the light of these three conflicting philosophies of life our task is threefold.

This anti-Christian, anti-Jewish, and anti-human Totalitarian system must be defeated and crushed not just because it is a political or economic system contrary to ours, but because it is anti-human, and it is anti-human because it is anti-God, hence our war against it is not in the name of democracy, but in the name of humanity.

We must fearlessly admit that we are not fighting the war to keep everything just as it is, for the materialism, selfishness, and godlessness which would eat away the vitals of American traditions, justice, and equality we can and should scrap. Then, having recovered our allegiance to God's moral law, we may be worthy of our mission to lead the world to the peace born of the justice and charity of God, for "Unless the Lord build the house, they labour in vain that build it. Unless the Lord keep the city, he watcheth in vain that keepeth it" (Ps. 126:1–2).

This war is incidental to the great decision the world must make: whether man is a tool of the State as Totalitarianism believes; or whether man is an animal as the secularist tradition of the Western world and too many Americans believe; or whether man is a creature made to the image and likeness of God as the Christian believes.

There is the essence of conflict.

We have a double enemy in the war, not a single one. We must defeat the active barbarism from without, and we must defeat the passive barbarism from within. We must use our swords with an outward thrust against Totalitarianism and its hard barbarism; but we must also use the sword with an inward thrust to cut away our own soft barbarism.

In personal language, each of us must say: I must fight the enemy of man, and I must fight myself when I am my own worst enemy. We have a war to win; and we have a revolution to win. A war to win by overthrowing the power of the enemy in battle; a peace to win by making ourselves worthy to dictate it.

Victory on the field will conquer the hard barbarism. Repentance and catharsis of spirit alone will conquer the soft barbarism. Guns, ships, planes, dynamite, factories, ships, and bombs will put down the first evil. Prayer, sorrow, contrition, purging of our hearts and souls, meditation, reparation, sacrifice, and a return to God will alone accomplish the second. If we merely defeat the hard barbarism and lose to the soft, we will be at the beginning of cyclic wars, which will return and return until we are beaten and purged and broken in the creative despair of getting back to God.

This is the true revolution. All the other revolutions of the twentieth century have been from without; this time we want a revolution from within. The revolutions which shook Europe during the last twenty-five years only shifted power from one class to another, and booty from one pocket to another, and authority from one party to another. This time we want a revolution that will change hearts! A revolution like the one pictured in *The Magnificent* which was a thousand times more revolutionary than the Manifesto of Karl Marx in 1848. The trouble with all political and economic revolutions is they are not revolutionary enough! They still leave hate in the heart of man!

24

The Things We Are Fighting For

Of these dogmas or philosophies of life struggling for mastery in this war, we here discuss the first, the anti-Christian Totalitarian world view.

This anti-Christian, anti-human, anti-democratic Totalitarian ideology exists in four forms widely scattered throughout the world:

In a historical form, as the revival of the imperial traditions of the ancient Roman Empire, which is Fascism.

In an anthropological form, as the glorification of the Nordic race, which is Nazism.

In a theological form, as the identification of divinity with a dynastic house, which is Japanese imperialism.

In an economic form, as the proclamation of class struggle on the anti-religious basis of dictatorship of the proletariat, which is Marxian Socialism.

In the Christmas (1942) encyclical, the pope condemned these four forms as a "conception which claims for particular nations, or classes ... the norm from which there is no appeal."[45]

Not one of these four forms exists in a state in the political sense of the term; rather each is a philosophy of life working through a unique party

---

[45] Piux XII, Christmas Message on the Internal Order of States and People (December 25, 1942).

which acts as a substitute for the State. All agree in investing primitive ideas of class, race, nation, and blood with a divine significance.

Furthermore, they demand power over the total man—the whole man, body and soul, and aim at control over the most intimate regions of the spirit. In this sense they are religions; only secondarily, are they systems of politics. Because they are religions they persecute Jews and Christians, for in their eyes these are rival religions. In fact, they claim more than Christianity, for Christianity left to Caesar the things that were Caesar's, but these new false religions insist that even thing things of God belong to Caesar.

How did these pseudo-mysticisms originate? In their European form they arise in part as a reaction against the excesses and defects of the secularist and materialist culture of the rest of the Western world, just as a man might foolishly burn his barn to get rid of a few rats. Anyone who looks at history in the perspective of the last few hundred years will see in it a progressive repudiation of Christian principles in social, political, and economic life, which repudiation produced first our present non-religious civilization; then an anti-religious civilization (Communism), and finally by reaction the anti-religious one of Nazism against which we are struggling.

Once upon a time there was a Christian culture. It was not a perfect culture, because Christianity was never meant to be perfected in this world. It flowered during the Middle Ages. Chesterton once said that these are called the "Dark Ages" by those who are in the dark about them. The basis of its civilization was that law, education, politics, economics, social service, arts, crafts, labor, and capital were all built up in a hierarchical fashion like a pyramid, with God at the peak. Everyone, whether he was a scholar or peasant, lord or serf, sinner or saint, recognized the Lord as the One to whom he would one day return to render an account of his stewardship. Thus all life was impregnated with morality; economics and politics were branches of ethics; men were one because there was one Lord, one Faith, one Baptism.

This great civilization went into decline partly through the rebirth of pagan ideas and partly through the moral decline of the individuals. There then began what might be called the Era of Substitution in which men sought other bases for moral unity than the Church. Among these substitutes were the Bible, reason, and individual self-interest. Our present non-religious secularist culture grows from these roots.

The first substitute, the Bible, had the great advantage of still keeping society together on the basis of the supernatural and the moral inspiration of Christ the Son of God. But it was unable to maintain that unity long, first of all, because, when every man became an infallible interpreter of the Book, there were as many religions as heads; and because once the Book was detached from the Board of Editors which guaranteed its inspiration, and from a Supreme Court which interpreted it, it became rather the basis of discord than of harmony.

Men then set about for a new bond of cohesion and they found it in reason—not reason illumined by faith, but reason divorced from faith, but reason divorced from faith. The so-called "Age of Reason" was really an Age of Unbelief for its strongest protagonists were corrosive men like Hume, Kant, and Voltaire, who measured the growth of reason by its alienation from God who alone could guarantee its deliverances and its conclusions. The sovereignty of reasonable people replaced the sovereignty of God. All principles were rejected except a few self-evident ones which, it was hoped, would preserve the brotherhood of man without the Fatherhood of God.

But reason could not hold society together for everyone soon became his own interpreter of reason, as everyone once before was his own interpreter of the Book. As Dean Swift so well described it: "Wisdom is a hen, whose cackling we must value and consider, because it is attended with an egg; but then, lastly, 'tis a nut, which unless you choose with judgment, may cost you a tooth, and pay you with nothing but a worm."[46]

Finally there came the last and final substitute: the enthronement of individual self-interest, which is known as liberalism. Men once said, we will not have the Church of Christ rule over us, and then later on added, we will not have the Word of God rule over us; then, we shall rule ourselves by our own reason; now they finally decided to rule themselves on the basis of their absolute independence of God.

---

[46] Dean Swift, *A Tale of a Tub*, in *The Choice Works of Dean Swift in Prose and Verse* (Boston, MA: De Wolfe and Fiske, 1876), 197.

The three most important principles of this liberal culture were:

Economically: leave every man free to work out his economic destiny as he sees fit, and the general good of all will result. Upon this non-moral principle modern Capitalism is grounded.

Politically: in order that the individual may be free from restraint in his economic exploitation, the State must have only a negative function like a policeman whose business it is to prevent others from meddling in our affairs, and particularly to preserve property rights.

Socially: freedom means the right to do whatever you please. A man is therefore most free when he is devoid of all restraints, discipline, and authority. Personality is self-expressive when it is unhampered by law.

The Era of Substitution has behind it three great revolutions: the religious revolution which uprooted man from responsibility to a spiritual community; the French Revolution which isolated man from responsibility to a political community or the State; and the Industrial Revolution and liberalism which isolate man from all responsibility to the social community or the common good. Such is the essence of our secularist culture: the supremacy of the individual man. Torn away from his roots in God, his roots in law, and his roots in a brotherhood of men, it naturally led to the anarchy of the jungle and the oppression of the weak and the unfortunate, and a society which was nothing but a criss-cross of individual egotism, where each man was a wolf to his neighbor. And when these egotisms became nationalized and militarized they came to a head in the First World War. Thus did a secularist age, which began with the dream of a universal brotherhood without God, end in a series of frustrated strifes in which men of different races and nations were tempted to deny the last vestige of humanity.

But we failed to learn our lesson after the First World War. We were very much like man after the Flood. Immediately after the deluge, man built for himself the Tower of Babel, by which he affirmed that through his own power and without God's help, he could climb to the Heavens. So too after the First World War, which was a deluge, not of water but of blood, man still continued to affirm that by his own power he could build a new world without duties to God and His moral law. One of the babels produced by human pride was the League of Nations which sought to build a world society not on the moral law, but on the balance of power. Nothing better reveals its inadequacy than the fact that in nineteen years of its existence, 4,568 treaties of peace were signed before it; and the year before this war broke out, 211 treaties of peace were signed. These were enough to last until the crack of doom, if nations really believed in what they signed! Nations entered into international agreements in the same spirit a modern man marries—namely: prepared to get a divorce on the grounds of incompatibility when something more attractive comes along.

But something unusual happened after the First World War among certain nations of the world. Namely, a reaction against individualism and all its works and pomps.

In three countries revolution broke loose; the revolutions of Nazism, Fascism, and Communism. These revolutions were not simply imposed upon the people by cruel dictators. The masses are not stupid; the leaders could never rise to power unless the masses felt that the revolutions were correcting some dreadful abuses.

In every revolution there are two elements: protest and reform. The protests of these revolutionists were right; the reforms were wrong. The appeal of the revolution consisted in its protest against the errors of our secularist culture with its glorification of the individual. Lenin went before the world and said:

> Can you not see that an economic system which allows every man to do what he pleases, means that the strong shall be pleased and the weak shall be crushed: such so-called economic freedom will mean in the end the concentration of wealth in the hands of the few and the impoverishment of the masses. There must be a re-ordering of economic life so that all the economic resources of a nation are bent to the good of all.

And in saying this Lenin was right! But though his protest was right, his reform was wrong, for he went to the other extreme and substituted privilege of power for privilege of money, and cured the abuse of property rights by the destruction of all rights.

Mussolini went before his masses and argued: "Can you not see that any political system which asserts that the individual must be kept free from all State control, and which makes the State a policeman, means in the end that the State leaves the weak unprotected against the strong? The State must protect the weak against the strong." In saying this Mussolini was right! But like all reformers he went too far. He got rid of the policeman-State by making the State a nurse and thus extinguished individual freedom and democracy altogether. Such is the error of Fascism: the State is all!

Hitler in his turn argued: "Can you not see that if you define freedom as the right to do whatever you please you will end in anarchy? There must therefore be a restoration of law and authority." And in saying this Hitler was right! But he went too far, as reformers do, and restored law at the expense of freedom. Freedom, which under liberalism meant the right to do whatever you please, now became freedom to do whatever you must instead of being what we must make after this war, the freedom to do whatever you ought. Thus did slavery return to the world.

The strength of these Totalitarian systems was that they supplied some kind of an answer—false though it was—to the hidden dominance of the lord of finance, to the indifference of democracies to absolute values, and to their claim that the body politic must have precedence over private gain. In the end, however, none of these solutions achieved their goals because none of them understood the nature of man as a creature, endowed with rights because possessing a soul and saddled with duties made by God.

The ills they attempted to cure were basically due to the de-Christianization of society. But through a false diagnosis, they attempted to arrest de-Christianization by anti-Christianizing the world. Because Capitalism, indifference, and financial oligarchy sprang up in a civilization whose roots were Christian, they made the mistake of thinking that these evils were due to Christianity. Hence they said: "Religion is the opium of the people." What they failed to see was that, on the field of Western civilization where grew the wheat of Christianity, some enemies came by night and sowed weeds and thistles. The solution of the problem was not in uprooting the wheat of Christianity but in burning the weeds of our indifference to it.

The story of the last few hundred years is the story of the prodigal son. Western civilization left the Father's house with some of the spiritual substance it had preserved during one thousand six hundred years of martyrdom and hard thinking. We are now far enough away from those days to see that it has spent all the capital which it had: the belief in the Divinity of Christ, the inspiration of Sacred Scriptures, the moral law, and the existence of God. Finally it reached the stage where, like the prodigal, it fed on husks as a substitute for the bread of the Father's house—the husks of liberalism, materialism, agnosticism.

The prodigal was right in being hungry; that is the way God made him. The Totalitarian States were right in being hungry for law, the common good, and authority. They were wrong in eating the husks of Fascism, Nazism, and Totalitarianism. The right way to look on Totalitarian systems is as so many convulsive attempts to arrest the disintegration of society, as the awakening of the conscience of the world against an acquisitive society founded on the primacy of profit, and as a final reminder that man cannot be godless.

Because the enemy is demonic in his philosophy of life, it might be well to recall the words of our Lord as to how he can be defeated. The disciples on one occasion tried to cast the devil out of a boy possessed. Our Divine Lord did so immediately. The disciples came to Jesus privately and said: "Why could not we cast him out?" He said: "Because of your unbelief.... This kind is not cast out but by prayer and fasting" (Matt. 17:19–20). This service they have done us did we but have the eyes to see. They have the great value of reminding us that unless we get back again to God and His moral law, we shall revert to barbarism.

Now that we have suggested the nature of Totalitarianism's origin, as a reaction to fundamental defects in our civilization and as false attempts to arrest its disintegration, we now consider its doctrines.

Totalitarianism has three negative dogmas: it denies the value of a person by affirming the primacy of the mass, the race, the class. It denies the equality of man, and it affirms that evil is the method and the goal of the revolution.

The basic principle of democracy is the sacredness of the individual as a creature endowed by God with inalienable rights. The basic principle of

Nazism and other Totalitarian systems is that the individual has no rights except those given him by the Party or the State. In America, freedom resides in man; in Nazism, freedom resides in the race. In America, man endows the State with rights which he received from God; in Nazism, the State endows man with rights which it got from Hitler. One of the best expressions of this Totalitarian idea—that the individual has no value because all value resides in collectivity—is to be found in that influential German, Karl Marx, who in 1843 rejected the democratic conception of man saying: "That each man has a value as a sovereign being is an illusion, a dream and a postulate of Christianity which affirms that every man has a soul."[47]

Later writing in the first edition of *Das Kapital*, he further developed the idea, "If I speak of individuals, it is only in so far as they are personifications of economic categories and representatives of special class relations and interests."

In plain language, this means that Marx had no use for the individual worker or proletariat as such. The person in himself has no value; he has value only as a representative of a revolutionary class. Once the person ceased to be a member of that class, he ceased to have value. This disposal of the human person, as such, is the first dogma of all Totalitarian systems. It explains why the individual Jew has no value or rights in Nazism, because he is not a member of the revolutionary race; it explains Fascism which affirms: "Society is the end, individuals only the means and the instruments of social ends." It explains the wanton disregard of individual life by the Japanese imperial government and the statement of the Japanese educators: "The individual is not an entity but depends upon the whole arising from and kept in being by the State." These low and unspiritual views of man are the beginning of slavery.

Persons lose their identity in Totalitarianism very much like grapes in a wine press; they continue to exist only in the wine. As Hitler wrote in *Mein Kampf*: "There is only one sacred right, and this right is that the blood is preserved pure." Such is the basis of the cruelty of the Nazis to

---

[47] Karl Marx, in Karl Marx and Friedrich Engels, *Collected Works*, vol. 1 (Moscow: Progress, 1975), 590.

those who are not of their blood, for example, the Poles. "If," said Hitler, "I am willing to spend the flower of three million of the German race in war, why should I care about extinguishing the scum of seventeen million Poles?" And if Europe today is in chains, it is not because Nazism is cruel in war; it is because Nazism is wicked in principle; it denies the value of man! Against this absorption of man by the State, the present Holy Father said: "The State may demand the goods of its citizens and if need be its blood, but the soul redeemed by Christ—never!"[48]

Next, Totalitarianism denies the equality of man:

American democracy is founded on the principle of the essential spiritual equality of all men. When President Roosevelt was asked at the end of October 1942, to whom his four freedoms were meant to apply, he answered: "To everyone, all over the world." This is in keeping with that great Christian message St. Paul delivered to the proud Athenians on the hill of the Aeropagus: "God, who made the world, and all things therein.... And hath made of one, all mankind, to dwell upon the whole face of the earth ... For in him we live, and move, and are; as some also of your own poets said: For we are also his offspring" (Acts 17:24, 26, 28).

Totalitarianism, on the contrary, denies the basic equality of all men as children of God. Men are equal only on condition that they belong to a certain class, a certain race, a certain dynasty, a certain nation. Hitler, therefore, proclaims the superiority of the German race over all the peoples of the earth with the possible exception of the Japanese, for Hitler has discovered that one of the Japanese sun-gods is a first cousin of the German god Wotan.

The persecution of the Jews therefore is not because, as he first claimed, they were too wealthy but simply because they were not Nordic. "As for the Jews," he writes in one of his early decrees, "they have simply been placed outside the law" as if any signing of a law could make a man a monkey. Once their equality was denied, their properties were dispossessed. "As a foundation for a new currency, the property of those who are not Jews

---

[48] Pius XII, Encyclical on the Unity of Human Society *Summi Pontificatus* (October 20, 1939), no. 66.

and not of our blood must do service."[49] According to the same principle a Protestant Pastor Niemoeller and the Catholic bishops and priests, such as Bishop von Galen of Munster, are denied equality because they put loyalty to Christ above to Christ above loyalty to the führer.

This silly idea of the superiority of the German race, with its anti-Semitism and its anti-Christianity, has had a long history in Prussia in such men as Fichte, Herder, and Treitzwscke. It was no mere accident that when Hitler came into power, one of his first official acts was the ordering of the singing of *Die Meistersinger* of Wagner in the Opera of Berlin. The reason for this choice was because that glorified Hans Sachs, the poet of racism and, in tribute to him, Hitler ordered that all the Party congresses of the Nazis should be held in the city of the birthplace of Sachs. For that reason they have all been held in Nuremburg.

Neither was it an accident that he called the forts erected opposite the Maginot line after Siegfried, the Nordic hero whom Wagner popularized in his opera, and to whom Hitler compared the German people. It will be recalled that Siegfried, thanks to a bath in dragon's blood, was made invulnerable except on his back, where an oak leaf had attached itself. Appealing to this myth, Hitler declared that the superior German race could never be defeated; it could only be betrayed like Siegfried, by a stab in the back.

Neither was it an accident that in his attachment to Richard Wagner, who accustomed three generations of Germans to the myths of the Nordic and pagan past of Germany, Hitler should have built his nest at Berchtesgaden. For, in his prose works, Wagner wrote that Germany has already had one reincarnation of Siegfried in Frederick Barbarossa who established the first Reich (Bismarck's being called the second). Wagner said that a day would come when this Siegfried-Barbarossa would have a third reincarnation, a "hero who turns against the ruin of his race"[50]—the hero wondrously divine, and when he comes he will make his home over

[49] Adolf Hitler, *The Speeches of Adolf Hitler, vol. 1: April 1922–August 1939*, ed. Norman H. Baynes (New York: Oxford University Press, 1994), 108.
[50] Peter Viereck, *Metapolitics: From the Romantics to Hitler* (New York: A.A. Knopf, 1941), iii.

the spot where the bones of Barbarossa and Siegfried now are supposed to lie buried—in Berchtesgaden—where Hitler has his home.

This barbaric racism, which denies the equality of all men, is less a science or even a philosophy than it is a religion—an anti-Christian mysticism which adores a tribal blood as sacred; a narcissistic self-worship with a supreme diabolical conceit, which in the language of Alfred Rosenberg "represents the mystery which has overcome and replaced the old Sacraments of the Church."

Totalitarianism is wicked because it makes evil the method and the goal of the revolution.

The inspiration for this idea is due principally to Frederick Wilhelm Nietzsche who gave what might be called the moral code of Nazism, understanding moral here as immoral. Nazism is not negative like Communism. Communism is antireligious: Nazism is not; it is very religious except that its religion is diabolical. There is only one world to describe how it grafted violence onto legality and that is in the phrase of Rauschning: "The Revolution of Nihilism." And such it is! The following of blind irrational myths; the complete turning upside down of traditional morality; the enthronement of the will to power. It is almost pointless for us to argue against the Nazis on the ground that they are cruel and unjust, or because they have built their system on another basis than that of justice and righteousness. We are not talking about the same things. What justice is to us, that injustice is to the Nazis.

The inspiration for this idea is due principally to Nietzsche who sought to found a basis for morality other than that of Christianity, which he called slave morality, and by so doing to release the pent-up energies of the will to power. "Morality must be shot at," as he put it. Then adding, "We are probably also the first who understand what a *pagan faith* is ... to value all higher existence as *immoral* existence."[51]

From this principle he gives what he calls a new table:

---

[51] Friedrich Nietzsche, *The Will to Power*, in *The Complete Works of Friedrich Nietzsche*, vol. 15, ed. Oscar Levy, trans. Anthony M. Ludovici (New York: MacMillan, 1924), 407.

Become hard.... Man must be trained for war and woman for the relaxation of the warrior; all else is folly. You should love peace as a means to a new war; and the short peace more than the long. I do not exhort you to work, but to fight. Ye say that a good cause will sanctify war! I tell you, it is a good war that sanctifies every cause.... My code is the code of Dionysius; sensuality and cruelty. There is the struggle: Dionysius or Christ.

Add these three ideas together: the denial of the value of the person which the German Marx proclaimed; the denial of the equality of all men which the German philosophers proclaimed and which Wager set to music; and the primacy of irrational power, lust, and cruelty which the German Nietzsche affirmed, and you have the thing we are fighting against. It is not a nation; it is not a state; it is a spirit, the spirit of antichrist, the last and awful perversion of a community that turned its back on God and to whom Satan showed his face.

Let no one stultify himself by believing that Totalitarianism as we have defined it, in any of its forms can be Christianized or democratized or humanized; for here we are dealing not only with wicked men who could be converted through God's grace but also with a wicked ideology that makes conversion impossible. Erring sheep can be brought into the sheepfold of Christ, but evil philosophies which are like wolves cannot. By their very nature they are anti-Christian because they exalt the herd recognized by the State, over the person whose value comes from God. That is why Totalitarianism persecutes the Church. Persecution could be avoided only by emptying Christianity of Christ, man of his soul, and the soul of its justice and charity.

The evil ideology we are fighting today is in revolt against both humanity and Christianity. Over a century ago, a German Jew, Heine, by name, warned the world of how terrible Germany would be gathering up the full fruits of its Kant and Fichte, how it would revive the spirit of the ancient Germans "which does not fight in order to destroy or conquer but simply for the sake of fighting." Christianity—and this is its fairest merit—has in some degree subdued that brutal Germanic joy of battle, but it could not destroy it; and when the cross, that restraining talisman, falls to pieces, then will break forth again the ferocity of the old combatants, the insane berserker rage whereof northern poets have said and sung. The talisman is rotten, and the day will come when it will pitifully crumble to dust. The old stone gods will then arise from the forgotten ruins and wipe from their eyes the dust of a thousand years, and at last Thor with his giant hammer will leap aloft and he will shatter the gothic cathedrals.

> When ye hear the trampling of feet and the clashing of arms, ye neighbour children, ye French, be on your guard.... Smile not at my counsel, at the counsel of a dreamer, who seeks to warn you against ... Kantian, or Fichtean, or Philosophies of Nature. Smile not at the fancy of one who forsees in the region of reality the same outburst of revolution that has taken place in the region of intellect. The thought precedes the deed as the lighting the thunder. German thunder is of true German character: it is not very nimble, but rumbles along somewhat slowly. But come it will, and when ye hear a crashing such as never before has been heard in the world's history, then know that at last the German thunderbolt has fallen. At this commotion the eagles will drop dead from the skies, and the lions in the farthest wastes of Africa will bite their tails and creep into their royal lairs. There will then be played in Germany a drama compared to which the French Revolution will seem but an innocent idyl. At present, it is true, everything is tolerably quiet, and though here and there some few men create a little stir, do not imagine that these are to be the real actors in the piece. They are only little curs chasing one another round the empty arena, snapping and barking at each other till the appointed hour when the troop of gladiators appear, to fight for life and death.[52]

The war is exploding the fallacy that it makes no difference what you believe. It does make a tremendous amount of difference what we believe,

---

[52] Heinrich Heine, *Wit, Wisdom, and Pathos from the Prose of Heinrich Heine*, ed. and trans. J. Snodgrass (London: Alexander Gardner, 1888), 140.

for we act on our beliefs. If our beliefs are right, our deeds will be right. The evil of the Nazis is that they practice what they preach. If twenty years ago we educated ourselves along the line of Christian morality to see the utter moral evil and logical absurdity of these ideas, we would not now have to sacrifice our lives to bolt them from the earth. What we were once tolerant to as a wicked idea, we must now be intolerant to as a deed.

We were indifferent to good and evil; we ignored what happened to the soul of man, to his thinking and his purpose. These states then came on the scene to say that his soul, his thinking, and his purposes must be under the domination of the State.

These demonic forces replaced the spiritual anarchy of bourgeois civilization with a semblance of order; they found substitutes for the doubt, skepticism, and sophistication of an irresponsible intelligentsia in the certitude of an absolute authority embodied in a social philosophy. They proved that any world view is better than no world view: and that a regime that possesses some authority is better than a system of no authority. And in doing so, they thrust the issue before us very clearly; it makes a war of a difference what you believe. This conflict is not between men and nations; it is not only a war—it is a revolution!

What has the Western world to offset this evil? Presently it is depending on what Professor Sorokin has called a "sensate culture": a pragmatic, liberal, and humanistic philosophy of life which affirms the doctrine of the sovereign ego as the ultimate ground of certainty. Such a philosophy is in reality a staff that will pierce our hands. To that point we now move forward.

25

Barnacles on the Ship of Democracy

The second worldview locked in this world conflict is the non-Christian or secularist view of Western civilization. By secularist ideology, we mean the attempt to preserve human and democratic values on a non-moral and nonreligious foundation. Secularism means the separation of the parts of life—for example, education, politics, and economics and family—from their center, which is God. Each department of life is considered as having absolute autonomy and in no way can be brought under the sway of ethical principles or the sovereign law of God. Secularism reaches its peak when men say, "business is business," and "religion is religion," as if the way a man worked or the pay he gave to workers had nothing to do with conscience and the moral fibre of a nation. Secularism affirms an absolute irrelevance of the moral to the secular, denies a religious culture, and, if there were one, denies it could be superior to an anti-religious culture. It was the secularist culture St. Paul condemned when he declared the Romans to be guilty in the sight of God: "They are inexcusable. Because that, when they knew God, they have not glorified him as God, or given thanks; but became vain in their thoughts, and their foolish heart was darkened" (Rom. 1:20-21). Every form of modern secularism implies self-glorification as St. Paul here described it. Rationalism, for example, glorifies human reason by detaching it from the eternal reason of God. Political positivism of modern law glorifies the State as the source of law.

At first it may seem unfair to characterize our present Western civilization as secular. It may be objected that there are millions of Jews, Protestants, and Catholics who are leading lives in close union with God. This, of course, is true. But here we are speaking not of a multitude, but of a spirit; not of numbers, but of influences; not of a minority, but of a temper. There is no doubt that a doctor could find some very healthy organs in an incurably cancerous patient, but "cancerous" and not "healthy" would be the accurate description of such a patient. So with the secularist tradition of Western civilization: strong religious lives exist in it, but they are like a Church in a modern factory town: they exist alongside of other influences, but they do not create the spirit of Western civilization, nor mold it into a definite philosophy of life. A Bible and shoe can be in the same box, but there is no casual connection between the two.

In like manner, modern Western civilization acknowledges that some respectability attaches itself to these devout souls, but it assumes and more often insists, that religion is for personal use, not social expression. Religion is regarded only as a pious appendage to life, not its soul; it sugar-casts political and economic activity, but does not infuse it. As Peguy has said: "Never has the temporal been so protected against the spiritual; and never has the spiritual been so unprotected against the temporal."

If anyone doubts the validity of this distinction between the individual Christians living in the Western world and the spirit of the Western world, let him suggest, for example, that the modern youth be given a religious and moral training in our schools. Immediately, the prophets of doom would arise in loud protest, cloaking hatred of religion under the pretext that there is "not sufficient time for religion," or that "we want no union of Church and State," or "religion is all right for the individual if he needs it, but it has no relation to politics or economics."

We must add to the distinction already made between the individual and society, the more important one between what is the good and the bad in any civilization, just as we distinguish between man and his disease. We regard the disease as evil, but the man as good. In an impersonal order, we make a distinction between the ship and its barnacles. The ship in its passage through the seas, develops barnacles which impede the free passage of the ship through the waters; it must occasionally be taken to dry dock to have the barnacles knocked away.

The ship is good; the barnacles are bad. Now the Western civilization, or what some call democracy, may be likened to a ship. America, in particular, is a good ship. It carries the precious cargo of the belief in inalienable rights and liberties, the value of the human person, representative government, and equal opportunities. It is freighted down also with the precious cargo of the four freedoms about which our president spoke: freedom of religion, freedom of speech, freedom from want, and freedom from fear. It is freighted down also with the cargo of the right of sanctuary, for America has been in the past and is now a sanctuary for the persecuted as no other land on the face of God's earth has been a sanctuary. Finally, this ship is good for it is freighted down with the precious cargo of all those values which make us proud to call ourselves "Americans."

But it happens that this admirable ship of democracy has, in the course of the last century or more, accumulated certain barnacles. These barnacles are to be understood in terms of certain false assumptions which have too generally influenced much of our Western world. They have produced what Sorokin calls a sensate culture, that is a culture in which the material and sensible values of life are divorced from their spiritual foundations. There is a grave danger that unless these barnacles are removed, the ship may sink.

These barnacles constitute what we have already called the passive or the soft barbarisms from within, and they are a danger to Western civilization—not quite as open as Totalitarianism, but just as insidious. All religious groups have warned us of the possibility of defeat from within through this materialism which, though it does not persecute religion, nevertheless abandons it.

The American Institute of Judaism, for example, on December 25, 1942, made this significant statement:

The failure of men to recognize the implications of the sovereignty of God and the sanctity of human life has resulted in moral disruption and worldwide devastation. Misreading the findings of the sciences, both physical and social, men have given their allegiance to false philosophies, spiritual and moral values have been divorced from human life and materialism has been made supreme in the affairs of men. In order to rebuild our broken civilization the spiritual teachings of religion must become the foundations of the new world order and the dynamic force in a just and enduring peace.[53]

The Malvern Conference of the Church of England, on January 10, 1941, issued the same warning:

The war is not to be regarded as an isolated evil detached from the general condition of Western civilization during the last period. Rather it is to be seen as one symptom of a widespread disease and maladjustment resulting from the loss of conviction concerning the reality and character of God, and the true nature and destiny of Man.

The Federal Council of Churches of Christ of America, in the same spirit on April 15, 1941, stated:

We are well aware of the fact that in times like these Christians desire to be practical.... The Commission shares the desire, and has the intention to be practical, but we strongly disagree with the view that Christian principles have no practical relation to present-day problems. On the contrary, we trace many of our present troubles to political planning which was fatally defective precisely because it ignored Christian principles. We are confident that for the future only frustration can result if such precepts continue to be ignored.

Pius XII, addressing himself to the world in his first encyclical said that a loss of God had created a vacuum which no national or international myth could fill.

In this atmosphere of alienation from God and de-Christianization, the thinking and planning, judgment, and actions of men were bound to become materialistic and one-sided, to strive for mere greatness and

[53] "Statement by American Institute of Judaism," *New York Times*, December 25, 1942.

expansion of space, a race for a quicker, richer, and better production of all things which appeared to be conductive to material evolution and progress. These very symptoms appear in politics as an unlimited demand for expansion and political influence without regard to moral standards: in economic life they are represented by the predominance of mammoth concerns and trusts, in the social sphere it is the agglomeration of huge populations in cities and in the districts dominated by industry and trade, an agglomeration that is accompanied by the complete uprooting of the masses who have lost their standards of life, home, work, love, and hatred. By this new conception of thought and life, all ideas of social life have been impregnated with a purely mechanistic character.

Returning now to our theme: the ship is good, and the barnacles are bad; let us discuss the barnacles. These barnacles might be called superstitions or dogmas; in any case they are assumptions of sensate culture which the press, education, and public opinion accept as unchallenged truths.

The Superstition of Progress

The superstition of progress asserts itself in some such fashion as this in our classrooms, best-sellers, and high-class journals: Man is naturally good and indefinitely perfectible, and thanks to great cosmic floods of evolution will be swept forward and forward until he becomes a kid of a god. Goodness increases with time, while evil and error decline. History represents the gradual but steady advance of man up the hill of the more abundant and happy life. No special institutions, no moral discipline, no divine grace are necessary for the progress of man; for progress is automatic, due to the free play of natural forces and the operation of freedom in a world released from the superstation of religion. Because evil and sin are only vestigial remnants from the bestial past, evolution and science and education will finally eradicate them.

This superstation of progress is false because it completely ignores the goal and purpose of progress. The modern world confuses motion with progress: instead of working toward an ideal, it changes the ideal and calls it progress. If every time an artist looked up he saw a different person sitting for the portrait, how would he ever know he was making any progress in painting? As Chesterton said: "There is one thing that never makes any progress and that is the idea of progress."

Progress in an indefinite future, but not beyond history, makes present moral lives meaningless and endows them with no other value than that of so many sticks to keep the cosmic bonfire blazing for the next generation. When the only kind of happiness men can enjoy is one which they celebrate in the distant future on the graves of their ancestors, then indeed their happiness is the happiness of gravediggers in the midst of a pestilence.

As Berdyaev so well expressed it:

Both from the religious and ethical point of view this positivist conception of progress is inadmissible, because by its very nature it excludes a solution to the tragic torments, conflicts and contradictions of life valid for all mankind, for all those generations who have lived and suffered. For it deliberately asserts that nothing but death and the grave awaits the vast majority of mankind and the endless succession of human generations throughout the ages, because they have lived in a tortured and imperfect state torn asunder by contradictions. But somewhere on the peaks of historical destiny, on the ruins of preceding generations, there shall appear the fortunate race of men reserved for the bliss and perfection of integral life. All the generations that have gone before are but the means to this blessed life, to this blissful generation of the elect as yet unborn.... Thus the religion of progress regards all the generations and epochs that have been as devoid of intrinsic value, purpose or insignificance, as the mere means and instruments to the ultimate goal.

It is this fundamental moral contradiction that invalidates the doctrine of progress, turning it into a religion of death instead of resurrection and eternal life. There is no valid ground for degrading these generations whose lot has been cast among pain and imperfection beneath that whose pre-eminence has been ordained in blessedness and joy. No future perfection can expiate the sufferings of past generations. Such a sacrifice of all human destinies to the messianic consummation of the favored race can only revolt man's moral and religious conscience. A religion of progress based on this apotheosis of a future fortunate generation is without compassion for either present or past; it addresses itself with infinite optimism to the future, with infinite pessimism to the past. It is profoundly hostile to the Christian expectation of resurrection for all mankind, for all the dead, fathers and forefathers.

This Christian idea rests on the hope of an end to historical tragedy and contradiction valid for human generations, and of resurrection in eternal life for all who have ever lived. But the nineteenth-century conception of progress admits to the messianic consummation only that unborn generation of the elect to which all preceding generations have made their sacrifice. Such a consummation, celebrated by the future elect among the graves of their ancestors, can hardly rally our enthusiasm for the religion of progress. Any such enthusiasm would be base and inappropriate.[54]

The doctrine of progress confuses mechanical advancement with moral betterment. There is no denying the material order, but mechanical development does not necessarily imply moral development. Progress in "things" is not necessarily progress in "persons." Planes may go faster, but man does not became happier. Progress in medicine is not necessarily progress in ethics, and mastery over disease is not necessarily mastery over sin. Conquest of nature does not mean conquest of selfishness. Scientific advancement is no guarantee of moral betterment. Greater power over nature can increase our potentiality for evil. Put the forces of evil in charge of radio, the press, and the new inventions and you corrupt or destroy a nation. Mechanics is one thing, freedom is quite another. Moral optimism, based on mechanical progress and the assumption of the natural goodness of man, understands neither the heights to which man can climb through the grace of God, nor the depths to which he can fall through the abandonment of a divine life

---

[54] Nikolai Berdyaev, *The Meaning of History*, trans. George Reavey (London: Geoffrey Bles, 1936), 188-190.

purchased through a Cross. The conquest of nature does not parallel our conquest of evil. We are equipped like giants to subdue the environment of the air and the sea and the bowels of the earth, but we are as weak as pigmies for the conquest of ourselves. The greater power which science has put into man's hands can, unless his will is right, increase his potentiality for evil, as the present chaos so well bears witness. Time does not always operate in favor of human betterment; because a man is sick, time does not necessarily make him better. Unless evil is corrected, time operates in favor of disease, decay, and death.

The superstition of progress denies human responsibility. When human goodness is attributed to automatic laws of nature, but never to good will; when evil is explained in terms of environment, heredity, bad milk, insufficient playgrounds, and those naughty ductless glands, but never to a perverse order, then the world is most in danger of losing freedom when it talks about it.

Someone was recently horrified at the immorality of young girls between the ages of fifteen and seventeen and suggested that the solution to this problem was to "build more dance halls where they sold soft drinks."

If we attribute evil to external circumstances, and believe that we can cultivate virtue by a swing band and soda pop, we will have become a nation where there is no freedom because there is no responsibility. Evil is not in the absence of opportunities for amusement. Evil is in the will, and in the heart and in the decisions of each and every one of us. Youth can be vicious with dance halls; it can be virtuous without them, but youth will never be good unless its will is ordered to the moral law of the all-holy God. The confusion of the idea of progress with the idea of evolution kills the value of intention and the fruits of high resolves. True progress is ethically and not cosmically conditioned; it depends not on the refinement of luxuries, but in their deliberate control through human intention. There is really therefore only one true progress in the world and that consists in the diminution of the traces of Original Sin.

Historical facts do not support the utopian illusion that goodness increases with time. What happens in reality is something quite different. Evil grows along with the good. The history of the world is rather like a tension between good and evil than an escalator which keeps going upwards.

The kingdom of heaven is likened to a man that sowed good seeds in his field. But while men were asleep, his enemy came and over-sowed cockle among the wheat and went his way. And when the blade was sprung up, and had brought forth fruit, then appeared also the cockle. And the servants of the goodman of the house coming said to him: Sir, didst thou not sow good seed in thy field? whence then hath it cockle? And he said to them: An enemy hath done this. And the servants said to him: Wilt thou that we go and gather it up? And he said: No: lest perhaps gathering up the cockle, you root up the wheat also together with it. Suffer both to grow until the harvest, and in the time of the harvest I will say to the reapers: Gather up first the cockle, and bind it into bundles to burn, but the wheat gather ye into my barn. (Matt. 13:24–30)

Nothing better proves the fallacy of progress than to recall the interval between modern wars. It has been a common fashion for the utopians to explain wars away as "falls in the evolutionary process," or as "necessary incidents in the evolution from savagery to civilization," or as "survivals of the animal in civilized man." But history does not prove we are making progress; instead of evolving from savagery to civilization, we seem to be devolving from civilization to civilization, we seem to be devolving from civilization to savagery. The interval between the Napoleonic War and the Franco-Prussian War was fifty-five years; the interval between the Franco-Prussian War and the First World War was forty-three years; and the interval between the First World War and this one was twenty-one years. Fifty-five, forty-three, twenty-one years—and each war more destructive than the former, and at a time when man materially had more to make for happiness than any other period of history. Is that progress? Shall we not learn from our modern history its record that man, once he forgets his God, has also an increasing capacity for evil?

The sad and tragic fact is that modern man under sufficient stress, and even amidst comforts spiced with lust, will do deeds of evil as terrible as anyone recorded in history. Barbarism is not behind us; it is beneath us. And it can emerge at any moment unless our wills, aided by the grace of God, repress it. The modern superstition of man's indefinite perfect-ibility, without God's sustaining graces, forgets the historical data before our eyes, that history is creating ever-increasing possibilities for chaos and wars. Our mechanical progress in moving quickly can go hand in hand with power to do more evil. Let no one deny it: our scientific progress has outstripped our moral progress. We are a more comfortable people than our ancestors, but we necessarily a happier people? The myth of necessary progress is exploded. But that is no reason why the liberals who were so optimistic about progress, like Bertrand Russell, should now fall into a Hellish despair. Because the evil in the world does not involve right does not mean there is no right. It only means that we have to put the evil right, and in order to do this we may have to learn the lesson of a cross and the toil of Gethsemane. Neither is the solution to be found among those Fas-cist intelligentsia who appeal to the authority of H. G. Wells and requite in the darkness of their souls: "Men are borne along through space and time regardless of themselves, as if to the awakening greatness of Man."[55]

The answer is somewhere else. Maybe we had better get back again to God.

The Superstition of Scientism

By the superstition of scientism we do not mean science, but rather that particular abuse of it which affirms that the scientific method is, as John Dewey put it, "The sole authentic mode of revelation." For the modern sensate mind, to understand is to measure; to know is to count. The senses are the only sources of knowledge. Hence any knowledge derived from any source other than counting and experimentation is illusory. Sensible knowledge is the final arbiter of experience. Science says "this," or science says "that," is the last word to be said on any subject. Hence there is no place for values, tradition, metaphysics, revelation, faith, authority, or theology. God has no purposes in the universe; first of all because there is no God, and secondly because there are no purposes. Scientism does not say we

[55] H. G. Wells, *The Work, Wealth, and Happiness of Mankind*, vol. 2 (London: Heinemann, 1932), 812.

ignore purposes in our laboratory, but rather we eliminate purposes from the universe. The greatest obstacle to progress, according to Dewey, is the survival of old institutions such as the Church, and the best guarantee of freedom in the world is the spread of the scientific method. Wherever there is science there is freedom, he declares. Or, as Russell puts it, wherever there is science there is culture. Such is the superstition of scientism.

Science is a very valid and necessary way of knowing, but only of knowing those things which are subject to experimentation and to the methods of a laboratory. The great values of life such as justice, truth, and charity are beyond such an experimentation. No one yet has ever been able to put a mother's love into a test tube, and yet who will deny its reality? Nor can we throw a man into a caldron to boil to see if he gives forth the unmistakable green fumes of envy and jealousy.

Once the modern mind denied that man was a creature made in the image and likeness of God, it naturally fell into the error of saying that man was made in the image and likeness of the beast. Man then ceased to be studied theologically or philosophically, and began to be studied with the other sciences of nature, biology, physiology, and physics. But this identification of man with nature deprived man of all value. Once you make man a cog in a test astronomical machine, or a molecule in a spatio-temporal continuum, or an enlarged cell of some original protoplasmic stuff, you deny that man has a right to be treated differently than anything in nature. But, if man is not different from nature, then what value has man? If there is no specific difference between a man and a horse, then why not yoke man to the plow of Nazism or the tractor of Marxian Socialism, or make him an instrument of the State as the Fascist intelligentsia teach today?

The answer to this superstition of scientism, which makes man meaningless by making him one with nature, is not in the repudiation of science but in the recognition that there are higher values beyond the ken of science. Professor Hocking, of Harvard University, speaking of scientism says,

This desiccated picture of the world is a damnable lie—for values are there; values are among the inescapable facts of the world—and whoever disseminates this death's-head worldview in the schools and colleges of this or any other land is disseminating falsehood with the brow-beaten connivance of a whole herd of intellectual sheep, and of culpable guardians of the young.... This is one of the insights with which the new era of History begins.[56]

Scientism has ruined higher education in the United States by prostrating itself before the god of counting, and by assuming that anyone who has counted something that has never been counted before is a learned man. It makes no difference what you count, but in the name of Heaven, count! A certain Western university has awarded a doctor of philosophy degree for a thesis on the "Microbic Content of Cotton Undershirts." A Midwestern university has counted the ways of washing dishes; and some eastern universities have counted the infinitives in Augustine, the datives in Ovid, and the four ways of cooking ham; while another counted the "psychological reactions of the post-rotational eye-movement of squabs."

These subjects seem amusing when extracted from the context of universities, but the universities unfortunately take them seriously. The result is we are giving our students theories, opinions, and facts which will be out of date before the ink on the diploma fades; but we are not equipping them for life by proposing its high purposes. In the madness of specialization we have come to know more and more about less and less, but in the meantime we have lost ourselves in the maze of numbers. Fed with huge quantities of undigested facts, our judgment has become hampered and we have only unrelated bits of information instead of wisdom which alone is true knowledge. Go into any parochial school in the United States, take out a child in the first or second grade, and ask him: "Who made you?" "What is the purpose of life?" "Are you different from an animal?" Any such child aged seven or eight could answer the question of the purpose of life. But ask a Ph.D. graduate, who has counted the microbes on cotton undershirts, why he is here or where he is going; he could not tell you. He would not have a five-cent-gadget in his house five minutes without knowing its purpose, but he would live ten, twenty, or sixty years without

[56] W. E. Hocking, *What Can Man Make of Man* (New York: Harper, 1942), 33.

knowing why he is here, or where he is going. What is the use of living unless we know the purpose of being a man? It is not true, as is so often asserted, that modern youth is revolutionary because he has lacked sufficient economic advantage. Never in the history of the world did youth have so many advantages. The modern youth is revolutionary because he has no purpose in life and hence doubts the worthwhileness of living amidst plenty. Anything that loses its purpose becomes revolutionary. When a boiler loses its purpose it explodes; when a man loses his purpose he revolts.

It is true, as Dr. Dewey has said, that the use of the scientific method is the guarantee of freedom? What country, before this world war began, was generally recognized as the most advanced in the scientific method? To what nation of the world did our American universities look as the paragon of scientific perfection, and from which did they draw their greatest scientific inspiration? It was from Germany. And yet there is no country in the world where freedom is more universally suppressed.

It is true, as a Mr. Russell affirms, that if you spread science you spread culture? We gave Japan science. But will these philosophers of the superstition of scientism dare assert that culture went with it? The scientific method did not bring to a benighted people an increase of tolerance and kindness and brotherhood. They have proven what we ought to recognize; namely, that a high degree of scientific advancement can exist with utter and absolute moral depravity.

We are paying the penalty for divorcing our science from God. Nature, which science studies, belongs to God, And when man turns against God, nature or science turns against man. Francis Thompson beautifully spoke of this when he found that the whole world turned against him because he would not answer the call of God:

I tempted all His servitors, but to find
My own betrayal in their constancy,
In faith to Him their fickleness to me,
Their traitorous trueness, and their loyal deceit.[57]

---

[57] Francis Thompson, "The Hound of Heaven."

That is the true story: nature will be false to anyone who is untrue to its Maker. I am free to break the law of gravitation but if I do, the law breaks me. The law still stands. I am free to ignore God the Creator of nature, but if I do, nature will wreck me. For years science has been discovering the wonders of nature, finding in the tiny atom a miniature of the great solar system. But, instead of glorifying God for the order, law, and harmony they found in His universe, scientists vainly assumed that because they discovered the laws they were the authors of the book of nature, instead of only its proofreaders. Tearing nature away from God, nature now turned against man; refusing to serve God, nature refused to serve man. The result is that science which was supposed to be our servant is now our master. Why do millions in the world shrink in terror from a machine in the air? Why does man use his technique to destroy man? Why do children crouch in dread and mothers dig like moles into the bowels of the earth as bombs fall from the skies, as all Hell is let loose, if it is not because something has gotten out of our control?

Science has become a source of destruction, because we refused to use it as a means for lifting us to God. It is not that God has punished man for his ingratitude to nature; it is rather that nature, in unconscious loyalty, has punished man for his disloyalty. No creature can be used for the happiness of man, which has alienated itself from the service to its Creator.

Something else that we have forgotten in our glorification of science as the only true knowledge, is that science itself has no morality. An isosceles triangle for example is no more moral than a square; vitamins may be more hygienic than the pointer-readings, but they are not more ethical. The morality of science is derived from the purpose for which it is used. But in denying all purposes in life, we have made science its own justification. If there is no higher knowledge than science, how will we know what is good or bad? Hitler, using science, spreads tyranny on a vast scale and suppresses human rights and liberties through new weapons which science puts into his hands. How shall we say he is immoral and we, who use science to defend liberties, are moral, unless there be a standard outside of both? Cannot we see that by making science an ultimate, we have deprived ourselves of criterion by which to judge our cause from theirs? Divorce the products of science from the higher objectives of human life which reason and faith reveal to us, and you have a mad world wherein "humanity preys upon itself like monsters of the deep."

The Superstition of Relativism

The superstition of relativism tells us there is no distinction between truth and error, right and wrong; everything depends upon one's point of view. All values are relative and depend entirely upon the way people live in any generation. If in the twentieth century they live monogamously, then monogamy is right; if in the future, they live polygamously, then polygamy is right. Whatever the best way to find it out. When expedient, moral conventions can be accepted; when a hindrance, they can be rejected. There are no objective moral standards; no absolute distinction between good and evil. Everyone is his own lawgiver; everyone is his own judge. Tolerance is the greatest virtue and tolerance means indifference to truth and error, right and wrong. Such is relativism.

The superstition of relativism, or the notion that there is no absolute distinction between right and wrong, stems in this country from the philosophy of pragmatism. This philosophy denied that God was an absolute; it judged truth not by its consistency, nor its correspondence with reality, but by its utility. In the words of one of its best-known exponents: Truth is to be judged by its "cash-value in terms of particular experience."[58] "The gods we stand by are the gods we need and can use."[59] "'The true,' to put it very briefly, is only the expedient in the way of our thinking, just as 'the right' is only the expedient in the way of our behaving. Expedient in almost any fashion."[60] In order words, whatever succeeds is right.

This particular philosophy was born of an excessive adoration of the scientific method. Science evolved practical prescriptions for dealing with

---

[58] William James, *The Varities of Religious Experience* (New York: Longmans and Green, 1920), 443.

[59] James, *The Varities of Religious Experience*, 331.

[60] William James, *Essays in Pragmatism*, ed. Alburey Castell (New York: Hafner, 1948), 170.

particular problems; when the practical problems changed, the prescription changed. This method was practical in dealing with phenomena, but the philosopher enlarged it to apply to all truth. Nothing was considered immutable or changeable. Everything was relative to a point of view. Not being able to apply his method to religion and morals, instead of acknowledging the insufficiency of his method, the pragmatist denied the value of religion and morals.

The pragmatists thus assume that the spiritual and moral needs of man and a nation needed no other foundation than that of the utilitarian activities associated with earning a living. Ideas thus were regarded as instruments of power. These ideas—that there is no absolute distinction between truth and error, right and wrong, that morality is determined by the subjective outlook of every individual and is devoid of all objective standards—are taught in many secular colleges and universities in the United States. A distinguished professor in a Midwestern university revealed that there was not a single student in his class who could give a rational justification for democracy. The students justified democracy solely on the grounds of expediency and the fact that it had the greatest power; none saw any intrinsic value in democracy. Very few saw the evil implications in a morality of self-advantage, and some who did were reluctant to abandon it in a world where success was the measure of greatness. It took a great catastrophe to bring home its falsity. And this is how it happened.

What moral standards are the Japs violating, if the criterion of truth and righteousness is expediency? Why do we say that Japan has violated the conscience of the world, if the conscience of the world has no other measure than the useful? Incidentally, where was this moral conscience of the world before the war began? How shall the rightness of our cause be distinguished from the rightness of our enemies, if there is no objective standard outside of both? If there is no right and wrong, independent of the whims of individuals, how shall we defend ourselves against despotism? The ultimate bulwark of democracy is in the recognition of moral standards, so absolute that citizens are willing in the end, if need be, to give everything—even life—to maintain them. If there is no objective distinction between right and wrong, how can Hitler be wrong? How can he be right?

Our journalists, our educators, our movies, our best sellers, our forums, and even some of the churches have been sniping away for years at the moral law, knocking off first its application to politics and economics, and then to the family, then the individual. They have sneered at and ridiculed those who still held on to the moral law, calling them "reactionary," "behind the times," and labeling purity and truthfulness as "bourgeois virtues" in the language of Marx. They now say that all we need do about evil is to forget it, and that faith and morality can be brought back into civilization as one might buy a commodity at a drugstore.

We have an active barbarism to defeat on the outside, and we have a passive barbarism from within; the first is openly violent, the second is sinister and secretive. The first endangers or shores, the second pollutes our souls; the first would take away external liberties such as freedom of speech and press, and the second would take away internal liberty, or the right to call our soul our own. The first makes us stronger by the mere fact that we resist; the second makes us weaker by the mere fact that like a cancer we are blind to its dangers. We could defeat the enemy on the outside, and still completely collapse from the inside. We could win the war and lose peace: "Fear ye not them that kill the body, and are not able to kill the soul: but rather fear him that can destroy both soul and body in hell" (Matt. 10:28).

When Colin Kelly as a selfless pilot sank the first Jap ship of the war and in doing so lost his life; when Edward O'Hara shot down the first Jap plane; when Dick Fleming made himself the first human torpedo; when Daniel O'Callaghan became the first admiral to go down fighting on the bridge of the *San Francisco*; when Mike Moran became the first naval officer to sink six Jap ships in single combat; when Commander Shea became the first fighting man whose last letter to his son became a famous American testament on patriotism; when the five Sullivans became the first American family of boys to be snuffed out in this war; these men had no "opinion" about America's cause; they did not believe that the righteousness of the stars and stripes depended upon this subjective outlook. They believed in an absolute distinction between right and wrong, our cause and our enemy; in fact, so much did they believe in it that life was secondary to that cause.

And while these and millions of men in our armed forces believe in such an absolute distinction between right and wrong, our Fascist intelligentsia are telling us: "right and wrong are relative to expediency; it all depends upon your point of view." Nonsense! It does not! Our cause is right! It is right before God! It is right under God! And in God's name we will defend it!

The Superstition of Materialism

The superstition of materialism affirms that man has no soul, that there is no future life, and that man has no other destiny than that of the animals. Being devoid of spirit man may best be described not as a creature made to the image and likeness of God but as a "psychoanalytical bag with physiological libido," or a "stimulus response mechanism."

Since there is no future life, it follows that the good life consists in material improvement; that civilization and culture vary in direct ratio with wealth and the two chickens in every pot; that want is the greatest cause of misery and unhappiness, and that abundance is the surest guarantee of peace and happiness. Goodness, truth, honor, and beauty are natural byproducts of increase of national dividends. The end of life is the acquisition of money, the ceaseless enjoyment of pleasure, and the avoidance of sacrifice. Such is the superstition of materialism.

It simply is not true that peace follows material prosperity and unhappiness follows the want of it; rather unhappiness flows from loss of a goal and purpose of life through the denial of the human soul. It is not economic hardship nor political injustice which has driven modern man to revolutionary action: it is the horror of an empty sterile world. Men lived with only the necessities of life before, but they were never as revolutionary as they are today. Religious communities through the Church survive on the minimum of existence, with vows of poverty, chastity, and obedience, and where shall you find greater happiness? Glance around at those who possess abundance of material goods. Does happiness increase with wealth? There is more frustration among the rich than the poor. It is the former who are most addicted to selfishness, who are satiated and unhappy. Sin and evil do not disappear with the advent of gold. Society can become inhuman while preserving all the advantages of great material prosperity.

The materialist superstition that man has no other end than this life, and no other task than economic betterment, and that education must produce a race of doers rather than an "impractical" race of knowers, will eventually build a civilization in which we will have no standards to judge what is economically good or socially bad. The philosopher could make a good world without the economist, but the economist could not make one without the philosopher. By making acquisitiveness supreme, we lose all standards of knowing what is right or wrong, the injustices of capitalism; but they do not always realize that capitalism is maintained not only by capitalists but by those who, like some of themselves, would be capitalists if they could, and that these injustices survive, not merely because the rich exploit the poor, but because in their hearts too many of the poor admire the rich. They know and complain that they are tyrannized over by the power of money. But they do not yet see that what makes money the tyrant of society is largely their own reverence of it. And to complete Tawny's picture, if we make material standards the only standards, then we become incapable of judging the new acquisitive society which is arising—the acquisitiveness of power. As fortunes dwindle, as taxes eat up inheritances, and as bureaucracies begin to administer vast sums of money formerly administered by capitalists and bankers, envious, greedy, and lustful men will seek to become dispensers of that social booty, and who shall say that these new financiers of power are wrong? Given no standards other than materialism, wherein remorse is disjoined from power, and we will have a new capitalism—the capitalism of power, wherein the bureaucrats become the bankers.

> Bidding the law make court'sy their will;
> Hooking both right and wrong to the appetite,
> To follow as it draws![61]

The modern man wants back his soul! He wants the intelligentsia to stop the nonsense of regarding him as an animal, a libido, a toolmaker, or

[61] William Shakespeare, *Measure for Measure*, act 2, scene 4.

a voter and to begin to look at him as a creature made in the image and likeness of God.

It is pathetic to hear people asking: "What can I as an individual do in this crisis?" So many feel that they're like robots in a great machine, that they would like to get away from it all, even if it meant climbing back into the catacombs. Like the Jews in exile they hang their harps on the trees, and ask how can they a song without a soul.

In plain, simple language, all these individuals want their souls back! They want to be whole again. They are sick of being thrown into a Darwinian pot to boil as a beast, or into a Freudian stew to be squeezed between two conflicting slices of capital and labor. They want to possess that which makes them human, gives meaning to politics, economics, psychology, sociology; namely, the soul.

Listen to them:

I want my soul back; that I may be free from earth; that I may surrender it to Him. I want to hold my own life, as a responsible creature, in my own hands, that I may emancipate it not only from nature, but even from the man-made environment. Somewhere I am lost amid organized chaos. Everywhere I hear talk about freedom, but how can I be free unless I have a soul? Stones are not free; neither are cows or cabbages. From every side I am told I have no soul. If I have no soul, then I have nothing to lose, and if I have nothing to lose why should I feel unhappy when I sin?

In my misery I go to the modern world and it tells me that I need to be integrated with society, and hence I must throw myself into the vast social experiences and sociological adventurings. But society cannot help me, for it is in the same mess as I. Society is made up of millions of frustrated souls exactly like myself. How can it cure me, when it has the same disease? Then the world tells me I should have ideals, for no one can live without faith; give yourself over to aims, and you will find your soul. But when I ask whether these ideals are real, such as God and the moral law, I am told that they are myths; that it makes no difference whether there is a God, or Christ ever lived, or that there is any reason behind these ideals; but that they are just helpful fictions.

I am thus back to where I was at the beginning. I am told to have ideals and at the same time told that they are only fictions. I am not an animal, not a libido, not a proletarian, not an atom; I am something else, more and greater than these things. And I want to be more! I want back my soul![62]

To get back our souls we have to turn our backs on all the twaddle we have been fed for the last century about the nature of man. We might just as well put it bluntly, and say that what we call modern is only an old error with a new label. The modern view of man is wrong—completely and absolutely wrong, and if we go on following it we will end in blind alleys, frustrated hopes, and unhappy existences. It is not nearly as funny as we thought to make a monkey out of a man.

The millions of our boys on the battlefronts of the world fighting for their lives and for great moral issues, will recover their souls. Amidst wounds of death, fire, and shell, they will get close to the meaning of life and to that something within them that makes them human. They will be angry when they look back on the way some of them were educated. They will come to have not only the enemy they meet in battle, but the intelligentsia who told them they were only animals. They will begin to realize that these intelligentsia robbed them of their greatest possession—faith. For a while they will wander around the battlefields like Magdalene in the garden saying: "They have taken away my Lord; and I know not where they have laid him" (John 20:13). But when they do stumble on Him as Magdalene did when she saw the lived marks of nails, they will enter once again into the possession of the soul. And when they come marching home there will be a judgment on those who told them they had no soul; they will live like new men and they will give a rebirth to America under God.

Recovering our souls demands doing two things: turning our backs completely on the way the modern world thinks, and facing our Divine Original,

[62] See Hocking, *What Can Man Make of Man*, 52–54.

who made us and who alone can tell us what we are. Instead of drifting with the current into the abyss of hopeless paganism, we must learn to swim against it like the salmon black to the spawning ground where man is born again.

> It is the Soul's prerogative, its fate,
> To shape the outward to its own estate.
> If right itself, then all around is well;
> If wrong, it makes of all without a hell,
> So multiplies the Soul its joys and pain,
> Gives out itself, itself takes back again.
> Transformed by Thee, the world hath but one face.[63]

The Superstition of License

The superstition of license here means perverted freedom. It defines freedom as the right to do whatever you please or the absence of law, restraint, and discipline. A man is considered free when his desires are satisfied; he is not free when they are unsatisfied. The goal of freedom is self-expression. Such is the superstition of license.

This superstition is grounded on a false definition of freedom. Freedom does not mean the right to do whatever we please. If it did, it would be a physical power, not a moral power. Certainly, we can do whatever we please, but ought we? Freedom means the right to do whatever we ought, and therefore is inseparable from law. It was precisely because we made freedom consist in the right to do whatever we pleased, that we produced a civilization which was nothing but a criss-cross of individual egotisms in the economic, political, and international order. Communism, Nazism, and Fascism arose to organize that chaos and became as so many convulsive attempts to arrest a disintegration by the false method of going to the other extreme, by extinguishing all freedom in order to preserve law.

The solution lies along other lines, namely that we are most free when we act within the law and not outside it. An aviator is most free to fly when

---

[63] R. H. Dans, "Thoughts on the Soul."

he obeys the law of gravitation. As our Lord said: "The truth shall make you free" (John 8:32).

Nor is it true that freedom consists in the shaking-off of convention and tradition and authority. What is called self-expression is in reality often nothing else than self-destruction. The railroad engine that suddenly becomes so "progressive" that it will not follow the tracks laid out by an engineer of a previous generation soon discovers that it is not "free" to be an engine at all. If freedom means only the lessening of authority, then we shall have indeed the thrill of risk, but in the end we shall have no freedom. As Leo XIII expressed it, "liberty will ever be more free and secure in proportion as license is kept in fuller restraint."[64]

About the only curbs which the sensate man allows himself are those which contribute to his own physical well-being. Dieting is about the only discipline left, and dieting is not fasting. Dieting is for the body; fasting is for the soul. Moral restraints, spiritual discipline, ascetic life, denial of evil thoughts and temptations, restraint in the use of the legitimate pleasures of life—these things are meaningless to the modern man who feels he has sufficient warrant in throwing off moral standards for no other reason than because they are old. When we reach a point where we measure our self-expression by the height of the pile of our discarded disciplines, inhibitions, and moral standards then anyone who would die to preserve that disemboweled ghost of liberty is a fool.

Salvation lies in the fact that freedom exists for a purpose; that is, we have freedom to give it away. No one keeps his freedom. A man in love surrenders it to the woman he loves and calls it a "sweet slavery"; the modern man who has thrown off morality surrenders it to public opinion, becomes the slave of fashion and passing moods; the Christian who uses his freedom gives it to God, "to serve whom is to reign" and then purchases the slavery of the infinite in whom is love and life and truth. Every freedom is for the sake of bondage, and we are all in bondage—to a fellow creature, to the mob, to Hitler, or to God who alone can make us truly free.

[64] Leo XIII, Encyclical on the Nature of Human Liberty *Libertas* (June 20, 1888), no. 23.

That is why freedom for freedom's sake is meaningless. I want to be free from something, only because I want to be free for something. That is why freedom is inseparable from purpose. Freedom from restraint is justified only when it depends on freedom for something else. The fallacy of the superstition of license is that it makes us free just to be free, which is a meaningless and as unsatisfying as a cold in the head.

The superstition of license assumes that men will always do the right thing if they are educated; hence they need no restraint and no discipline. And here we touch on the basic weakness of sensate education; namely, it assumes that sin is due to ignorance and not to the abuse of freedom. When evil was attributed to the will, the school belonged to the Church. Now that we believe there is no sin, and that what we call evil is only want of enlightenment, the school stands in isolation from religion and morality. Schools once belonged to religious groups in order that moral training of the will might keep pace with enlightenment of the intellect. Now the universities have for the most part lost all concern for the will. When confronted with the problem of evil, they immediately rush to a conference to discuss greater knowledge, when what is really needed is more discipline.

The sensate culture is right in saying that sin is irrational because every sin is a violation of law of eternal reason, but the unreason or ignorance is not the citadel of sin. A man sins, not because he is ignorant, but because he is perverse. The intellect makes mistakes, but the will sins. A man may know all we teach him and still be a bad man; the intelligentsia are not necessarily the saints. The ignorant are not necessarily devils. Enlightenment and education can became the servants of a perverse will, and when they do it is like Hell being let loose. Unless a man's will has a purpose and it is a good one, education will do nothing for him except to fortify his own egotism.

There is an almost unpardonable naiveté about those who say that reason alone can conquer anarchic impulses. Rather, the reverse is true. Reason can be used just as easily to justify evil, to rationalize evil, to invent lethal instrument for the defense of those wicked tendencies in time of war.

Reason was made to lead us to faith as the senses were made to lead us to reason. Now when reason is torn up from its roots in God, how can we trust its conclusions? If chance, blind evolution, or chaos were its origin, then why should it now be expected to be anything less than chaotic, unstable, and fluid? An age which has put all its trust in enlightenment as the cure of evil has founded itself possessed of the greatest evil war in the history of the world.

These superstitions constitute the cult of our contemporary Western civilization. The chaos into which they have led us reveals their fallacies more effectively than any intellectual argument. The so-called progressive man, who today is bewildered, baffled, and depressed at the disorder in the world need only go into his own godless disordered interior life to find its secret; the man without moral standards and therefore chaotic is the miniature of the world without a moral standard and therefore at war.

If these superstitions still exercise some influence, it is only because of artificial respiration given them by two classes of reactionaries—economic reactionaries and intellectual reactionaries.

The economic reactionaries are those who believe that any system which enables them to get rich must necessarily be a good system; hence any change in the existing order they regard as radicalism, revolutionist, or Communism.

The intellectual reactionaries are the intelligentsia (we use that world to distinguish them from true intellectuals). By the intelligentsia we mean those who have been educated beyond their intelligence. Like the economic reactionaries they equate what they have with what is best, the difference being that their wealth is ideological, not material. Their clichés, catchwords, and ideologies have value only in a world of a chaos which produced two world wars in twenty-one years; but they would be without validity any other time or in any other order based on justice and charity. They would be just as out of place in such a world as a teeter-totter in an old folks' home. A high-school youngster who thinks the "Jersey Bounce" is the highest expression of music would be lost at a concert of Toscanini.

Despite these two reactionary forces, it should now be recognized that these superstitions have failed to provide an adequate dynamic for either peace or war. The longer we try to keep them alive, the ruder will be our awakening; the more terrible will be our judgment.

It is no answer to retort with the old cliche that religion has been the enemy of science, for he who has eyes can see that science today is the enemy of man. It is not religion which has tyrannized man. Science has its place in the world; this we not only admit—this we insist upon. But its place is not at the peak of the pyramid of knowledge where Descartes placed it when he enthroned mathematics, or where Kant placed it when he enthroned physics, and where Comte placed it when he enthroned sociology. That place belongs to theology, the one science which makes a university, for the wold *university* implies all knowledge and all sciences and all arts turn on one axis, which is God. Cardinal Newman in his masterly treatise, *The Idea of a University*, allowed the imagination to run riot by picturing a university of the future where there would be no theology. To bring home the horror of such a condition, he described it as follows:

> Henceforth man is to be as if he were not, in the general course of Education; the moral and mental sciences are to have no professional chairs, and the treatment of them is to be simply left as a matter of private judgment, which each individual may carry out as he will. I can just fancy such a prohibition abstractly possible; but one thing I cannot fancy possible, viz.: that the parties in question, after this sweeping act of exclusion, should forthwith send out proposals on the basis of such exclusion for publishing an Encyclopedia, or erecting a National University.[65]

But these conditions are upon us now, and so strongly entrenched is the opposition that to plead for a return of theology to university curricula would be to bring down upon one's head the wrath of those intelligentsia who still live in the Dark Ages and still feed on the superstition that the proper way to study man is to study nature. Some day under the pressure of catastrophe we will come to see that as science reveals nature, so theology reveals man. In that day, universities will be universities.

[65] John Henry Newman, *The Idea of a University*, (London: Longmans and Green, 1917), 54.

In this conflict we must not save everything just as it is nor seek to maintain the status quo, nor preserve an empire, nor get back the kind of a world that existed before this war began, for if we did we would be fighting to keep a world from whose womb came the satellites of antichrist: Hitler and Hirohito and others.

Some things are not worth fighting for. One of these things is an unredeemed, materialistic selfish order, organized on the basis of neglect of God and the abandonment of moral standards. The victors who won the war of 1918 lost the peace because they attempted to keep a world together on the basis of the outworn slogans and the really bad philosophy of the French Revolution. Our peacemakers, inspired more by the expiring convulsions of a liberal would born 150 years before, became blinded to the needs of a new world expressed in the protests of the revolutions of Germany, Italy, and Russia. We won the war because we were stronger; we lost the peace because we tried to keep everything together on the basis of the liberalistic, Capitalistic, individualistic, irreligious world of the outworn nineteenth century.

Napoleon carried the ideas of the French Revolution over Europe. Hitler carried the ideas of Marx over Europe. Both have done a service. Both swept away the litter of a bad world; one a monarchical world based on privilege of power, the other the Capitalistic world based on the privilege of money. Both are wrong. He who would will to keep either privilege of power or money will keep only the dynamite for the next world war. We are not out to preserve either the Marxian or French Revolution—we are at war this time to build an order not for the common man, spoon-fed by democracies, but for common service to a common good: a world of free men—free from economic want and therefore free to save their souls. This is worth fighting for!

When the ship is sinking, we must not think of the cargo. It is not the ship of democracy nor the ship of America, nor the ship of our four freedoms we must abandon. But the barnacles we must abandon. Our task is not the restoration of everything as it was; restoration could be our greatest obstacle to peace. It is regeneration we are seeking. No sane person would suggest that when this war is over London should rebuild its bombed buildings just exactly as they were, just as no sane person would suggest the restoration of a world which in fifteen years vomited three terrific revolutions: red, brown, and black. Nor would he suggest that we reestablish the same old boundaries, the same sovereignties, and the same anemic League of Nations. Blind indeed would anyone be who suggests that we preserve the present order. There is one other order and that is our hope—the Christian order which starts with man.

26

The Revolution of Man

For years Lenin, Mussolini, and Hitler were saying that the old order was dead. We ridiculed them, insisting that the liberalistic, Capitalistic, agnostic world of the nineteenth century with its business and education on the table, and its morals and religion on the sideboard to sugarcoat them when necessary, would never die. Lenin, Mussolini, and Hitler were right in saying that the old order was dead. But they were wrong in saying that the new order or the future would be theirs, namely, socialism of class, nation, and race. Our error has been to assume that the choice is between their new order based on Socialism, and our old order based on individualism. It is not. There is still another order of which the modern mind never thinks, because it has had no contact with genuine Christianity in over two hundred years, and that is the Christian order.

These Totalitarian heresies were protests against an old order, for example: Marxian Socialism reacted against defects in Capitalism; Fascism reacted against defects in parliamentarianism; Nazism reacted against defects in nationalism, as in the League of Nations. Because they were protests against an old order, they practically never embodied a wholeness of view; their character was determined by the errors they combatted. For that reason, Marxian Socialism is nothing but rotted Capitalism on a state basis; Fascism is nothing but rotted parliamentarianism on a one-party basis; Nazism is nothing but rotted nationalism on a racial basis. In each case, they took their position from the enemy. They were inspired more by a hatred of something they wished to overthrow than by a love of the new ideals which they desired to establish.

Because political and economic revolutions were rebellions against the last revolution, they tended to bestow an absolutely sacred character on previously neglected elements of the regime they sought to overthrow. That is why we have capital in the saddle in one revolution, labor in the saddle in the nest revolution, and poor John Q. Public hitchhiking but never getting a ride. We need an entirely different kind of revolution, one that will not keep its eye on the last revolution nor take its character from it, but will concentrate on man in its highest reaches and noblest destiny. This is the Christian revolution.

The Christian worldview differs from the Totalitarian and the old materialist culture of the Western world in one basic fact: it believes that it is man who makes society, and not society which makes man. That is why the first discussion of the Christian order must begin with man.

After all, what is the use of a revolution or a new system of economics or a new international society, unless we know the type of creature who will live in it?

For the last century the world has had a very distorted notion of man. In fact there were fashions in man as there were in clothes. Each fashion concentrated on one aspect of man to the neglect of all the others, like the five blind men who felt an elephant, each describing it different accordingly as he touched its trunk, the tail, the ear, and so forth.

In the days of Darwin, blind thinkers went to man and since he felt like an animal they said he must be an animal, and therefore should be treated as an animal. Thus we had jurists like Justice Holmes of the Supreme Court defining man as a "cosmic ganglion." If man is only a ganglion why should we go to war to prevent Hitler from making mincemeat of ganglia?

Then came the new fashion. Blind men felt man and found that he was made up of nerves, reflexes, and responses, so they defined man as a "physiological bag filled with psychological libido," as they consulted dream books after each fitful sleep to learn what Freud had to say about their sex life.

Then came another blind philosopher, that German who denied democracy because its foundation was Christian: Karl Marx. He discovered that man spent much of his time earning a living.

Universalizing this particular aspect, he gave us the economic man, for whom religion, culture, law, literature, and the arts were byproducts of his method of production. And thus did a German spawn Marxian Socialism.

Now we are at the beginning of a new fashion in men. With increases of taxes, decline in income, blind men discovered man lived in a State and was dependent on it for his ideas, his values, and thus was born the political man who has rights because the new lawyers told him the State gave him rights.

The partial views of men as expressed by Marx, Spencer, Darwin, and Freud never treat man as he is—really is. These views represent incidental activities erected into absolutes and are of much the same mental construction as would be shown by a dentist who thinks man is all teeth; or a manicurist who thinks he is all bands; or a pedicurist who thinks he is all feet; or a phrenologist who thinks he is all bumps.

Man, of course, is each of these things: he is biological; he is psychological; he is economic, and he is political, but he is none of these things exclusively nor is he all of these added together, any more than a baby is the sum of all the chemicals in a laboratory. We have taken man apart and looked at all the pieces, but like children with toys we cannot put him together again. In our fever for psychoanalysis, we have neglected psychosynthesis.

Because the modern man is part-man, Christianity was watered down to suit these partial aspects. The result was that some did away with Heaven and Hell to suit economic man; some did away with sin and guilt, right and wrong to suit psychological man; others did away with theology and revelation to suit the Darwinian man; still others did away with the soul to suit political man and finally whittled away every trace of life until nothing was left.

The Christian view of man admits that man has ganglia, does dream, experiences libidos, works and talks politics, but it insists that man is exclusively none of these things. It begins by asking what is it that makes man different from anything else in the world; and answers an intellect and a will—an intellect by which he can know truth and a will by which he may choose goodness. Next, it says, since he is different from an animal he must have a different purpose than an animal, just as a monkey wrench must have a different purpose than a monkey. This purpose will obviously be in keeping with what is highest in his life, namely, an intellect and will. Man therefore wants life—not for two more days, or two more months, but undying life. He therefore wants truth—not the truths of geography to the exclusion of science, nor of art to the exclusion of history, but all truth without a mixture of error. He therefore wants love, not love for a limited period of time, but an eternal ecstasy of love without the shadow of hate or satiety. This eternal life, truth, and love for which he seeks is God. God therefore is his final and ultimate end. Therefore politics, economics, education, rationing, parliaments, parties, bureaucrats, governments, and social security are only means to that end and derive their morality from it. This is the foundation of the Christian order.

In order to understand man, one must begin with God, even more than to understand a sunbeam one must begin with the sun. God is the Creator of the world. He was not forced to create, any more than a poet is forced to write. He created freely out of the fullness of His Love. All good things diffuse themselves. Because the flower is good, it diffuses itself in perfume; because man is good, he gives; because God is good, He creates.

Among the creatures which He made, man was the peak of visible creation and for him all visible creation existed. This one creature He made free, in order that he might be capable of love. No one can be forced to love; to be forced to love anyone is Hell. Being made in his image and likeness, God intended that as man came from Love, so he should go back to Love after an earthly pilgrimage wherein he could freely say yea or nay to the courtship of the Divine Heart.

But in making man free, God made it possible for man to rebel. Man could be a traitor; he could be a soldier or he could be a deserter. Weighing all the possibilities, God chose to endow man with the power of rebellion in order that there might be meaning and purpose in allegiance, when he freely chose to give it.

In our language, God took the risk, and man, misinterpreting freedom as the right to do whatever he pleased, decided that he would be more free outside the law than within it. Instead of using creatures as a means to God, man decided to use them as an end and thus made gold, or the flesh, or power, the goal of living. He furthermore decided that instead of recognizing God as His Creator, he would make a declaration of independence and affirm himself as God. He thus committed the sin of lust by turning to creatures as an end, and the sin of pride by turning from God as his final end. Becoming hardened in his pride and lust, society became a confusion of conflicting self-centers instead of a fellowship of love which God intended it should be. The original freedom which was meant to be for God, and in God, became perverted to mean freedom from God.

This rebellion against God caused a fundamental disharmony inside man, for though he denies God, he still is God's creature. The prodigal son among the swine was still the son. Animals cannot rebel against their nature because they are not free, but man can rebel against his nature. He can deny his origin and his purpose, but he can never escape it. He could never lose the image in which he was created; he could never be free from his dependence on God. One can never be godless without God. Man could deface and mar the image but he could not destroy it; the great mosaics of Christ on their ceiling of the St. Sophia in Constantinople were defaced by the Turks who could never succeed in destroying them. Man thus became a twisted distorted creature, wanting God because he was made in His image by Him and for Him, and yet hating God because man defaced that image. Destined for eternity, he has longings for eternal life and truth and love; but repudiating eternity, he tries to capture this life, and truth and love, where it is not—in the transitory fleeting shadow of time. Having lost the great gift of God's grace, he became not just a mere man but like a king in exile, dispossessed of a royalty and a stranger in a land that was meant to be a home.

That primal sin of human nature disturbed the equilibrium of human nature; as man rebelled against God, man rebelled against himself; his senses revolted against his reason; his flesh against his spirit; and even creatures seeing that their master had turned against God, now turned against their master. That is why there is not a one of us who does not feel that as St. Augustine put it, "Whatever we are, we are not what we ought to be."

This permanent wound in human nature cannot be explained away by biological evolution, as we tried to do a few years ago, because its essence is not the will to survive but pride which biology cannot touch. Selfishness is the root of the inexplicable tragedy of the world, namely: man's proud unwillingness to accept the absolute authority and the claim of God on whose image he has been made. This is the mystery of iniquity! The optimism of the doctrine of progress, that man becomes better and better as time goes on, cannot stand up under the facts of history which reveal ever-increasing potentialities for chaos and war. Neither is there justification for the pessimism of Luther who said that man was intrinsically corrupt, nor for the pessimism of Hobbes who said man was "solitary, poor, nasty, brutish and short." Man's sin did not make him utterly leprous and unclean, but it did impair his nature by breaking off relationship with Divine Love, darken his intellect, weaken his will, and make him personally more prone to sin.

The condition of regenerating a world is in recognizing the abysmal depths of evil in the heart of man, and realizing that public enemy number one is neither ignorance, nor falls in evolution, nor bad government, nor ductless glands, but sin—apostasy from God.

This explains to some extent "how we got this way," but it is not the final world on the Christian doctrine of man.

God's love is limitless. As Love at the first moment of time could not keep the secrets of His Power and Goodness but told them the nothingness in creation, and later on could not keep the secrets of His Wisdom and told them to a chosen race in revelation, so now Love completely surrenders Himself by appearing in the form and pattern of man as the person of Jesus Christ, true God and true man.

Man was made originally to the image of God. Now that the image was defaced, who could better restore it than the Original Image according to which he was made? Thus the love that was spurned and rejected now appears in history as a Redeemer. The bridge between man and God had been broken down; only one who was both God and man could rebuild it. Being man, He could act as a man and for man; being God, His redemption of man would have an infinite value.

Coming among sinful men, He allowed all their sins to come to a head and to do its worst against Him, namely put Him to death. Sin could do no more. But in attempting to kill God, which is the nature of sin, sin really wrote its own condemnation on the pages of history. For in rising from the dead by the power of God, He made the disaster of sin the beginning of its conquest, and the occasion of a new and regenerated humanity under His headship which is the Kingdom of God.

If the Cross ended His life, if His Calvary was a hopeless fight against sin, then the pathos of our misery would be deepened and the riddle of our life darkened. But having met the enemy and overcome the worst, He becomes not only a Savior but a final authority who can tell us the way out of all the mad chaos of this hour. Thus we are confronted again with the original problem of creation: the problem of "either-or." Either we surrender our life and our will to Him and find peace, or we will repudiate Him wildly, completely, and hatefully and end in cyclic wars. Either we will love Christ or we will love antichrist.

There is no more compulsion in this choice than in Creation. Man is still free. As in the beginning, he was free to accept God or reject Him, so now in history he is free to accept God's Son, Jesus Christ, or the Cross, whereunto that Great Figure is nailed. Hands that are dug with steel cannot fashion a lash to break our wills. Feet that are pierced with nails cannot hunt us down as unwilling prey; lips that are bruised and parched can issue no dictatorial commands; eyes that are clotted and closed cannot make chains to enslave and imprison. His very flag is the flag of freedom, or better still the banner of love. He can only wait for us! But oh! How He waits: arms outstretched to embrace; heart open to love! No one else in all the world ever founded a religion wherein a welcome was extended to as sinner, while he was yet a sinner. But He does. "When as yet we were sinners … Christ died for us" (Rom. 5:8–9). All others are merely teachers; they tell us to wash ourselves righteous and then go to God. But He as a Savior, bids us come dirty that He might have the joy of washing away our sins. Everyone else demanded that we have a newness of life; He gives it, for there is no life apart from Him. Others make sin the condition of unacceptance; He makes sin the condition of *acceptance: O Felix Culpa.* "O Happy Fault that has won for us so loving, so mighty a Redeemer."

Such is the gesture of God's mercy on fallen man. Instead of restoring man to what he had been, God did more. He stooped down from Heaven, undoing the pride of Babel with the humility of Bethlehem, taking man unto His arms and drawing him to His Heart in an embrace so close that the gulf between the Creator and creature was bridged in a union as intimate as the branches and the vine.

Now contrast the modern pagan view of man. If this life is all, why not get all we can and by whatever means we can? Why be faithful to one spouse if a more attractive one comes along? Why raise children and subject oneself to pain and confinement? Why be temperate and chaste and generous except in those moments which please us, or when satiety overtakes us, or when expediency demands it? Why should not the Capitalist be greedy, the worker avaricious, the man on relief slothful? Why bother with distinctions between right and wrong, good and evil? Why not have a "progressive education" which would do away with restraint, discipline, and authority? Why not substitute hygiene for morality? Why not make law the instrument of power? Why not be anti-Semitic, anti-Christian? Why not, as a well-known American journalist did, define freedom as the right to tell everyone who opposes our individual whims and fancies to go to Hell?

A pagan who does none of these things is an inconsistent pagan, a cowardly pagan, a pagan half-afraid through Christian influence that he may be wrong. As G. K. Chesterton put it:

> Now who that runs can read it,
> The riddle that I write
> Of why this poor old sinner
> Should sin without delight?
> But I, I cannot read it
> (Although I run and run)
> Of them that do not have the faith,
> And will not have the fun.[66]

It is simply impossible to have millions of men in the world living according to their pagan principles, and not produce the modern chaotic

---

[66] G. K. Chesterton, "The Song of the Strange Ascetic," in *The Collected Poems of G. K. Chesterton* (New York: Dodd and Mead, 1911).

world in which we live. This idea of a "Heaven here below" is the surest way to make a Hell upon earth. The universe thus becomes a multiplicity of self-centered little deities; the coat of arms of each is a big letter *I*, and when they talk their *I*s are always getting closer together.

In the light of the foregoing explanation of man the choice before the world is this: Will we build a new order on the Totalitarian assumption that man is a tool of the State? Or will we retain the old order of the secularist culture of the last two hundred years, that man is only an economic animal? Or will we build a new order on the Christian assumption, that man is a creature made to the image and likeness of God and therefore one for whom economics, politics, and society exist as a means to an eternal destiny beyond the historical perspective of planets, space, and time?

The post-war planners are still assuming with Marx that man is essentially economic, or with Darwin that he is essentially animal, or with Freud that he is essentially sexual, or with Hitler that he is essentially political. Hence they think that all we have to do is to change an economic system, or form new parties, or give more sex instruction, or greater license to the breakup of the family and we will have peace.

These planners think they are practical, because they talk in terms of money, trade, international police, and geographical areas of influence and federated states. The truth is they are just as impractical as men who might legislate for squirrels by passing laws about nuts. Squirrels eat nuts, and man lives economically; but, as nuts do not explain squirrels, so neither does production explain man. Because the planners do not understand the nature of the one for whom they are planning, their plans are going to lead us into a phase of history where "eldest Night / And Chaos, ancestors of Nature, hold / Eternal anarchy, amidst the noise / Of endless wars."[67]

Given the errant impulse, the frustrated selfish existences, the distorted human goals which these partial views of man engender, there is only one way to arrest that chaos, and that is by organizing it, and the organization of chaos is Socialism. The individualism and egotism which a distorted concept of man begets leave him alone and isolated, and to overcome this

---

[67] John Milton, *Paradise Lost* (London: Bell and Daldy, 1861), bk. 2, p. 53.

isolation there is only one non-Christian solution possible: the subordination of those rebellious atoms to a compulsory principle in the hands of the State. Socialism is the secularized, atheized version of a community and a fraternity of man which Christian love alone can engender. It is the new form into which man will bring his tortured and isolated personality, in vain quest for peace. By abusing his freedom under liberalism, man, unless he returns to a knowledge of his true nature, will fall under the compulsion of Socialism. He will think less and less of freedom, though he may talk much about it, for a man talks about his health when he is unhealthy. His end will be the trading of his freedom for a false security from the wet nurse of the State.

The old order of liberal individualism is dead. Man will either become the subject of a non-divine evil will embodied in Socialistic bureaucracy, or he will submit himself to the higher Divine Principle for whom he was made and in whom he alone can find his peace. He no longer will be free to decide whether he will or will not live under authority. From now on it is a question of under whose authority he will live, the authority of a Socialistic State, or the authority of God reflected in a State which recognizes each person as endowed with rights and possessed of a value which no power can disinherit.

The Western world must learn that Totalitarianism cannot be overcome by Socialism, by laissez-faire Capitalism, by individualism, or by any combination of these, or that what has gone wrong is not the means of living, but the ends. The economic and political chaos of the modern world can be overcome only by a non-political, non-economic, non-Marxian, non-Freudian concept of a man and society. This does not mean that politics and economics are of no value; they are. But it means they are of secondary value for, unless we know the nature of the creature for whom politics and economics exist, it is just as useless to meddle with them as it is to fool with a blast furnace unless we know its purpose. Unless we restore the Christian concept of man, and thus build a human rather than an economic order, we will be forced into Totalitarianism in the hour we are doing our most to combat it.

What is the objection to the basic Christian principle that we build for the whole man as a creature of God instead of for the Darwinian, Freudian,

Marxian man? The answer is on the tongues of all the reactionaries: "Christianity does not suit the modern man." Certainly it does not. And for the reason that the modern man is not man; he is part-man, a dissected man.

But Christianity does however suit man in his entirety, or human nature as it is, composed of body and soul and made to the image and likeness of God, with horizontal relations to the right and left in space and time, and yet never wholly explained by these, because identified with something prior and more fundamental, namely vertical relations with God, His Creator and Redeemer in whom is his peace and his joy.

Up until now it has been said Christianity does not suit the modern man, therefore scrap Christianity. Now let us say, Christianity does not suit modern man, therefore let us scrap modern man.

Maybe there is nothing wrong with Christianity after all; maybe—may we dare suggest it—there is something wrong with us. Maybe there is something wrong with John Dewey and nothing wrong with St. John; maybe there is something false about H. G. Wells, and nothing wrong with Gertrude Stein, and something right about St. Gertrude; maybe there is something wrong with progressive education and nothing wrong with the Light of the World who said: "Suffer the little children, and forbid them not to come to me" (Matt. 19:14). Maybe science cannot be a substitute for morality; maybe morality is not identical with self-will; maybe the goal of life is not to get 7 percent on mortgages; maybe the goal of economics is not for management to be responsible to bondholders, but to be responsible to the common good; maybe self-expression raised to a national form could end in Nazism; maybe we have been wrong. Maybe, we had better get back to God! We have given the Darwinians their chance; we have given the Marxists their chance; we have given the Freudians their chance; we have given the Hitlerites their chance. Now, let us give man a chance.

27

Man's Christian Character

Why have not the moral forces of a nation, such as education, the press, radio, the clergy, and social reformers been more insistent on developing a new order instead of patching up an old one? Perhaps the principal reason is because they have been getting behind certain movements instead of ahead of them. The first thought that comes to a particular group who wishes to further legislation in their favor, is to wire educators, clergymen, actors, and social workers to sign their names sponsoring their cause. There are at least five hundred such professional signers in our country who keep their fountain pens uncapped for such cheap publicity. It is just this irrational mentality, which substitutes imitations for thinking and which pushes some group or class instead of leading the common good, that has paralyzed the regeneration of society.

A few generations ago it was a fashion to get behind Capitalism as political parties were formed to support their legislation. Now it is the fashion and mood to get behind labor which develops its own parties, while the common good is ignored. Each class demands its rights in the name of freedom, forgetting that as Lincoln once said: "Sheep and wolves never agree on the definition of freedom."

The Christian solution is to be neither behind capital nor labor exclusively, but to be behind capital when Marxian Socialism would destroy private property, to be behind labor when monopolistic Capitalism would claim the priority of profits over the right to a comfortable wage, and to be behind the common good when either capital or labor would injure it.

If we are behind either capital or labor, at what point will either stop in their demands? Or is there a stopping point? Did capital ever decide for itself when it was in the saddle that it would take no more than 10 percent profits? Capital took all the profits the traffic would bear. Now that capital is unseated and labor is riding the economic horse, what limits does labor set itself? Is there a wage beyond which it will not ask? Are there certain minimum hours below which it will not work? They too will get all the traffic will bear. When self-interest and class interest become the standard, then who shall say there is a right and wrong? As the old Chinese proverb put it: "No good rat will injure the grain near its hole."

This brings us to a consideration of the economic and political principle of the Christian order. The Christian order starts with man; all other orders start with a class. Capitalism and Communism, for example, though opposite in their directions, like branches of a tree, are nevertheless rooted in the same economic principle that a class takes all. Communism is only rotted Capitalism. Under Capitalism the employer takes all; under Communism the worker takes all.

The basic principle of the Christian order is this: economic activity is not the end of life, but the servant of human life. Therefore, the true primary end of economic production is profit but the satisfaction exists for production, and production for finance. The Christian order reverses it: finance exists for production, and production for consumption. This demands a revolutionary change of the whole economic order because it affirms the primacy of the human over the economic. Its starting principle is that the right of a man to a living wage is prior to the right of returns on investments.

From this basic principle the Christian economic charter draws the following conclusions: when an industry cannot pay a wage sufficient not only for a moderately confortable life but also for savings, the difference should be made up either by industry pooling a percentage of all wages paid, or in default of this, by the State.

Neither the Capitalists' right to profits nor the laborers' right to organization are absolute and unlimited; they are both subjected to the common good of all. Both the right to profits and the right to organization are means, and as means they are to be judged by the way they promote the true ends of life: religion, general prosperity, peace, and happy human relations. These rights therefore can be suspended for the common good of all.

The consumer must not be treated as the indispensable condition of unlimited demands by labor or unlimited profits by capital, but as the person whose interest is the true end of the whole process.

The distinction between capital and labor, which is based on whether one buys labor or sells it, must be broken down. It must give way to a union of capital and labor on the basis of the common service they render to the nation. To ask which is more important to a man is to ask which is more important—the right leg or the left. Since they both have a common function, they should function together. Conflicts between capital and labor are wrong, not because they hold up the delivery of goods, but for the moral reason that they create distorted personal relationships, as the quarrel of a husband and wife disrupts the good of the family.

The wage contract whenever possible should be modified somewhat by a contract of partnership between employer and employee so that the wage earners are made shares in some sort in the profits, management, or ownership of industry. Since both produce a social wealth there is no reason why both should not share in the wealth produced. A worker in a factory has more right to the profits of his industry than a man who clips coupons. The only way to make labor responsible is to give it some capital to defend; and the only way to make capital responsible is to make it labor for its right to possess it. Did anyone ever hear of an artist agitating for a seven-hour day? Why not? Because his work is his life. Today men do not work; they have employment. Work is a divine vocation; employment is an economic necessity. A laborer will sit down on someone else's tools, but no artist will sit down on his paintbrushes. The reason is that the artist's work entails responsibility. That is why those who are exclusively getting behind either Capitalists to defend them against labor racketeers, or behind labor to defend them against economic royalists, are delaying the day of economic peace and contributing to a future economic conflict which the Communists seek to thrust upon this country. The Christian solution is to unite them on the basis of a common task.

28

Political Charter

The primary end of political and social life is the conservation, the development, and the perfection of the human person as a creature made to the image and likeness of God. Hence the State exists for man, not for the State.

The political and social activity of the State is directed primarily not to any one class, or party or race or group, but to the common good of all, by creating those external conditions which are needed for the material, intellectual, and religious development of man.

The State, in the just fulfillment of its rights and in the exercise of its authority, will always recognize its responsibility to the Eternal Judge before whose tribunal every wrong judgment and every revolt against morality will receive one day its just retribution and judgment.

The State while justly altering an acquisitive society which made profits primary to the human, must avoid falling into the opposite extreme of substituting for the acquisitiveness of money an acquisitiveness of power.

Democracy should be extended, not curtailed. For many decades political power was controlled to a great extent by organized capital, by merchants, lords of finance, and industrialists. Today the stage is being prepared for the control of political power by labor. A class transmission of power is opposed to the basic principles of democracy. The Christian concept of politics is that government exists for the common good of all. If democracy is to be made effective the holders of economic power whomsoever they be must be made responsible to the community. They are its servants, not its masters. There once was a day when capital appealed to government to protect it; now labor appeals to government to protect it, and the only bond which unites them is their unconscious opposition to the common good.

The Christian would seek the broadening of democracy. Presently there is political democracy with a representation based on geography, that is, on population and on states which constitute the House and the Senate, which must be continued. But why should there not be industrial democracy wherein there will be not only a geographical but vocational representation, namely one based on the work citizens contribute to the general welfare. There are already a number of natural bonds existing between employees and employer, for example, those who engage in mining, transportation, communication, building, and the like. The railroaders, even though they be separated, talk a common language because they have a common task. Men are more naturally united on the basis of their work than on the basis of their congressional district. This is not saying that the present methods of representation should be abandoned. They should not. It is only saying that democracy should be extended to recognize these vocational groups. No citizen ever enthuses about meeting a fellow citizen from the same congressional district, but a railroad man from San Francisco and a railroad man from New York have common interests. Why should there not be a recognition of these various unions or organizations; and when we speak of unions, we mean here employers and employees, within the same vocational group.

At the present time men are bound together according to the position they occupy in labor market, that is, whether they buy labor or whether they sell it, which is the basis of the conflict of capital and labor. This opposition can be done away with by recognized groups on the basis of the diverse functions they exercise in society. Just as men who live near one another naturally unite themselves into municipalities, so too those who practice the same trade, or profession, economic or otherwise, should form vocational groups.

When America was a young country, representation on the basis of individuals was sufficient; but now it has grown together like a body. It is no longer composed of individuals or cells; it has spontaneously formed natural unities. The body grows from individual cells and forms organs, for example, heart, lungs, cells, which mediate between the cells and the head. Our notion has grown into such a network of relationships, associations, and fellowships. It is in these that the real wealth of our nation consists. Why should not these industrial units, made up of the employers and the employees in the same profession or vocation, be recognized? Who has more to do with the common good, in a material way, than they? And would not their recognition by government do away with pressure groups in our legislation? The way to make democracy work is to make it democratic.

Representative democracy is today based on hardly anything more than mechanical divisions of geography and population. The result being that there is too great a gap between the work performed by citizens and the contribution of that work to the nation as a whole. Too many citizens feel their vote means little; they have no consciousness of being politically represented, since the primary earthly interests of a man are his occupation and his livelihood.

The reason the existence of these groups is ignored is because we have not been thinking on Christian principles, but rather on the principles of rationalism, which thought of everything as being either particular or universal. Hence we had first a society based on individualism, and now in some parts of the world a society based on collectivism, as if there were no alternative. There is an alternative in the human body, between the head and the cells, namely, the organs. There is also an alternative in political life, namely this network of social relationships, based on the common task of employers and employees in a common calling.

The great revolutions which have swept the world since the First World War were in their higher reaches, strivings for fellowship — Communism basing it on the class, Fascism on corporations, and Nazism in race or blood. All three were wrong because they were too exclusive, because they derived their unity from a dictator, instead of from themselves — and because they liquidated all opposition, for example, kulaks, Italian liberals, and Jews, The national craving of man of fellowship and unity, America can supply on democratic principles, that is, on the basis of a common service to a common cause. The nation would then be made up of a series of unities. A member of each particular group, for example, mining, farming, dairying will do all that he can for his own group while recognizing that the self-interest of his own group will be subject to the greater interest of the nation of which he is a part.

One of the greatest enemies of democracy is a Fascism which refuses to recognize that these employer-employee units have arisen spontaneously in society. Fascism imposes leadership on such associations from above. Democracy, on the contrary, insists that being natural associations they should choose their own leadership. No dictator at the top of the pile shall organize or lead them; they organize and lead themselves.

A nation will then be made up of circles of loyalties. Just as a member of a family has a duty to submerge his individual assertiveness for the good of the family, so too these natural associations of men will have their present self-assertiveness merged by recognizing the prior claim of the nation. The nation would then be not only a union of states, which it must remain, but also a community of communities, each community of which is free to guide its own activities, provided it falls within the general order of communal life and does not injure the freedom of other communities.

In other words, the Christian principle in the economic and political order seeks to end the conflict between capital and labor by making them co-partners in a common responsibility. The principle will not be, "What do I get out of this?" but, "What service can I render to my country?" Freedom, fellowship, service: these are the basic principles that man is a creature of God, destined after a life of free service to enjoy eternal fellowship with Divine Love.

In order to build up a new world, we must begin thinking in a new way. Just as Totalitarianism cannot be defeated by thinking down the same roads which led to it, so neither can the selfishness, the egotism, and the class conflicts of our social order be conquered by patching up the principles which produced it.

We must rethink on the Christian principle that production exists primarily for consumption. The old liberal principle that workers are "hands" must give way to the Christian principle that workers are "persons," and therefore may never be permitted to sink below the human level. The old liberal principle that finance may determine production must give way to the Christian principle, that the hungry and the needy and the common good must determine production. The old liberal idea that culture is a product of economies, must give way to the Christian idea that economics is a byproduct of culture, and that unless our morals are right our economics will be wrong. The old liberal idea which recognized only the individual and the State must give way to the Christian idea which recognizes intermediate groupings, in each of which a man can feel that he counts for something, and that others depend on him, and he on them. The old liberal idea that the State is only a policeman protecting property must give way to the Christian idea that the State is a moral person, protecting persons and communities of persons. The old liberal idea that representation is limited to individuals in geographical areas must be supplemented by the Christian idea that representation must include the various groupings of men on the basis of the service they render to the nation. The old liberal idea that freedom is to be used for self-interest must give way to the Christian idea that freedom is justified only when it expresses itself in fellowship, as the eye is free to see only when it functions within the body and not outside it. The old liberal idea that democracy is political must be supplemented by the Christian idea that it is also economic, and that just as men have something to say about the country where they vote, so they shall have something to say about the place where they work.

Why is it so important that we start with an entirely new set of principles, and a new standard of values? Because, if we do not, we will end only by shifting power and booty from one party and class to another, instead of working for the good of all.

This war is the end of the economic man and by the economic man is meant the man whose basic principle was the primacy of profit. Unless we accept Christian principles based on the primacy of the person and the common good, we will end in the enthronement of political man. This is where the irreligious revolutions of both Marxian Socialism and Nazism ended: in the substitution of the acquisitiveness of power for the acquisitiveness of money. And the political man whose god is power can be just as lustful, just as avaricious, as the economic man whose god is money. The decent human person has little to choose between the two.

Either we will restore Christian order based on the dignity of the human person, or we will shift from a regime dictated by economics to one dictated by politics. This is the tendency in world politics as the State shifts from its original basis of popular sovereignty to a Totalitarian basis in which the State is an end in itself.

There are four steps upwards to the modern Socialistic State. The first was the false principle of the sixteenth century that the religion of the State was the religion of its prince, by which national churches were substituted for a Catholic or universal Church. The second step was the Age of Reason in which the State became secularized by divorcing politics from ethics, and economics from morality. The third step was Marxian Socialism in which the Church was liquidated by the State. And the fourth step is Nazism where the State is substituted for the Church.

Nothing so proves an utter and absolute ignorance of the facts of history than to be fearful of the union of the Church and the State. Rather all the facts point to the danger to the State absorbing the Church. It was Christ who said: "Render therefore to Caesar the things that are Caesar's" (Mark 12:17). It is the new State which says: "Render to Caesar the things that are God's."

The omnipotent State of political man has only one enemy, the Church. It knows it cannot absorb man totally, until it suppresses the Church which says that the soul belongs to God. That is why it persecutes the Church.

Education is incapable of stopping the omnipotent State because education will belong to the State. Einstein is our witness that when political power substituted itself for economic power, the universities and the schools failed because they were already part of that world. Only the Church defended man. He said:

> Being a lover of freedom, when the revolution came to Germany I looked to the universities to defend it, knowing that they had always boasted of their devotion to the cause of truth; but no, the universities immediately were silenced. Then I looked to the great

editors of the newspapers whose flaming editorials in those days gone by had proclaimed their love of freedom; but they, like the universities, were silenced in a few short weeks....

Only the church stood squarely across the path of Hitler's campaign for suppressing the truth. I never had any special interest in the Church before, but now I feel a great affection and admiration because the Church alone has had the courage and persistence to stand for intellectual truth and moral freedom. I am forced thus to confess that what I once despised I now praise unreservedly.[68]

This war is an expression of a world disease. It will avail us naught to give old order artificial respiration, for we are doing it to a corpse. Let us wear no window's weeds of mourning because our superstitions are being carried to the grave. Rather should we be putting on our wedding garments to court a new world and a new order, in a renewed Divine Justice.

If the old world of politicians who promise to the electorate everything it wants, from pillaging the treasury to new tires and more sugar, is passing;

if the old world of Capitalism, which thinks that property rights mean the right to accumulate profits uncontrolled by the common good and the rights of organized labor, is dead;

if the old world of labor organizations which thinks there is no minimum two hours of work and no maximum to salary demands, and which would paralyze a national industry for five days, because of a five-cent transportation charge, is dead;

if the old world where a college education was a social necessity, instead of being what it ought to be—an intellectual privilege—is dead;

if the old world of social Christianity which emptied religion of God, and Christianity of Christ, and which thought the whole business of religion was to drive an ambulance for social workers or

---

[68] Albert Einstein, *Albert Einstein: The Human Side*, ed. Helen Dukas and Banesh Hoffman (Princeton, NJ: Princeton University Press, 1989), 93–94.

to pipe naturalistic tunes for the intelligentsia who said they were only animals, is dead; let it perish!

We are a creative people; we are responsive to human rights and need as no nation in the world is responsive; we have tremendous powers of renewal. We must not delay the reconstruction, for when the boys come home from the battlefronts of the world they will share none of the old ideas. Every one of them will want a job and they will have a right to one, whether they belong to a union or not; they will not admit that joining a union is the only condition on which a man may work. Every one of them will want a living wage and the right to raise a family in comfort and decency, and they will not admit that these personal and family rights are subject to and conditioned upon bondholders receiving 6 percent interest on their investments. Every one of them will have lived through a day when capital ruled and when labor ruled; and because they fought for neither, while at war, they will fight for neither in peace. But they will fill up a great vacuum in our economic and political life, as they fight for the common good in which the uncommon man of Capital and the common man of organized power will be both subject to the resurrection of a justice under God. And with God on their side—who can stand against them!

29

Conspiracy against Life

The Christian order demands the restoration of that area of life which is life-growing, life-sustaining, and life-forwarding, namely: the family. As from the impoverishment of cells in the body there flows the tragedy of death, so from the disintegration of the family there springs and spreads the dry-rot of the body politic, the nation, and the world. As the family is the school of sacrifice wherein we first learn to bear each other's burdens, so the decay of the family is the unlearning of those sacrifices which bring on the decay of a nation as it faces the miseries and horrors of life.

That the family is disintegrating in our national life, no one will deny. The modern husband and wife, like isolated atoms, resent the suggestion that they should lose their identity in the family molecule. It is each for himself as against all for one and one for all. And when there is an offspring, never before have children been so distant and so separated from their parents. The family hardly ever meets. The family that once had permanent headquarters, now has none, as the mother assumes she contributes more to the nation by making bullets than by raising babies. About the only time the family meets is after midnight, when the home becomes a hotel, and the more money they have the less they meet. Less time is passed together than is spent at a motion picture, or a beauty parlor. Courtship takes place outside the home, generally in a crowded room with a long ceiling, amidst suffocating smoke, while listening to a tom-tom orchestra glamoured by a girl who invariably cannot sing. The wife listens to radio serials with their moans, groans, and commercials, wherein triangles are more common than in a geometry book. She reads magazine articles by women who never stay at home, saying that a woman's place is in the home. The family Bible recording dates of birth and Baptism is no longer existent because few read the Bible, few give birth, and few are ever baptized. The intelligentsia love to read George Bernard Shaw on the family: "Unless woman repudiates her womanliness, her duty to her husband, to her children, to everyone but herself, she cannot emancipate herself." And as for Catholics there is hardly a Catholic man or woman in the United States today over fifty years of age who cannot remember that in the days of his or her youth the Rosary was said every evening in the family circle and everyone was there. How many do it now?

The two most evident symptoms of the breakdown of the family are: divorce and voluntary or deliberate sterility, that is, broken contracts and frustrated loves. Divorce destroys the stability of the family; voluntary sterility destroys its continuity. Divorce makes the right of living souls hang up the caprice of the senses and the terminable pact of selfish fancy; while voluntary sterility makes a covenant with death, extracting from love its most ephemeral gift while disclaiming all its responsibilities. It is a great conspiracy against life in which science, which should minister to life, is used as it is in war—to frustrate and destroy; it is a selfishness which is directed neither to saving nor to earning, but only to spending; it is an egotism, which because it admits of no self-control, seeks to control even the gifts of God; it sees sex not as something to solder life, but to scorch the flesh; it is a denial that life is a loan from the great bank of life and must be paid back again with the interest of life, and not with death.

It is a world wherein musicians are always picking up their bows and violins, but never making music; a world wherein chisel is touched to marble, but a statue is never created; a world where brush is lifted to canvas, but a portrait is never born; a world wherein talents are buried in a napkin as life plays recreant to its sacred Messiahship. It is therefore a world wherein the thirst for love is never satisfied for never will they who break the lute snare the music.

We as Christians have argued with those who believe in divorce and the mechanical frustration of love, but our arguments convinced no one. Not because the arguments were not sound. That is the trouble. They are too good! Good reasons are powerless against emotions. Like two women arguing over back fences, we are arguing from different premises. The majority of people who are opposed to the stability and continuity of family life, for the most part do not believe in the moral law of God. They may say they believe in God, but it is not the God of Justice. Few believe in a future life, entailing Divine Judgment, with the possible sanction of eternal punishment. Even professed Christians among them, when confronted with the text: "What therefore God hath joined together, let not man put asunder" (Mark 10:9), will retort that God never intended that it should be so.

They argue from the need of pleasure, the necessity of avoiding sacrifice, and the primacy of the economic. We argue from the eternal reason of God rooted in nature, the teachings of His Incarnate Son, Jesus Christ the Redeemer of the World.

There is absolutely no common denominator between us. It is like trying to convince a blind man that there are seven colors in a spectrum, or like arguing with a snob that a ditchdigger is his equal.

Instead then of arguing against the modern pagan who believes in the disruption of the family, let us assume that his premises are right, namely, man is only an animal; that morality is self-interest; that if there is a God, he never intended that we should not do as we please, that every individual is his own standard of right and wrong; that the amount of wealth one has must be the determinant of the incarnations of mutual love; that when we die that is the end of us, or if there be a Heaven we all go there independently of how we conduct ourselves in life.

Now, once you start with these principles, then certainly divorces are right; then certainly avoid children; then certainly shirk sacrifices. If we are only beasts, and love is sex, then there is no reason why anyone should assume responsibility.

But why not go all the way? By the same principle anything is right if I can get away with it. If the bonds between husband and wife are revocable at will and for the advantage of self-love, why should not the treaties between nation and nation be revocable at the will of either partner? If a husband may steal the wife of another man, why should not Germany steal Poland? If the possession of a series of lust-satisfying partners is the right of man, why should not the possession of a series of slave colonies be the right of a nation? If John Smith can break his treaty to take Mary Jones until death, who shall say Italy is wrong in breaking its treaties with Ethiopia, or that Japan is wrong in seizing Manchuria? If this life is all, if there is no moral order dependent on God, then any man is a fool for being true to his contract.

Why not do away with all business credit? Why should the government pay us for the bonds we buy? Why should we not repudiate our loyalty and trust? What guarantee have we of credit, when the most vital of all compacts can be "sworn" with reservations? Why should not international treaties be like marriage treaties: "not worth the paper they are written on"?

If divorces from marital contracts, why not divorces from international contracts? If in domestic society moderns sneer at marital fidelity as "bourgeois virtue," what right have they to ask that "bourgeois virtue" should be recognized in world society? "if the trumpet give forth an uncertain sound who shall prepare for battle?"

If the economic is primary to the human, then why should not the Capitalist be more interested in profits, than in the right of subsistence of his workers; then why not artificially limit children for the sake of the economic and the financial? If a man outgrows his clothes why should he not starve himself; if he lacks bread, why should he not pull out his teeth; if there is not enough room on a ship, why not like mutineers at sea throw sleeping comrades to the sharks? In each case it is the same principle: the primacy of the economic over the human.

We are at war with Hitler because he makes the human secondary to the racial. What is so different to making the human secondary to the economic? If Marxist Socialism says that only those belonging to a certain class shall live, and Fascism that only those belonging to a certain nation shall live, and, if we say that only those who have a certain bank account shall live or have the right to live, we are emptying and in the end no one will be permitted to play a piano unless he does it in a grand salon, nor shall anyone have the right to drink cocktails unless he is in evening clothes. Such snobbishness is anti-democratic. It is wicked, because it exalts the economic over the human.

Some time ago a Nazi soldier in occupied France took his French wife into a hospital. Seeing a crucifix on the wall, he ordered the nun to take it down. She refused! He ordered her again saying that he did not want his child ever to look upon the image of a crucified Jew. The nun took it down under threats. The father's wish was fulfilled to the letter. The child was born—blind. Now shall we say only those of an economic status have the right to bring children into the world, as the Nazi said that only those of certain race had a right?

And so we go back to the beginning. If we are only animals and not moral creatures of God, then certainly act like animals; then certainly permit divorces, and a pharmacopeia of devices, prophylactic and eugenic, to cultivate the animal that man is; make it a universe where the ethics of man are no different from the ethics of the barnyard and the stud.

Some day because of the refusal to live for others, to the full extent of our capacity, there will be the haunting conscience. As John Davidson puts it:

> Your cruellest pain is when you think of all
> The honied treasure of your bodies spent
> And no new life to show. O, then you feel
> How people lift their hands against themselves,
> And taste the bitterest of the punishment
> Of those whom pleasure isolates. Sometimes
> When darkness, silence, and the sleeping world
> Give vision scope, you lie awake and see
> The pale sad faces of the little ones
> Who should have been your children, as they press
> Their cheeks against your windows, looking in
> With piteous wonder, homeless, famished babes,
> Denied your wombs and bosoms.[69]

---

[69] John Davidson, *Mammon and His Message*, act 2, scene 1, in *God and Mammon: A Trilogy: Mammon and His Message* (London: Grant Richards, 1908), 32–33.

In contrast to this pagan view of life, the Christian principles governing the family are these:

Marriage, naturally and supernaturally, is one, unbreakable unto death: Naturally, because there are only two words in the vocabulary of love: *You* and *Always. You*, because love is unique; *Always*, because love is eternal. Supernaturally, because the union of husband and wife is modeled upon the union of Christ and His Church, which endures through the ageless-ness of eternity.

The foundation of marriage is love, not sex. Sex is physiological and of the body: love is spiritual and therefore of the will. Since the contract is rooted not in the emotions, but in the will, it follows that when the emotion ceases, the contract is not the vicissitudes of passion. A lifetime is not too long for two beings to become acquainted with each other, for marriage should be a series of perpetual and successive revelations, the sounding of new depths, and the manifestation of new mysteries, At one time, it is the mystery of the other's incompleteness which can be known but once, because capable of being complete but once; at another time, the mystery is of the other's mind; at another the mystery is of fatherhood and motherhood which before never existed; and finally there is mystery of being shepherds for little sheep ushering them into the Christ who is the door of the sheepfold.

Love by its nature is not exclusively mutual self-giving, otherwise love would end in mutual exhaustion, consuming its own useless fire. Rather it is mutual self-giving which ends in self-recovery. As in heaven, the mutual love of a Father for Son recovers itself in the Holy Ghost, the Bond of Unity, so too the mutual love of spouse for spouse recovers itself in the child who is the incarnation of their lasting affection. All love ends in an incarnation, even God's.

Procreation then is not in imitation of the beasts of the field, but of the Divine God where the love that vies to give is eternally defeated on the love that receive and perpetuates. All earthly love therefore is but a spark caught from the eternal flame of God.

Every child is a potential nobleman for the Kingdom of God. Parents are to take that living store from the quarry of humanity, cut and chisel it by loving discipline, sacrifice, mold it on the pattern of the Christ-Truth until it becomes a fit stone for the temple of God, whose architect is Love. To watch a garden grow from day to day, especially if one has dropped the seed himself and cared for it, deepens the joy of living. But it is nothing compared to the joy of watching other eyes grow, conscious of another image in their depths.

At a time when the first wild ecstasies begin to fade, when the husband might be tempted to believe that another woman is more beautiful than his wife, and the wife might be tempted to believe that another husband would be more chivalrous—it is at that moment that God in His Providence sends children. Then it is, that in each boy, the wife sees the husband reborn in all his chivalry and promises; and in each girl, the husband sees his wife reborn in all her sweetness and beauty. The natural impulse of pride that comes with begetting, the new love that over blooms the memory of a mother's pain as she swings open the portals of flesh, and the joy of linked creatures in each other's fruit, are as so many links in the rosary of love binding them together in an ineffable and unbreakable union of love. Deliberately frustrate these incarnations of mutual love and you weaken the tie, as love dies by its own "too much."

Since nature has associated private property in a very special manner with the existence and development of the family, it follows that the State should diffuse private property through the family that its functions may be preserved and perfected.

If the bringing of children into the world is today an economic burden, it is because the social system is inadequate; and not because God's law is wrong. Therefore the State should remove the causes of that burden. The human must not be limited and controlled to fit the economic, but the economic must be expanded to fit the human.

Since the family by nature is prior to the State, and more sacred than the State, it is the duty of the State to establish such external conditions of life as will not hamper a Christian home life.

The head of the family should be paid a wage sufficient for the family and which will make possible an assured, even if modest, acquisition of private property.

The State should defend the indissolubility of the marriage ties rather than weaken the sanctity of contracts, for divorces are in the highest degree hostile to the prosperity of families and of States, springing as they do from the depraved morals of the people.

Such is the Christian position concerning marriage, and one that is, outside of the Church, almost universally misunderstood. It is so often said: "They can divorce and remarry, because they are not Catholics," or "the Catholic Church says that deliberate frustration of the fruits of love is wrong." No! No! No! Divorce and voluntary sterility are not wrong because the Church says they are wrong. Why does the Church say they are wrong? The Church says they are wrong because they are violations of the natural law, which binds all men. There is not one God for Catholics and another God for Hottentots. And all who violate the natural law will be punished by God. A modern pagan is no more free to break God's law than a Catholic.

But why does almost everyone outside of the Church associate the objection to divorce and voluntary sterility with the Church? Because the Church is today alone defending the natural law. If a time ever came when the Church alone defended that natural truth that two and two make four, the world would say: "It is a Catholic doctrine." As the natural law continues to be defended only by the Church, a day will come when Catholics will have to be prepared to die for the truth that it is wrong to poison mother-in-law and that apples are green in the springtime.

Sometimes nations and people learn through experience that a violation of the natural law is wrong. Such expressions as "crime does not pay," or, "you cannot get away with it," or "it pays to live right," mean that, having burned our fingers, we learn that it is in obedience to law, and not in rebellion against it, that we find peace.

No country better illustrates this than Russia. In the first flush of its atheistic Marxian Socialism, it denied the necessity of marriage, established abortion centers, ridiculed fidelity and chastity as a "bourgeois virtue," compared lust and adultery to drinking a glass of water, after which you could forget the glass in one instance, and the person in the other; introduced postcard divorces, which required only that you send a notice that you were no longer living with a certain party, and all obligations thereby ceased.

Now, like a man who violates the natural law by overdrinking and then learns to respect the law through ruined health, so too Russia, by violating the natural law of marriage, has learned through its tragic effects to respect it. In 1934, without even cracking a smile, the Russians repudiated their Communistic immorality by a complete somersault, as the government declared "divorces and remarriage were a petty bourgeois deviation from Communist ideals." Divorces where made more difficult; fees for divorces were increased, so that, "silly girls would think twice before marrying a man with twenty or thirty records." Postcard divorces were abolished. Frequent remarriage after divorce was legally identified with rape and punished as such. Abortion clinics were eliminated; desertion was considered "bourgeois." On November 29, 1941, a tax was imposed on single persons and childless married couples, and a decree of June 27, 1936, which sought to increase the size of the family, set up a system of payment to parents on the basis of the number of their children. Premiums were paid to mothers for every child after the sixth, and payments increased with the eleventh and subsequent children. Under this law a billion and a quarter million rubles were paid out by the government in the first nine months of 1941.

In 1919, Russia regarded the Christian concept of purity, chastity, and marriage with its unbreakable union, its forbidding of divorce and deliberate control of the number of children in a family, abortion, and the like, as "bourgeois virtues." But the Russia of today we find looking on divorce, voluntary sterility, desertion, abortion, and the breakdown for family life as "bourgeois vices." Such change reveals not only the inner inconsistency of Marxian Socialism, but more than that, how Russia has apparently learned something that we in America have not yet learned, namely, that you cannot build a strong nation by disintegrating the family. It is conceivable that, in this respect, Russian family life may stand higher in the eyes of God, than America's.

If some of our "pinks," intelligentsia, fellow travelers, and Reds, who are under orders to bore into civilian defense to disrupt this country, would keep up-to-date, they might learn that they are trying to impose upon America the very scum which Russia rejected. History testifies that the prosperity of the State and the temporal happiness of its citizens cannot remain safe and sound where the foundation on which they are established, namely, the moral order, is weakened and where the very fountainhead from which the State draws its life, namely, wedlock and the family, is obstructed by the vices of its citizens.

A downward step in the stability of the family was taken on December 21, 1942, when the Supreme Court of the United States held that a divorce granted in Nevada must be accepted by every other state. There were only two dissenting votes, one by Mr. Justice Murphy, the other by Mr. Justice Jackson. The latter wrote the dissenting opinion, calling the Court's decision "demoralizing."

A few of his many objections against the majority opinion may be cited: (a) "The Court's decision … nullifies the power of each state to protect its own citizens against the dissolution of their marriages by other states." (b) "To declare that a state is powerless to protect either its own policy or the family rights of its people … repeals the divorce laws of all the states and substitutes the law of Nevada to all marriages, one of the parties of which can afford a short trip there." (c) "Settled family relationship may be destroyed by a procedure that we would not recognize if the suit were one to collect a grocery bill."

The universalizing of easy divorce means that the institution of marriage is slowly degenerating into State-licensed free love.

Legalized polygamy and polyandry are recognized now on condition that husbands or wives, as the case may be, do not harness other wives or husbands together to the coach of their egotism, but that they hitch them up in tandem fashion, or single file. To the extent that the courts disrupt this natural unity of a nation, they will incapacitate themselves for international fellowship. For if we destroy this inner circle of loyalty through disloyalty, how shall we build up the larger international circles of loyalty from which world peace is derived?

Without realizing it we may be getting back to a condition which shocked Caesar. Plutarch tells us that one day Julius Caesar saw some wealthy foreign women in Rome carrying dogs in their arms and he said: "Do the women in their country never bear children?" Apparently, even in those days, maternal instincts which should have been directed to children were perverted, in certain cases, to Pomeranians.

Men and women of America, raise altars to Life and Love while there is time! If the citadel of married happiness has not been found it is because some have failed to lay siege to the outer walls of their own selfishness. The purpose of war is not for the loot of the private soldier, neither is the purpose of marriage for the loot of life. Like apostles, husband and wife have been sent out two by two, not that they might only eat and drink, buy and sell, but that they might enrich the Kingdom of God with life and love and not with death.

The soil that takes the seed in the springtime is not unfaithful to its Messiahship of harvest, so neither may husband and wife play recreant to the responsibilities of life. The fires of Heaven which have been handed down to them as an altar have not been given for their own burning, but that they may pass on the torch that other fires may climb back into the Heavens from which they came.

Marital love is happiest when it becomes an earthly trinity: father, mother, and offspring, for by filling up the lacking measure of each in the store of the other, there is built up that natural complement wherein there love is immortalized in the offspring. If love were merely a quest or a romance, it would be incomplete; on the other hand, if it were only a capture and an attainment, it would cease to rise. Only in Heaven can there be combined perfectly the joy of the chase and the thrill of the capture, for once having attained God, we will have captured something so infinitely beautiful it will take an eternity of chase to sound the depths. But here on earth, God has given to those who are faithful in the Sacrament, a dim sharing in those joys, wherein two hearts in their capture conspire against their mutual impotence and recover the thrill of chase in following their young down the roads that led to the Kingdom of God. It was a family in the beginning that drew a world of wise men and shepherds, Jews and Gentiles to the Secret of eternal peace. It will be through the family too that America will be reborn. When the day comes when mothers will consider it their greatest glory to be the sacristans of love's fruit, and when fathers will regard it their noblest achievement to be stewards of love's anointed ones, and when children realize that nature sets no limit on the number of uncles one might have, but that a man can have one mother—then America will be great with the greatness of its Founding Fathers and the greatness of a nation blessed by God.

30

Democracy in Education

Just as Christian principles demand that democracy be extended economically so as to give both capital and labor a share in the profits, management,
and ownership of industry; and that democracy be extended politically by a
recognition of those naturally formed associations in social and economic
life, so too, the Christian order demands education be made more democratic, by widening its influence so that it satisfies not only the atheist, but
also the believer. At the present time only group education really caters to
is the group that neither practices nor believes in any religion.

Once upon a time religion was considered indispensable to learning;
now learning dispenses with religion. Once man had to know why he was
living in order that he might know how to live; now he is told how to live
without ever knowing why.

We are in a condition of society where the school has replaced the
Church in education, and we are coming to a condition where the State
replaces the school. Such is always the logic of history; when the family surrenders its rights, the State assumes them as its own. In order to avoid the
condition, the new order must integrate in some way religion to education.

Mr. Walter Lippmann, addressing the American Association for the
Advancement of Science on December 29, 1940, stated:

> The prevailing education is destined, if it continues, to destroy the
> Western civilization, and in fact, is destroying it.... The plain fact

is that the graduates of the modern school are actors in the catastrophe which has befallen our civilization.... Modern education is based on a denial that it is necessary, or useful, or desirable for the schools and colleges to continue to transmit from generation to generation, the religious, and classical culture of the Western World.... By separating education from the classical, religious tradition the school cannot train the pupil to look upon himself as an inviolable person because he is made in the image of God. These very words, though they now sound archaic, are the noblest words in our language.

And more lately still on July 4, 1942, he wrote:

In the American schools and colleges, we have gone very far towards abandoning the idea that an education should be grounded upon the deliberate training of the mind and upon a discipline in the making of moral choices.... So when this war is over, we have a rendezvous with ourselves to consider as a matter of high priority, the restoration and the reconstruction of American education.

President Hutchins of the University of Chicago, in June 1940, said:

In order to believe in democracy we must believe that there is a difference between truth and falsity, good and bad, right and wrong, and that truth, goodness and right are objective (not subjective) standards, even though they cannot be verified experimentally....

Are we prepared to defend these principles? Of course we are not. For forty years and more our intellectual readers have been telling us that they are not true....

In the whole realm of social thought there can be nothing but opinion. Since there is nothing but opinion, everybody is entitled to his own opinion ... if everything is a matter of opinion, force becomes the only way of settling differences of opinion. And of course, if success is the test of rightness, right is on the side of the heavier battalions.

Our great country was founded on the principle of the separation of Church and the State, and we have no desire to change this principle; but our country was not founded on the principle of the separation of religion and the State.

It was intended that no particular religion should be the national religion, but it was never intended that the nation should be devoid of religion. This is evident both from the words of great Americans and from the tradition of our government.

As George Washington said:

Of all the dispositions and habits which lead to political prosperity, religion and morality are indispensable supports. In vain would that man claim the tribute of patriotism, who should labor to subvert these great pillars of human happiness.[70]

We ought to be no less persuaded that the propitious smiles of Heaven can never be expected on a nation that disregards the eternal rules of order and right which Heaven itself has ordained.[71]

The United States Supreme Court, on February 29, 1892, after an elaborate review of legal decisions, laws, and constitutional history declared: "The reasons presented affirm and reaffirm that this is a religious nation."

And Abraham Lincoln once said:

It is the duty of nations as well as of men to own their dependence upon the overruling power of God; to confess their sins and transgressions in humble sorrow, yet with the assured hope that genuine repentance will lead to mercy and pardon; and to recognize the sublime truth, announced in the Holy Scriptures and proven by all history, that those nations only are blessed.[72]

[70] George Washington, *Washington's Farewell Addres to the People of the United States, 1796* (New York: Houghton Mifflin, 1913), 16–17.
[71] George Washington, First Inaugural Address, New York City, April 30, 1789, in *Inaugural Addresses of the Presidents of the United States* (bicentennial ed., Washington, DC: United States Government Printing Office, 1989), 3.
[72] Lincoln, Proclamation of a National Fast Day, March 30, 1863.

The First Amendment to the Constitution forbids the establishment of any religion as a national religion; this was because there was an established religion in eight of the thirteen colonies — Congregationalism in three; Episcopalianism in five. Furthermore, the same amendment ordered that Congress shall make no laws prohibiting the free exercise of religion. It did not, as for example, article 124 of the Soviet constitution, reserve the right to the State to propagandize for atheism and deny it to religion.

Similar provisions for religion are found in the state constitutions, most of which legislate against a union of the Church and the State, but none of which legislate against the union of religion and the State as their distinction between the word *sectarian* and *religion* proves. That attitude of the Founding Fathers is well expressed in the Ordinance of 1787 providing for the development of the Northwest, which the Ordinance clearly associated religion with education: "Religion, morality and knowledge being necessary to good government and the happiness of mankind, schools and the means of education shall be forever encouraged."

Coming up to the present, The White House Conference of 1940 stated: "The child ... needs to have a personal appreciation of ethical values consistent with a developing philosophy of life.... Here the potent influence of religion can give to the child a conviction of the intrinsic worth of persons and also assurance that he has a significant and secure place in an ordered universe."[73]

President Roosevelt has said:

"We are concerned about the children who are outside the reach of religious influences and are denied help in attaining faith in a ordered universe and in the Fatherhood of God."... Practical steps should be taken to make more available to children and youth through education the resources of religion as an important factor

---

[73] As quoted in *Proceedings of the White House Conference on Children in a Democracy: Washington, D.C., January 18–20, 1940* (Washington, DC: United States Government Printing Office, 1940), 29.

in the democratic way of life and in the development of personal and social integrity.[74]

It was assumed in American tradition that education would be moral and religious. It was left to the freedom of the religious groups to undertake education. The State would favor no particular religion, but it would welcome any religion. For that reason all the early colleges of the United States were founded with a distinctly religious basis: Harvard, Yale, Princeton, Columbia, Pennsylvania, Brown, Rutgers, and Dartmouth. Harvard was founded in 1636 to save churches from an illiterate ministry. William and Mary was founded in 1693 for the same purpose. Yale in 1701 declared its aim was to prepare young men for "Public employment both in Church and Civil State." Columbia was established in 1753 with the chief objective "to teach and engage children to know God in Jesus Christ." Of the 119 colleges founded east of the Mississippi, 104 were Christian and all of them were primarily for Christian purposes. Of 246 founded by 1860, only seventeen were state universities. The academy, the precursor of our modern high school which had its rise about 1750, and its highest development in 1850, was definitely religious in character.

Very few of these early colleges and universities have retained religion as an integral part of education. An investigation made some years ago recalled that some colleges had reduced the number of students believing in God from one in five at entrance, to one in twenty at graduation. Dr. Alexander Meiklejohn blames the decline of religion in these institutions on the churches which have surrendered their fundamental beliefs.

It is a curious feature of this revolutionary transfer of power from church to the state that, for the most part, it has happened with the consent, and even on the initiative, of the churches themselves. Slowly, it is true, especially in England, and reluctantly in many cases, these churches have deprived themselves of one of their most cherished prerogatives. We Protestants have torn our teaching loose

---

[74] As quoted in *Proceedings of the White House Conference on Children in a Democracy*, 30–31.

from its roots. We have broken its connection with the religious beliefs out of which it had grown.[75]

But while these great institutions which once were religious have now become secular, one cannot point to a single Catholic college or university founded by Catholics one hundred or one hundred and fifty years ago which is not now as Catholic as ever.

Congregationalists had 700 churches ministering to the needs of the early American youth at the time of the American Revolution; Baptists had 421; Episcopalians had 300; Presbyterians had 417; Lutherans had 60; Dutch Reformed had 82; and the Catholics had 52. In each and every instance, religion and education were synonymous to these groups. Certainly no one will deny that the Catholic Church has consistently kept education and religion together. The Catholic Church today has 10,459 schools, 83,515 religious themselves.

In other words, only the Catholic colleges and universities and other Church colleges are in the spirit and tradition of the Founding Fathers. We have kept the Faith with America. And we are not saying this boastfully, but regretfully. A great burden has been placed on us which we cannot bear. The other churches were supposed to help carry this burden of preserving the religious and the moral foundations of the country. They have shirked the burden. Today we are left practically alone.

John Erskine, after saying that "where morality—that is, personal obligation and responsibility—is not taught from the home up, the educational system first becomes an expensive folly, then an organized racket," he goes on to say:

Before I attempt to make good this charge, let me notice two exceptions. Military schools, particularly the academies at West Point and Annapolis, teach responsibility and train character.... The other exception which in justice should be named, is the Roman Catholic

---

[75] Alexander Meiklejohn, *Education between Two Worlds* (New York: Routledge, 2017), 7.

Schools. They too inculcate a system of personal ethics; they too educate their students in matter of character.[76]

Are we not complaining against the Nazis today because they will not allow the Jew, the Protestants, and the Catholics their freedom to educate their youth? Yet under the present system a religious education by Jew, Protestant, or Catholic cannot be given except under the prohibitive system of building their own schools.

Education as it is presently constituted is not the bulwark of the nation. Washington said that it should be; but it is not. And the reason is because the college, in taking over the function of the Church, failed to supply a body of beliefs which could sustain the nation in time of trouble. Religion has a social function; that is, to give citizens a set of principles, a hierarchy of value, fundamental convictions and beliefs, and a set of moral standards.

We need these standards and beliefs today, but who shall say what are the beliefs of an educational system? There is no agreement on principles and no uniform set of values. In time of peace the only universal agreement was a negative one, namely, that the Church is nonessential; and in time of war, another negative one, a hatred of Hitler. Education now affirms that the function which was once performed by religion can be better performed by a school without religion.

The result is that in time of a crisis such as this, we lack a positive belief and a unifying inspiration of sacrifice. As Calvin Coolidge said in May 1928, "Unless our people are thoroughly instructed in [religion's] great truths they are not fitted to understand our institutions or to provide them with adequate support."[77]

We are at a stage like unto that developed by Dostoevsky in his *Crime and Punishment*, in which he describes the world as having been desolated by a microbe which affected the intellect and the will rather than the body. The effect of being poisoned by these bacteria was that one imagined there was no law or authority outside himself; that he was the final standard

---

[76] John Erskine, *My Life as a Teacher* (Philadelphia, PA: J.B. Lippincott, 1948), 27.

[77] Calvin Coolidge, *Mr. Coolidge's Address on Secondary Education* (Berkeley, CA: University of California Press, 1929), 13.

and arbiter of right and wrong; and that all his scientific conclusions and judgments were absolutely right, because they were his.

Whole populations became infected, and no one could understand anyone else; each considered himself as the possessor of the greatest truth: greatest truth; and when someone insisted on his great truth, another would throw his arms in the air and complain about the stupidity of the first. Not only could no one agree with anyone else, but there was no outside standard by which they could be judged, no moral judgments by which to arbitrate a dispute. The result was that there was only chaos in the world, which ended in a great strife in which every man rose up to kill his brother.

And this picture is fairly accurate. No one in his right mind will admit that universal education has brought us freedom from evil.

One unforeseen stumbling-block has been the inevitable impoverishment in the intellectual results of Education when the process is reduced to its elements and is divorced from its traditional, social and cultural background in order to make it "available" for "the masses." ... The possibility of turning Education to account as a means of amusement for the masses—and of profit for the entrepreneurs by whom the amusement is purveyed—has only arisen since the introduction of Universal Education of an elementary kind; and this new possibility has conjured up a third stumbling block which is the greatest of all; for it is this that has cheated our educationalists, when they have cast their bread upon the waters, of their expectation of finding it after many days. The bread of Universal Education is no sooner cast upon the waters of social life than a shoal of sharks rises from the depths and devours the children's bread under the philanthropists' eyes. In the educational history of England, for example, the dates speak for themselves. Universal compulsory gratuitous public instruction was inaugurated in this country in A.D. 1870; the Yellow Press was invented some twenty years later—as soon as the first generation of children from the national school had come into the labour market and acquired some purchasing power—by a stroke of irresponsible genius which had divined that the education philanthropist's labour of love could be made to yield the newspaper king a royal profit.[78]

Ignorance is not the cause of evil; hence universal education of the intellect alone will not remove evil. It is not the educated who are the good. In fact, the great marvel about St. Thomas is that in being so learned, he was also so very saintly, and not the other way round. What is the use of piling up knowledge, unless we know what we are going to do with it? Facts are for the purpose of feeding values and the moral ends of living; but when our education is devoid of these things we leave the facts hanging in mid-air. If they are taken into the mind, they remain as so much undigested knowledge which through constipation mars mental and moral judgments. We are all agreed that the young should know something, but there is no agreement as to the one thing everyone ought to know.

Upon what principles shall we proceed?

First, educate the whole man, not the part man. The whole man is not only economic, nor political, nor sexual, but is moral. Because he is moral, he is economic, political, and social, and not vice versa. The education of the whole man entails education on three levels: man must be informed about what takes place on the sub-human level, and thus become acquainted with the natural sciences; he must become acquainted with what takes place on the human level, and hence know the humanities and metaphysics. Finally he must become acquainted with what takes place on the supra-human level, and hence be taught something about God and the moral law and his eternal destiny.

Secondly, as a basic principle of the rights of education, the family, because instituted by God, has a priority of nature and therefore of right over civil society. Existence does not come from the State, hence the parents' rights of education is anterior to a right of civil power and the State. The State derives its power to educate from the family; the State does not give it to the family.

---

[78] Quoted in Toynbee, *A Study of History, vol. 4*, 193–194.

Third, restore education back again to the churches and to religion. We are at present in an era of transition in education, and coming into an era wherein education will belong to the family which insists on religion, or to the State which will exclude it. No one wants education to be the unique and fundamental right of the State because such is the essence of Nazism. As H. M. Tomlinson put it in his *All Our Yesterdays*,

> My church is down (I hear him saying), my God has been deposed again. There is another God now the State, the State Almighty. I tell you that God will be worse than Moloch. You had better keep that in mind. It has no vision: it has only expediency. It has no morality, only power. And it will have no arts for it will punish the free spirit with death. It will allow no freedom, only uniformity. Its altar will be a ballot-box, and that will be a lie. Right before us is its pillar of fire. It has a heart of gun-metal and its belly is full of wheels. You will have to face the brute, you will have to face it. It lifted up. The children are being fed to it.[79]

Fourth, in a country such as this where there are different religious beliefs; it is the duty of the State to leave free scope to the initiative of the Church and the family while giving them such assistance as justice demands. As we stated before, the pagan element alone in our population is given the benefit of tax money. As Nicholas Murray Butler said: "Even the formal prayer which opens each session of the United States Senate and each session of the House of Representatives, and which accompanies the inauguration of each president of the United States, would not be permitted in a tax-supported school."

Just how the principle of freedom and equality of all citizens is to be worked out is the business of the State. But the suggestion of the principle is sound Americanism, as President Hutchins has so well said :

> The States may, if they choose, assist pupils to attend the schools of their choice. Since we want all American children to get as good

[79] H. M. Tomlinson, *All Our Yesterdays* (New York: Harper, 1930), 526–527.

an education as they can, since we know that some children will not voluntarily attend public schools, and since we are not prepared to compel them to do so, it is in the public interest to give States permission to use Federal grants to help them to go to the schools they will attend and to make these schools as good as possible.

We are at the crossroads of our national history. In the field of education we will either believe or we will obey. He who will not believe in truth must submit to power. Which will it be? Will we retain a set of beliefs in which we are all agreed, and on which we were all agreed when this country was founded, or, scrapping all beliefs, will we obey the State which will determine what these beliefs shall be and thus extinguish all freedom?

Let no one who hates religion falsely think that we can do without religion or that it can be banished from the earth. That is the false assumption under which modern pagans work. Nazism has revealed its fallacy better than any argument of mine. The choice is not between religion and no religion, but between two religions: a religion from God or a state religion with a Cross or religion with a double-cross.

We do not yet realize this truth, but it is an indisputable fact that a nation's education is far more important than a nation's government. Given one generation educated on the principle that there is no absolute truth or justice and our next generation will be a government of power.

There is no such this as neutral education; that is, education without morality and religion. Religion and morality are not related to education like raisins to a cake, but as a soul to a body. There can be a cake without raisins, but there cannot be a man without a soul. If education does not inculcate a moral outlook, it will inculcate a materialist or a Communist or a Nazi outlook. Neutrality is absolutely impossible in education. By the mere fact that religious and moral training is neglected, a nonreligious, non-morality and by consequence an antireligious and anti-moral ideology will be developed. "He that is not with me, is against me" (Matt. 12:30).

The old notion of "no indoctrination," really meant "no religion," but instead of "no indoctrination" of faith, it really meant "indoctrination of doubt and unbelief." And doubt is the accomplice of tyranny; if we educate pagans in one generation, we will educate barbarians in the next. As William Penn said: "Men must be governed by God or they will be ruled by tyrants."

The liberalism of the last century despised all dogmas, not realizing that in divorcing culture from dogmas it asserted a dogma—the false dogma that man has no soul, no supra-temporal purpose, no other goal than to make money, wed, and die. In Germany, in Russia, and in Japan, for years education has been built around a creed—either racial, atheistic, or dynastic. To it the young subscribed, they believed in it with creeds. Our educators at home regard it a waste of time to discuss whether children should be taught to believe in Him whose love is perfect freedom. The question before us as a nation is not whether religion shall be taught as one subject among many, but whether the integrating principle of all subjects will be derived from the spiritual and absolute Truth, or from the material and omnipotent State.

The modern world has confused the extension of education with intention, and by spreading it thin has sacrificed it depth. This does not mean that universal education is wrong. No! It is not the universality of it that is wrong, but its lack of a philosophy of life and a proper understanding of the man to be educated. The natural or "natural" man, as the intelligentsia call him, is antisocial and can be accounted on to abuse society for his own personal ends. The only way this egotistic impulse can be competed is by a renewal of his nature from above. This rebirth alone enables him to be a member of society without losing his personal dignity. There is no disputing the necessity of controlling selfish tendencies. The choice is in whether the State will control it by its omnipotence. The whole of civilized man is today confronted with this question: "To whom do you belong?" Education will give the answer.

Neglect conscience, and the majority makes right; neglect the absoluteness of divine truths which religion teaches, and you enthrone power as the only criterion of right and wrong. Neglect the training of freedom, as liberty within the law, as religion teaches, and you enthrone first a liberty without law which is anarchy, and then by reaction a law without liberty which is Totalitarianism. Neglect the principle that evil is rooted in a perverse will, which religion teaches, and you train the intellect to the neglect of the will and thus end in a system where reason is used to support the passions. Neglect the principle that the progress of man is conditional upon the progressive diminution of Original Sin, and you create a fatalistic belief in progress which is unable to stand either the shock of depression or the bloodshed of war. Neglect the idea that man was made of happiness as religion teaches, and exalt the idea that man was made to make money and you build a race of profiteers, but not a race of Americans.

The hour is past when anyone can say, "I belong to nobody, because I belong to myself." We will belong either to Caesar or we will belong to God. It was Christianity in the beginning that deprived Caesar of his unrestricted power over the individuals, and it was through the martyrs' blood that it was accomplished. It is through their blood today, that modern Caesars are challenged.

That America may be preserved from such a necessity, it must close the gap between the principle of democracy and its education. Our democracy is founded on the principle that our rights come from God: "The Creator has endowed man with certain unalienable rights." Education has a tendency to divorce these human rights from God. It cannot be done. If our rights come from God, no one can take them away—they are "unalienable," as the Declaration of Independence puts it. If they come from the State, the State can take them away.

Certainly, we have rights, but there are never any rights without duties. In fact, duties are opportunities for acquiring rights. Because God made us free, we have rights. Because God made us creatures, we have duties. For over one hundred and fifty years we have been celebrating the ten articles of the Bill of Rights. It is now about time to recall the Ten Commandments in our Bill of Duties!

Here is the dilemma facing this country. On the one hand, government admits that good citizenship is impossible without religion and morality, and that such an integration has been our philosophy of democracy from the beginning.

On the other hand, what encouragement is given by the states to foster religious and moral education? The White House Conference stated that of the thirty million children between the ages of five and seventeen, sixteen million receive no religious education. When you take out of this sixteen million, those who are being educated by the Catholic Church at its expense, the number becomes more staggering still.

If this condition existed in less important matters it would have been remedied long ago. If, for example, it had been discovered that the geography of Russia was left out of our schools how quickly it would be inserted. Why is nothing done about that which our tradition says is the indispensable condition of democracy? If the government has no scruples about spending millions for boon dogging, why should it scruple about saving morality and religion?

Any doubts about the importance of religion to resist political slavery can be dissipated by inquiring into the forces which resisted it in our modern crisis. When Hitler came into power in 1933, the first to capitulate were the professors, and the one force which never capitulated was religion, such as the Catholic bishops and Pastor Niemoeller. It was the professors who allowed the independent administration of the universities to be abolished, the universities offering no objections to State elected *Rektoren* and *Dekane* who were forced upon them. It was bitter disappointment for all who considered the German universities the defenders of rights and justice, but when one considers the extremes to which specialization had been carried, and a unified philosophy of life so universally abandoned, there was no one idea around which they could rally.

Given a crisis in any country in the world in which Totalitarianism in any form threatens the liberty of its citizens, the first to capitulate will be the nonreligious educators. How could it be otherwise for, without a faith, how could they oppose a faith? It will be only those schools which give a moral and religious training which will challenge the right of the State to dominate the soul of man.

That is why the safeguard of American democracy and freedom is in the extension of religious and moral training, and not in its suppression through excessive burdens. There is no reason in the world why any school in the United States which teaches religion and morality should be penalized for being patriotic, or for giving to the nation the two supports without which, as Washington told us, a nation cannot endure.

The prime purpose of education is the making of a man and it is impossible to make a man without giving him the purpose of being a man. Unless we make sense out of life, we fail in education. Life can be bearable without football, without fraternities, without junior proms, without moving pictures, without a cheap press, without a cocktail hour, but life cannot be bearable unless a coordinating and evaluating principle is given to these and all other activities of life. So long as we educate without defining the purpose of life and the standards of life and without developing a sense of right and wrong, we are losing our souls.

It is up to America in these days, when an old order is passing away, to decide whether we shall allow our soldiers to die for the defense of Christian liberty and justice on the battlefields of the world, and at the same time allow our schools to kill that Christian heritage in the minds of the young. There is something very contradictory about our war cry that we are fighting to preserve a Christian civilization, and a continuance of an education which ignores or destroys it. It is not fair, it is not democratic, it is not American to cater only to the non-religious. A government "of the people, for the people, and by the people" should respect the will of those who believe in religion and morality, even though they be in the minority, for democracy is not the preserver of minority privileges, but the preserver of minority rights.

No signer of the Declaration of Independence was educated in a non-religious school. For a century the United States did not have a single president who was educated in a nonreligious school. The only time the State now recognizes religion is when it builds a chapel in a penitentiary. Would it not be a good idea to give a religious training before men get into the penitentiary?

Centuries ago the Light of the World rebuked those whom He called to be teachers, because they ignored little ones: "Suffer the little children, and forbid them not to come to me: for the kingdom of heaven is for such" (Matt. 19:14). That Master is crying out to them now. Hitler has said: suffer the little children to come unto me, for of such is the essence of Totalitarianism. There is the dilemma: the children of America will belong either to God or to the State.

31

The Need of an Absolute

How to overcome this evil we are fighting against? In order to answer this question one must know the strength of the enemy. In all human forces there are two factors: physical and psychological. The first is the ability to fight; the second is the zeal with which one fights. A weaker weapon in the hand of a man who has a great passion for his cause, will overcome a stronger weapon in the hands of a man who has little or no faith in his cause, or who does not know what he is fighting for.

From a purely material point of view, our enemies are well-armed — technically perfect. But their great strength lies in a psychological factor; they believe in an absolute. They have a dogma, a creed, a faith, a religion. Call it a pseudo-mysticism, for that is what it is, but it is still a religion in the sense that it gives the people a faith and a loyalty around which they can rally. That pseudo-religion may be centered about a race, an emperor, a Caesar, or a corpse, but in its essence it is the same: the affirmation of another absolute than God.

Thanks to it, they have an impetus for action which is wanting to those who are without faith. Not only do they have a passionate devotion to this absolute, but their bodies and their armies are steeled to such a passionate commitment to that faith, that they are willing to sacrifice everything for it, even life itself. Call it fanaticism, call it diabolical, the fact of the matter is that the Nazis are men of faith; they have faith in the primitive purity of their race, faith in the messianic call to be the master of the world. From that faith has come those un-Pentecostal fires which in the course of less than ten years swept them into the fury of the strongest army the world has ever seen.

It is no answer to say that their faith is false—certainly it is—it is like the faith of the demons in Hell. But without a faith nothing great can ever be accomplished. The faith of the demons inspires them to the ceaseless energy of the destruction of the Kingdom of God, as the faith of the saints inspires them unto its building.

Whence came this fanaticism for an absolute? It is the manifestation in a false form of the zeal which men should have for a true Faith. For the last two centuries it has been a fault of the Western world to ridicule zeal for religion. Tolerance which should have been applied to persons was transferred to truths so that we became indifferent to right and to truth and to error. The zeal which men should have for the true God, could not long be kept chilled and frozen by indifference and our so called broad-mindedness; it finally swept up through the surface and came out as fanaticism for false gods. The young people in these Totalitarian countries were dissatisfied with the husks of a secularized culture; they wanted an absolute that would command conviction, the hardy wine of sacrifice, a truth for souls and a fire for harts, and an altar for obligations, and they found it in a religion which is anti-religion. Their answer to a civilization that had forgotten the Christian religion was to be anti-Christian, to erect a counter-Church of the City of Man which would war against the City of God until the end of time. That is why the world today is in the peculiar mood of having more energy for the spread of the false gods of race and class and power than it has for the spread of knowledge of the true God of life and of love.

The human heart must have an absolute. As Voltaire has said: "If man had no God, he would make a God for himself." Deny man the right to make a pilgrimage to the shrine of a saint, and in fifty years he will be making pilgrimages to a tank factory. Deny man a God incarnate, and in a few generations he will adore the emperor as the incarnation of a sun god; deny man the right to worship one who rose from a tomb, and in a decade he will try to immortalize a corpse. The Totalitarian powers have convinced us that man cannot live without a religion, a faith, and an absolute. The question no longer is: whether we will or will not have an absolute; the only question is which absolute will we have?

This very enthusiasm for false gods is the explanation of their cruelty. There is nothing temporal that can bear the strain of being defied; it is like placing a marble bust on the stem of a rose; it distorts man like beating a cripple with his own crutches. Endow a machine with infinite power and it will kill you: endow a finite human being with the power of an infinite God, and he will slay you. "Absolute power," as Lord Action says, "corrupts absolutely." And as Chesterton said, speaking of the horrors of the new religion: "God is more good to the gods that mocked Him / Than men are good to the gods they made."[80]

When therefore a man with an eternal destiny is enlisted in the service of our earthly absolute, he becomes its fiercest and its most fanatical soldier. And therein is the Totalitarian strength — it is a religion — the animal religion of false gods to whom its devotees pray, in the language of Lady Macbeth:

Come you spirits ... and fill me from the crown to toe, top-full of direst cruelty! Make thick my blood: stop up the access and passage to remorse, that no compunctious visitings of nature shake my fell purpose, nor keep peace between the effect and it.[81]

Our problem is how to overcome that false absolute.

Not by hate. There is a group in our midst who, feeling the lack of a great crusading idea and sensing the need of zest in battle, offer the substitute of hate. They contend that the condition of victory is a hatred of the enemies. Hatred is a poor alternative for faith; it inspires men to fight more because their enemy is wicked, rather than because their cause is righteous. It looks to the poison of their own arrows, rather than the justice of their targets. Lamenting the wickedness of our enemies will make us cruel; but it will

[80] G. K. Chesterton, "The Towers of Time," in *G. K. Chesterton: Collected Works,* vol. 10: *Collected Poetry, Part 1* (San Francisco: Ignatius, 1994), 179.
[81] Shakespeare, *Macbeth*, act 1, scene 5.

never make us strong. I would rather think that our soldiers were inspired more by the country they loved than by a country they hated. If we spend our wartime setting on the eggs of hate, in vain will we expect to hatch the dove of peace. As Milton wrote: "For never can true reconcilement grow / Where wounds of deadly hate have pierced so deep."[82]

Neither shall this false absolute be overcome by force alone, for no idea can be killed by force. A false idea can be conquered only by a true idea; a false dogma, only by a true dogma. When Hitler says the power of money is dead, we must not counter with a defense of financial plutocracy, but with a new idea in which money shall be exclusively a medium of exchange; when Hitler says the power of monopolistic Capitalism is dead, we must not defend its abuses but counter with a new idea of economics based on the moral order.

Neither will we overcome the false absolute by indifference to any absolute, or by saying that we were fighting to preserve the *status quo*. A good simple soul on being asked the meaning of status quo, defined it rather correctly as the "mess we are in." We are not fighting to keep the world just as it was; if we were we would be fighting to preserve a world that produced a Hitler and Communism and Fascism. We are not fighting to keep just what we have, otherwise we would be defending our personal or sectional interests rather than the good of all.

No vague sentiments about liberalism; no catchword about freedom of the press; no great mass production however great the eight-hour sacrifice of those who make it; no American sportsmanship transplanted from a football field to a sea or a fox hole; no boasting and bragging, no complaining or haranguing of our public officials, and no change of legislators will carry us safely through this crisis, unless we are prepared to give up our coat in time of fire or cargo in the case of a sinking ship. The Savior was right when He spoke of the crisis that faced Jerusalem: "Let him not go back to take his coat" (Matt. 24:18).

Their strength is in their absolute; ours is in the want of it. Their force is their ideology; our weakness is the lack of it. They were sweeping ahead

---

[82] Milton, *Paradise Lost*, bk. 4, 86–87.

because they have sure dogmas; we were falling behind because we have none. The dynamism of a false paganism cannot be overcome by the irreligion of a democracy. The enthusiasm for false gods cannot be drowned by an indifference to the true God. No secularized, nonreligious theory of political freedom is strong enough to overcome them. A people who lack the strength of an ultimate conviction, cannot overcome their faith or their false absolute. The effective answer to a false religion is not indifference to all religion, but the practice of a true religion. Their Totalitarian, false religion can be overcome only by a total true religion. If they have made a politics into a false religion, we shall have to see that religion has something to say about politics.

Unless there is a positive conviction to pit against the assaults of the demon, the citadel of the soul will fall. In other words, what we need above all things is the offensive of a great idea.

Is there a place of an absolute in American democracy? There are those who say that democracy by its nature is relative — indifferent to all ideas, as equally valid and therefore it can have no absolute. This is not true. Democracy is based on a political and economic relative, but on a theological absolute. That is so say, it is tolerant of all political and economic policies and suggestions which contribute to democracy, but it is not tolerant about the foundation of democracy.

If we doubt this we need only read the Declaration of Independence which affirms that the "Creator has endowed man with certain unalienable rights." The State is not autonomous, but subject to a higher law. Power thus becomes responsibility. God is the absolute in democracy. Democracy will rest on this divine foundation, or it will be laid to rest. There are no rights of man without duties to God, and if we doubt it, then point to any Totalitarian system which denies the rights of man and I will show you they also deny duties to God. Democracy, the value of a person, liberty, and like, are fruits that grow on the tree of belief in God.

These Totalitarian powers have thrown down the challenge to us by reminding us that we cannot preserve the fruits of moral order unless we keep the roots. Trying to preserve freedom and democracy without God, in whom they are grounded, is like preserving the false teeth of a drowning man, we will save his teeth; and if we save our souls in God, We will save our democracy and freedom, but not otherwise.

We cannot equate democracy with Christianity, but we can see that democracy can grow only the seeds which Christianity planted, and indeed from which it has historically spring.

The world today is choosing its Absolute. The Totalitarian system has chosen its false gods. The only other alternative is the true God. There are only two ideas in all the world. If men do not adore the true Absolute, they will adore a false one. Hitler and others have gone before the world with a new order—and that it is; new, not only in its politics and economics, but new in its foundation, its religion, its cruelty, its pragmatism, and its force. We cannot conquer that new order by seeking to preserve an old order from which it came. The one and only effective means is to build a new order ourselves—one grounded on the true absolute of God and on His principles of justice and morality.

Idolatry can be overcome only by worship and to worship is to quicken our conscience by the moral law of God, to enlighten our mind with the truth of God, to strengthen our will with the grace of God, and to open our heart to love of God, and to dedicate our purposes to the sovereign will of God. Only faith can prevail against a faith.

32

The Roots of Democracy and Peace

The word *crisis* in Greek means judgment. A crisis in history is therefore a "verdict of history" upon the way any given civilization has lived and thought, married and unmarried, bought and sold, prayed and cursed. That we are at such a crisis in history today is a commonplace. That this crisis is due to the progressive repudiation of Christian culture and the moral law is unfortunately not the thought of the "common man." It is still too universally believed that a shifting of political and economic forces, or a new banking system, will cure our ills. The heart of the crisis is not in these epiphenomena; it is rather in the abdication of conscience.

We are at the end of an era of history, just as definitely as Rome was at the end of an era when Alaric knocked at its Salarian gates. The difference between that crisis and ours is that in the case of Rome a material civilization was collapsing and a spiritual about to emerge. In the present instance, it is the spiritual which is being submerged and the material which is in the ascendancy.

The story of Western civilization, like the dramas of the Periclean Age, can be divided into three stages. First there was a Christian civilization. Then there followed what might be called the Era of Substitution; in the last four hundred years of the latter era civilization has been trying to find a substitute for the regency of the moral law of God in the hearts of individuals and in the councils of nations; among these substitutions were the divine right of kings, the common will, human reason, the natural law understood as physical law, and finally individual self-interest. The third and final stage, which is now being ushered in, is probably an era of cyclic wars where the issue will not be between nations but between ideological absolutes. The wars of religion of the sixteenth century have now reached their logical conclusion in the wars of anti-religion.

Our so-called liberal civilization which is dying, is only a transitional phase between a civilization that once was Christian and one that is anti-Christian. It has no stability of its own, being based for the most part in successive negations of the Christian philosophy of life. It will end either in a return to the Christian tradition or in revulsion against it. This alone constitutes the crisis of democracy; it will either return to its roots or die.

The practical atheism and indifference of the Western world was preparation for Communism, as Communism is the negative side of Nazism. Liberalism affirms that it makes no difference whether or not you believe in God. Communism answered; it makes a world of difference, because there is no God. Nazism retorted: Communism, you are wrong in saying there is no God. There is a god, but that god is not the God of Justice, he is the god of the German race. Nazism would probably have never come into being had not Communism cleared away the "debris of Christianity," and Communism would never have come into the world if it had not already been "etherized" by millions of individuals. Marx merely socialized individual atheism, turning the atoms of atheism into the molecule of Communistic atheism.

The Western world of the democracies is therefore partly the cause of this crisis in the sense that it was indifferent to the moral law, but it also provides the remedy in reacting against the terrible evils it has begotten. The spectacle of seeing its retail repudiation of the moral law worked out in a wholesale fashion has scandalized it, and caused it to react. Never before has the cause of democracy been so coincident with Christianity.

We are fighting not to preserve democracy as a particular system or form of government but democracy as a principle, that is, one which recognizes the intrinsic value of man regardless of race, color, nation, or class, More exactly, we are fighting not to preserve democracy but to preserve the roots of democracy.

We are not fighting to preserve the liberal concept of freedom, which understands freedom as the right to do whatever you please; we are not fighting to preserve the Marx-Engels-Hitler concept of freedom as the right to do whatever you must; but rather we are fighting to preserve the Christian concept of freedom, which is the right to do whatever you ought. Freedom from something is meaningless without freedom for something, and that ultimate something is God.

We are not fighting to preserve or create a material equality, which considers men equal when their stomachs are filled with the same brand of caviar or their vaults with the same quantity of bonds. We are fighting to restore a spiritual equality which denies that any shall ever be treated as a means or an instrument, and which affirms that all men are equal because there is a common denominator outside of men which makes men equal: that is, God. The liberal idea of equality was based on free trade, free money, and equal opportunity to run an economic race; the Christian concept of equality is based on free men and the equal opportunity of all men to live well, even though they are too weak, too crippled, or too old, to enter the economic race. We are fighting for peace; but what is peace? The best definition of peace the world has ever had is the given by St. Augustine: "Peace is the tranquility of order." It is not tranquility alone, for thieves dividing their loot, or the corrupt politician enjoying his spoils may be tranquil. Peace adds to quietude the idea of "order," which implies a hierarchy or a pyramid in which each thing is in its proper place and fulfills its proper function. There is order in the bodily organism. The head and the feet are not equal in dignity, but they are at peace when each acts according to its nature; their inequality is of function and therefore involves no injustice. The feet were made for walking, not for thinking. It would be a very perverted egalitarianism which would demand what we be fair to our head and walk on it as much as we do on our feet.

Since peace is inseparable from justice and charity, it follows that peace is conditioned upon a moral authority. This brings us back to the theme that a moral authority is needed today. This no one will deny. Minds are not universally perverse, but they are confused—they know not what is right. The criterion of right is agreement with a will or intention. For example, an engine works well when it conforms to the intention which the engineer had in designing it; a pencil is good when it writes thus fulfilling the will of its maker.

In like manner, right for man means acting in accordance with the Will of God or the intention God had in creating him. Holiness consists in fixation to that Divine Will. It happens that, since God made man free, man may follow another will than God's Will; for example, his own will, like the prodigal, or the popular will like Pilate. Unfortunately, too many in our day choose the second standard and identify right with the will of the majority, or mood of the masses, or the spirit of the world.

The millions of the world who keep their fingers on the pulse of public opinion and follow every theory, every vogue, have no standard of right and wrong. A thing cannot measure itself; a tape measure must be outside the cloth; a speedometer must not be a brick in the roadway; a judge must not be a shareholder in the corporation whose cause he judges. In like manner the judgment of the world must be from outside the world. Such a standard is the need of authority, an authority that does not, like some politician, find out what the people want and then give it to them, but which gives them what is true and good whether it is popular or not. We need someone to be healthy when the world is sick; someone to be stretcher-bearer when the house is burning; someone to be right when the world is wrong.

A sword can put an end to the war, but it cannot create peace. Peace does not come from the womb of silenced batteries, but from a justice rooted in the eternal law of God. As Pius XI said: "To create the atmosphere of lasting peace, neither peace treaties, nor the most solemn pacts, nor international meetings or conferences, nor even the noblest and most disinterested efforts of any statesman, will be enough, unless in the first place are recognized the sacred rights of natural and divine law."[83]

This moral basis of peace has been to great extent neglected in the past. Modern wars therefore came less as a surprise to the Church than to the world. For example, when in 1894, Leo XIII warned that the "armed peace

---

[83] Pius XI, *Caritate Christi Compulsi*, no. 26.

which now prevails cannot last much longer."[84] Who among the prophets of progress and Darwin and the brave new world of Huxley believed that new war would come twenty years almost to the day after the Holy Father foretold it?

When on December 23, 1922, while our optimists were still feeding themselves on Rousseau and the natural goodness of man and boasting that the war of 1914–1918 was a war to end all wars, how many heeded the words of the Holy Father that another world war near, and that the vengeance of Versailles was devoid of justice and charity? "Peace," he said, "was indeed signed between the belligerents, not in the hearts of men. The spirit of war still reigns in them, bringing always greater harm to society. Even though arms have been laid down in Europe you know well how the perils of new war are threatening."[85]

For many decades the world has resented the suggestion of an unarmed, responsible, supranational moral force as custodian of a fixed concept of justice. When the Hague Conference was held in 1889, there was a suggestion made that the Holy See be represented as a moral authority. Only one representative for the nations there present favored the inclusion; and that was the Queen of the Netherlands. In 1907 there was a similar exclusion of the spiritual authority of the Church.

Then came the world war and on April 26, 1915, the Secret Treaty of London was signed, article 15 of which reads: "France, Great Britain and Russia shall support such opposition as Italy may make to any proposal in the direction of introducing representatives of the Holy See in any peace negotiations or regulations for the Settlement of question raised by the present war." Article 16: "The present arrangement shall be held secret."

At the close of world war the Treaty of Versailles was signed, but its preamble was unlike all others, for by this time not only men but nations had apostatized from God. Every other treaty involving all the

---

[84] Leo XIII, Apostolic Letter on the Reunion of Christendom *Praeclara Gratulationis Publicae* (June 20, 1894).

[85] Pius XI, Encyclical Letter on the Peace of Christ in the Kingdom of Christ *Ubi Arcano Dei Consilio* (December 23, 1922), no. 20.

nations Europe had begun as the last such treaty—the Treaty of Vienna in 1815—had begun: "In the name of the Most Holy and Undivided Trinity." But this new one signaling the advent of a world made safe for democracy, but not Divinity, began, "In the name of the High Contracting Parties"!

When Benedict XV published his peace proposal during the last war, Ambassador Jusserand of France called on President Wilson and commented on the excellence of the proposals, to which the president retorted with ill humor—I am quoting verbatim—"Why does he want to butt in?"

But all that is in the past. What is the attitude of much of the world today in the midst of war? Note the change! For the past fifty years the world said: "We want no spiritual authority," but for the past two years it asks: "Why does not your spiritual authority have more authority?" The world that spent one hundred and fifty years exiling a spiritual force from international force has not kept peace in the house from which it was exiled. The very ones who some twenty years ago did all they could to make the Church weak, now bemoan because she is not strong. The world drove away the shepherd and his sheep and then complained it had no wool. It broke the signposts of peace which the Church erected and blamed the Church because the world lost the way.

What does the Christian spirit suggest to peacemakers? There should be an interval between the cessation of wars and the drawing up of a peace treaty. The ending of the war is distinct from making a durable foundation of peace. The first is to be dictated by the victors; the second is arrived at by consultation with the vanquished. The mistake made in the last war was to identify the two by drawing up the final treaty at the beginning. It allowed passions no time to cool, and gave no time to collect facts. So the Holy Father stated in his first encyclical:

> At the end of this war there will be fresh pacts, fresh arrangements of international relations. Will they be conceived in a spirit of justice and fairness all round, in a spirit of reconstruction and peace, or will they disastrously repeat our old and our recent errors? Experience

316

shows it is but an empty dream to expect a real settlement to emerge at the moment when the conflagration of war had died down.[86]

Nations must abandon the idea of their absolute sovereignty in order to give some sovereignty to the international order. The reason no penalties could be imposed on Japan in the case of Manchuria, and on Italy in the case of Abyssinia, was because the problem of sanctions was left to the sovereign States, thus depriving the League of sovereignty. No State wishes to use force even when it should, lest its own vital interests be affected. The common good of the world is not one of the vital interests of any individual nation. Article 13 of the League stated that in the case of disputes, the members would submit the matter to the League if "they recognized it to be suitable." In other words utility and not morality was the basis of whether or not a dispute should be adjudicated.

In order to have international sovereignty there must be recognized an authority above the nations. You can not pack up a suitcase if you go into it, and you cannot bind nations into a unity, unless there is a law and authority outside the nations. The problem of sovereignty thus gets down to something as basic as this: we will either obey one another's politicians, which will never be (for if we do not obey our own, why should we obey someone else's?), or we will recognize a supranational authority or the moral law of God.

Membership in the new international body should be based upon the acceptance of certain basic moral principles, such as the five enunciated in the papal program. Practically anyone could enter into the last League. "Any fully self-governing State, Dominion or Colony," the constitution stated, "may become a member of the League if its admission is agreed to by two-thirds of the Assembly." There was no criterion for admission, no required acceptance of common values; Russia with its atheism, Germany with its Nazism, Japan with its imperialism were all free to enter so long as they received sufficient votes. The only one who protested against Communistic representation in the League was De Valera. The result was

---

[86] Pius XII, *Summi Pontificatus*, no. 79.

that the League was a mechanical structure; it had no organic unity. No wonder it called itself "The High Contracting Parties." It was certainly not an organization of a common civilization and a common faith, sharing a common culture. It was only an artificial piecing together of mosaic-nations on the theory that the State is only the result of a contract.

The new League, or whether it is to be called, should have higher rates of subscription and admit only those who accept the moral conditions necessary for international peace and justice. Regardless therefore of how much Russia may aid the Allies, if at the close of this war it still insists on denying one of the four freedoms, namely religion, then it should not be admitted to the League. If it does fulfill the condition and grant freedom, then other things being equal, it should be admitted. In other words, the next world peace will not start with all the victorious nations, assuming that we win: it will start with the nations who believe in a moral order. There will be a moral subscriptions for admittance and not a numerical one.

The Christian spirit demands that this war shall not become the occasion for the expansion of imperialism, regardless of who is interested in doing so As a result of the last war, Great Britain increased its empire by 1,607,053 square miles with 35 million inhabitants; the Belgian Empire got 35,000 square miles with 3,387,000 inhabitants. Italy got none and America wanted none. It is very interesting that the difference between point number 1 of the papal plan for peace and article 4 of the Atlantic Charter is that the Holy Father grants "to all nations great or small, powerful or weak, right to life and independence." Article 4 of the Atlantic Charter conditions this upon "existing obligations." His Holiness says that no obligations shall stand in the way of their freedom and independence; the Atlantic Charter says that "present obligations" do so. Therein is the difference between morality and balance of power politics.

In order to bring home the importance of the moral basis for peace, we ask these questions: Why should any of the treaties or pacts signed at the close of this war be kept? What guarantee have we that they will be honored more at the close of this war than they were at the close of the last?

Some lawyers say that treaties should be kept because nations freely enter into them. But what is to prevent the same nations from freely walking out on the treaties, as Russia and Germany did in the case of Poland, Italy in the case of Ethiopia, and Japan in the case of China?

Another group holds that treaties are binding because it is advantageous to have them so. Then logic would suggest that as soon as they cease to be advantageous, they are no longer binding.

Another school of jurists argues that treaties should be kept because it is a custom. But does not modern history prove that it is more customary to break treaties than to keep them?

When one gets down to rock bottom, there are only two possible reasons for keeping treaties: either because of force or because of moral obligation. If force, then might makes right. If moral obligation, then the recognition of the natural law and a set of moral principles is superior to the sovereignty of any nation, existing before any nation began, and binding every nation even when its application goes against it. Perhaps it was a deep consciousness of this need that prompted President Roosevelt to say: "We are especially conscious of the Divine Power.... It is seemly that we should, at a time like this, pray to Almighty God for His blessing on our country and for the establishment of a just and permanent peace among all the nations of the world."[87]

---

[87] Roosevelt, *The Public Papers and Addresses of Franklin D. Roosevelt*, vol. 9, 328.

33

On Whose Side Are We?

Just suppose a sophomore was on his way home from an afternoon class convinced of the idea that there is no distinction between right and wrong. He would then be anti-Christian by conviction. Now suppose that he sees an innocent person assaulted, and immediately springs to his defense. He would thus disprove by practice what he believed in theory. He would be on the side of a absolute goodness through force of circumstances. We were like that student. Many Americans believed there was no distinction between right and wrong; thousands believed with Karl Marx, that man had no soul, and therefore democracy was wrong and Communism was right; tens of thousands believed that since there was no absolute truth, power was the determinant of truth. But suddenly when other nations began to put these ideas into practice, we became horrified; we were not shocked at their being retailed in America, but when our enemies began to hand them out in wholesale fashion we were shocked beyond expression. We had no idea that the philosophy of expediency was so wrong when a professor in a cap and gown taught it from a rostrum, but we began to realize how awfully wrong it was when a Jap practiced it from an airplane over Pearl Harbor. We began to see the fruits of godlessness in the persecution of Jews and Christians, in the denial of basic rights and freedoms, and in the glorification of power over truth.

Like a boy who, given to petty thievery, will sometimes be shocked back into honesty at the sight of a burglar going to jail for life, so America reacted. In the face of expediency and power, we said: "This thing cannot go on; it is too evil; too wicked, too cruel, too inhuman!" We arose to slay the beast. We are fighting for humanity. And since the cause of man is the cause of God, in battling against the dragon of evil, we found ourselves by force of circumstances on the Christian side!

Only a small percentage of Americans ever worship God on Sunday; one out of every six marriages end in divorce dispute God's law: "What therefore God hath joined together, let no man put asunder" (Matt. 19:6); too many have failed to teach their children to pray and to instill in their hearts the foundation of the virtues of purity and piety. Yes, we have broken God's law a million times and we shall have to do penance. But we have not, like our enemies, identified God with our wicked deeds, or enthroned a corpse as a substitute for the Living God, or made right synonymous with a race or a class or a nation. Our sins leave the way open for penance, amendment, redemption, and resurrection. God can use us through amendment as instruments for the restoration of His justice and goodness in the world. We have a greater potentiality for divine action than our enemies; He can lift us up because, though doing evil, we still believed in Righteousness above our heads. He can lay His absolving hand upon us as Magdalene at His feet; we can rise to proclaim the sweetness of the "passionless passion and wild tranquility" which is the love of God. As He took the bruised and rotted tree of Eden and transformed it into Calvary's tree of life; as He took the proud Eve and made her the instrument of the human race from begetting through His grace the New Eve of the Glorious Virgin Mary, so He in His mercy can use us as His instruments, if we but respond to His love for the restoration to a world order where shepherds need not be killed because they kneel at a crib, nor Johns be beheaded because they say divorce is wrong. In the sense that the weak, and the blind, and the deaf left the way open to His healing power, we too are on God's side!

Three scriptural figures represent our present position and our hope. Like St. Paul we should say that we are not deserving to be called an apostle;

for in our ignorance and like him we opposed the Divine. Our hands are not clean. But that will not prevent us, despite our unworthiness, from becoming good apostles, defending God's cause amidst opposition, putting on the armor of faith and the shield of salvation, so that in the end we may rejoice and say "[we] have laboured more abundantly" (1 Cor. 15:10) than those who never fell away.

We too are like Peter. We denied our Faith; we warmed ourselves by the fires of our complacency, we even cursed and swore that we knew not the Christ. But we never abandoned Him, nor set up a false god, nor in our sin, like Judas, despaired of His Mercy and Forgiveness. Rather, like Peter, despite our denials, when the test came and we were forced to take a side even in the face of death, we were found willing to die for the principle we had once rejected.

But better still, we are like Simon of Cyrene. As his name implies, he was not a native of Jerusalem. But like all mankind he was curious at the death of his fellow man. So he stationed himself by a Jerusalem roadside to watch what to him were three common criminals dragging their gibbets of death to the hill of the skull. He was perfectly indifferent about the whole spectacle—he was what we today call "broadminded." He saw no great issues involved; right and wrong was to him a question of a point of view. If anyone had told him that he was witnessing the greatest act of evil of all time—the Crucifixion of Truth, and that from the exhaustion of evil by that deed, life and goodness would come, he would probably have sneered as Pilate did: "What is truth?" (John 18:38).

But as he stood there an indifferent watcher of the great drama of redemption, the long arm of Roman law reached out in the first military conscription of the Christian ages and laid itself upon his shoulders saying: "Carry that man's Cross. Take it up." He did not want to do it; he had taken no sides. But he was forced to do it. In the strong language of Sacred Scripture he was "forced" (Mark 15:21).

Following in the footsteps of the Master with that queer yoke of the Cross upon him, he made a great discovery. He began to see that the yoke was sweet, the burden light. His two sons, Alexandrinus and Rufinus, became bishops and martyrs of the early Church.

That is America! Like Simon we stood as indifferent spectators on the roadway of our modern Golgotha. We saw the phenomenon of Totalitarianism arise, with its anti-Semitism, its "religion is the opium of the people," its anti-Christianity, its repudiation of the Sermon on the Mount. But we at first sight felt we should be broadminded about these things.

Then suddenly the invasion of Poland, the destruction of the Low Countries, the expulsion of the Jews and Christians, persecution, and the bombing of Pearl Harbor startled us out of indifference—almost in so many words we were told: "Take up your cross!" Carry the cross of justice, freedom and truth and law that are rooted in God. He did not want that cross of war. We did not ask for it. It was forced on us. But we took it. And like Simon we are trudging along the highway of the centuries carrying something whose meaning is not yet clear. We do not know who gave it to us; we do not yet know all of its meaning; we do not yet know we are carrying the Cross of Christ. That is America today.

This is the issue involved in this war, that is, the choice of absolutes. No one in the United States has put it as clearly as a recent Nazi book published in Berlin entitled: *God and Race: A Soldier's Creed*, by Theodor Frisch, in chapter 2 of which we read:

> Where there is a struggle there is a front. The fronts are evident; one is called Christ, the other Germany. There is no third front, nor is there any compromise, only one clear decision. Today is not a question of weakening Catholicism in order to reinforce Protestantism. Today every alien religion is replaced by a flame in the deepest depth of the German soul. Each epoch has its symbol. Two epochs and two symbols are now facing each other; the cross and the sword. Today Christianity is under the sign of the Cross; Christianity, but not the Christian. Our struggle against both, and the object of the struggle is German Community. No confession, not even a general Christian Church, but only one people that believes in God and itself!

That is one of the clearest expressions that has yet come from any nation in this world war. Truly indeed, it is a struggle of the Cross and the sword. We are on the side of the Cross; Hitler is on the side of the sword. May a day come when, as he reaches out his sword to us, we will be strong enough in virtue of recovery of the Divine: absolute, to seize the naked blade with our bare hands, pull it away from him and lift the sword high in the air with the hilt above and watch the hilt frame against the august blue of Heaven's sky the glorious symbol of the Cross of Christ!

SEVEN PILLARS OF PEACE

✠

(1944)

34

Preface

After the Treaty of Amiens in 1802 Napoleon I said: "What a beautiful fix we are in now: peace has been declared." This lament is true if by peace is understood the mere cessation of hostilities. No peace is true if it is *declared*. It is significant that in the Sermon on the Mount our Divine Savior said: "Blessed are the *peacemakers*" (Matt. 5:9). Peace is *made*: it is not declared. Later on, St. Augustine described such peace as the "tranquility of order."

With peacemaking rather than peace-declaring this book is concerned. It challenges the illusions of most planners today that military allies are necessarily political allies; it affirms that a common hatred can make nations *allies*, but only a common love can make them neighbors; it denies the primacy of action over reason, in the sense that the will of the State is that which makes a State right, it contends that utility does not establish justice, but it is justice which makes utility. Every right is useful, but not everything that is useful is right.

On the positive side it lays down seven basic conditions for world peace: (1) the unity of religious groups for social purposes; (2) the primacy of the moral law over force and expediency; (3) the greatest guarantee of economic freedom in the wider diffusion of property; (4) the State exists for the person, not the person for the State; (5) the natural unit of national life is the family, not an individual, nor a class; (6) the freedom of people must not be negative but positive; freedom from something is intelligible only in terms of freedom for something; (7) it is not geographical continuity but the recognition of a common moral principle which makes the world one. These are principles, not programs; principles not plans. Because this book deals with foundations of peace rather than with superstructure, it is called *The Seven Pillars of Peace*.

FULTON J. SHEEN
August 5, 1944

35

The Pillar of Good Will

Centuries ago out over the white chalk hills of Bethlehem there rang a song of angel voices: "On earth peace to men of good will" (Luke 2:14). Men of good will!

Three times recently we have heard echoes of that song to men of good will. One echo comes from Teheran, the other from the president of the United States, and the third from the Church.

The conference of Teheran declared: "We recognize fully the supreme responsibility resting upon us and all the nations to make a peace which will command *good will* from the overwhelming masses of the people of the world."

The president of the United States said: "The ninety percent who want to live in peace under law, and in accordance with moral standards that have received almost universal acceptance through the centuries, can and must find some way to make their will prevail."

Finally, the late Holy Father in addressing "all men of good will" pleaded: "In combating the violence of the powers of darkness ... we have high hopes that with those who glory in the name of Christian, all those also—and they comprise the great majority of mankind—who believe in God and adore Him, will effectively join."[88]

[88] Pius XI, Encyclical Letter on Atheistic Communism *Divini Redemptoris* (March 19, 1937), no. 72.

The Teheran Declaration spoke of "the overwhelming masses of the people of the world" as men of good will; President Roosevelt spoke of their being 90 percent; and the Holy Father spoke of their comprising "the great majority."

It may appropriately be asked: "If men of good will are the overwhelming majority, why does not good will prevail?" The answer of the Holy Father is: "Power is dissipated through disunion."[89]

Men of good will should unite because there is a *common enemy.* "The difficulties, anxieties and trials of the present hour," writes the pope, "make all believers in God and Christ share the consciousness of a common threat from a common enemy."[90] What is this common enemy? It is the forces that would destroy religion and moral law in favor of power and expediency.

The common enemy has three characteristics: it is atheistic; it is alien to our civilization; and it is a repudiation of the Christian tradition.

Twenty-five years ago atheism was an individual phenomenon; today atheism is social. The atheist, who once was a curiosity, is now a component part of some of the governments of the world.

A few decades ago Christianity's struggles were more in the nature of a civil war; that is, religious rivalries and contentions existed between Methodists and Presbyterians, Lutherans and Anglicans, and in a broader way between Jews, Protestants, and Catholics.

Today that simple condition no longer prevails. Christianity is no longer engaged exclusively in a civil war; it is face-to-face with an invasion, an incursion of totally alien forces who are opposed to all religion and all morality, whether they be Jewish or Christian. Once men quarreled because they wanted God worshipped in a certain way; now they quarrel because they do not want God worshipped at all. The wars of religion of the seventeenth century have become the wars against religion of the twentieth century.

We live in an age of revolution. But there is a vast difference between the revolutions of our times and those of the past. None of the previous

---

[89] See Pius XII, Encylical Letter on the Hundred and Fiftieth Anniversary of the Establishment of the Hierarchy in the United States *Sertum Laetitiae* (November 1, 1939), no. 42.

[90] Pius XII, *Summi Pontificatus*, no. 11.

revolutions repudiated the Christian tradition and the moral law. Certainly our American Revolution did not; neither did the English Revolution; nor even the French Revolution. Though there was a spasm of atheism about the French Revolution, its basic principles of liberty, equality, and fraternity were derivatives of Christian thinking.

But the three major revolutions of our times began by repudiation of the Christian tradition and the moral law. For the first time in 1900 years, a revolution attempted to seize neither political nor economic wealth, but the souls of men. If these revolutions did look to the past, it was not to a living or historic past, as a man might do who uses his memory; but to a primitive, prehistoric or barbaric past, as a man might do who sought to trace his ancestry to the baboon.

The Fascist Revolution, for example—at least in theory and in principle—skipped nineteen centuries of Christian tradition in Italy, and, for the inspiration of its new order, went back to the imperialism of fourteen hundred years of its Christian history and went back to the prehistoric Nordics, to Wotan and the forest nymphs of the Niebelungen saga, whence they sought to derive their messianic destiny. The Communist Revolution, at least in its beginnings, repudiated a thousand years of Christianity which was so deeply rooted in the Russian soul that the world for present and Christian (*krestianin*) were identical. And it gave the Russian people no ties with the past other than those primitive memories of prehistoric cutting and beating, symbolized by a hammer and a sickle. Even in the democracies some individuals and groups were measuring progress by the height of the pile of discarded moral inhibitions, and liberty by the absence of restraint and discipline and the abandonment of Christian morality. This substitution of emotional atavism for spiritual heritages, this amnesia which made men forget the traditions which made them great, has brought us to a day where we fear tomorrow because we have no yesterdays to light the way, and where we act like dull tragedians not knowing that the future holds because we have forgotten the past.

This universal, organized attack upon the moral foundations of society creates a problem. What are men of goodwill going to do about it? They must unite. There must be a common front against a common affront. The enemy is common to Jews, Protestants, and Catholics. It makes no distinction between them.

The crisis today is not religious, it is cultural. The coming of four-headed Totalitarianism created a new problem, for it divided men not on the basis of their religion, but on the question of whether rights were moral or physical, that is, whether they were God-given or State-given. The new decision which the enemy has forced upon us is: God or anti-God!

The principles which once were taken for granted, because beyond legal controversy or human manipulation, are today challenged. When Thomas Jefferson wrote the Declaration of Independence, he stated it was "self-evident" that man derives his rights and liberties from God, his Creator. When the Catholic hierarchy paraphrased that statement of Jefferson recently, a backwater press labeled it Fascism. The fact is that what was self-evident to our Founding Fathers, namely, that rights are God-given and not State-given, is not regarded as self-evident today.

The conflict has moved from the domain of the supernatural to the domain of the human; from the higher levels of Christian doctrine to the lower levels of the natural law. The struggle today centers not around belief in the Trinity or transubstantiation, but around the very minimal moral conditions for preserving even a vestige of civilization. Imagine a Catholic and a Protestant in a forest attempting to settle the problem of infallibility, not by argument but by muscular Christianity. They are suddenly attacked by a lion. What will they do? They will interrupt their controversy to do battle against their common enemy, of course, demonic, anti-human. The human must assert itself against the anti-human. Never before in the history of Christian civilization has the cause of God and man, of Christianity and democracy, been as nearly identical as at this very moment. At least faintly, men of good will have realized that the defeat of God is in every instance the defeat of man!

Men of good will must unite! The tragedy of our times is that the moral forces are disunited while the anti-moral forces are united. The State is becoming stronger, more centralized, as the spiritual forces are becoming more disparate. The Jews protest against the persecution of their people and sometimes ignore the persecution of Christians. The Christians protest the persecution of their own people and sometimes ignore the persecution of Jews. It should be elementary that, where basic rights are concerned, men of good will should be united. No man has a right to protest against a persecution unless he condemns it irrespective of where he finds it, and irrespective of who is persecuted. The choosing between Totalitarian barbarities has weakened the cause of democracy at the point where it should be strengthened. Some day I hope to see a parade in New York in which Jews will carry banners protesting against the persecution of Christians, accompanied by Christians bearing banners protesting against the persecution of Jews. Persecution is not exclusively anti-Semitic; persecution is not exclusively anti-Christian; persecution is anti-human.

Think not that this plea for unity is born of an admission of weakness, or because I fear that the Church or religion is in danger. Certainly, the Church is not in danger, for she has the divine assurance that Christ will be with her all days even to the consummation of the world. In vain will men look for the death of the undying, or the breaking of the Rock against which even the gates of Hell shall not prevail. The Church that survived Neros and Julians, Domitians and barbarian invasions, will also live to sing requiems over Hitler and his fellow dictators.

It is not the sanctuary that is in danger; it is civilization. It is not infallibility that may go down; it is personal rights. It is not the Eucharist that may pass away; it is freedom of conscience. It is not divine justice that may evaporate; it is the courts of human justice. It is not that God may be driven from His throne; it is that men may lose the meaning of home; it is not that the war may never end; it is that peace may never come. For peace on earth will come only to those who give glory to God! It is not the Church that is in danger, it is the world!

There is greater unity among the forces of evil than among the forces of good. To counteract the common danger there must be greater unity among men of good will. But what kind of unity? As Hamlet said: "Ay! There's the rub."[91]

Shall it be a unity for religious purposes or shall it be a unity for social purposes? Unity for religious purposes is commonly called union of churches and holds that the various sects should emerge into common

---

[91] Shakespeare, *Hamlet*, act 3, scene 1.

beliefs, rites, and forms of worship—broad and vague enough to be accept-able to all. Unity for social purposes, on the basis of certain moral principles necessary to guide the political, economic, and social life of our times.

Which shall it be? Absolutely not the first, that is, union of churches on the basis of the widest common denominator. And why not? Well, first of all because it does violence to truth. Religion must begin not by finding out what men want but what God wants. Unity must come not from below, that is, from men, for if the only way we can unite is by scrapping the few divine elements left in common, it would be better to live in isolation. If, as Christ said, "not a single iota" of the truth He gave was to be changed, then by what right do we sit in judgment on Divinity and say: "This much of your truth we will accept, because it pleases us, and this much we will reject?" We are not the creators of Divine Truth; we are only the trustees and the guardians. God's truths are not optional any more than the right to happiness is optional; they are not debatable any more than the multi-plication table is debatable. Any sect which starts with the assumption that it has rights over God's Truth proves that it is man-made, and a religion that is man-made can be man-unmade. But a Church which is God-made cannot be man-unmade.

In rejecting a union of churches purchased in compromise to truth and history, we pay tribute to the ideals of its advocates who seek to promote charity among all Christians; but perfect charity is impossible without the fullness of faith. Hence St. John, the great apostle of love, nevertheless forbade association with those who corrupted Christ's teaching: "If any man come to you, and bring not this doctrine, receive him not into the house nor say to him, God speed you" (2 John 1:10).

But there is still another kind of unity possible among men of good will, namely, a *unity for social purposes*. Outside of the Faith, where we are divided, there is a common ground where cooperation between men of good will is necessary and possible, namely, the preservation of the moral law in the political, economic, and international law. For example, we can be united for the defense of private property, for equality to all races, colors, and classes, for the betterment of the working classes, for freedom of conscience throughout the world, for a peace based on justice, and for the hundred and one other moral requisites of a social order, where men of good will can live short of a risk of martyrdom. It must, however, be understood that cooperation for the preservation of the moral basis of society must never be accepted as a substitute for religion.

There rests an obligation on all Christians to collaborate for the social good. It is easy for us to excuse ourselves from collaboration for social purposes on the grounds that politics are rotten or that Communists hold important posts in government, or that Capitalism is incurable and because of this to draw apart into a catacombic existence doing nothing except to cant the lamentations of Jeremiah.

It is incumbent upon us Christians to maintain fellowship across lines of conflict if the moral order of the world is to survive. This is sound Catholic and Protestant doctrine. When, for example, France was going through the struggles of monarchy and republicanism, Leo XIII appealed for joint action of Catholics and non-Catholics to save the "moral grandeur of France": "We ... exhort not only Catholics, but all Frenchmen of good will and good sense to put far from them every source of political dissension in order that they may consecrate their energies solely to the pacification of their country."[92]

A little later on, Leo XIII gave what he called a "practical rule," namely, "While holding firm to our dogmatic position and avoiding all compromise with error, it is Christian prudence not to reject, but rather to win over to us, the collaboration of all men of good will in the pursuit of individual and especially of social welfare."

Pius X urged Catholics "to cultivate that peace with their non-Catholic fellow citizens without which neither social order nor civil prosperity can be achieved."[93] Let therefore no Christian excuse himself from the duty of uniting with men of good will "towards the renewal of society spirit and in truth." The present pope condemned

[92] Leo XIII, Encyclical Letter on the Church and State in France *Au Milieu des Sollicitudes* (February 16, 1892), no. 4.
[93] Pius X, Encyclical Letter on Labor Organizations *Singulari Quadam* (September 24, 1912), no. 1.

those currents of thought which hold that since redemption belongs to the sphere of supernatural grace, and is therefore exclusively the work of God, there is no need for us to cooperate on earth.... If there ever was an objective deserving the collaboration of all noble and generous minds, if ever there was a spiritual crusade which might assume with a new truth as its motto: "God wills it," then it is this high purpose, it is the crusade, enlisting all unselfish men in all endeavor to lead the nations back from the broken cisterns of material and selfish interests to the living fountain and Divine justice.

That shall be the inspiration of this unity. All decent Americans are disturbed by the hate which war engenders; the Jews are worried about anti-Semitism; the Christians are disturbed by the radio commentators and journalists who nine out of ten give approval to those political or world forces which are definitely anti-religious. Up to this time men of good will have attempted to crush this spirit of hate by an appeal for tolerance.

It is our contention that we must find another inspiration for unity because tolerance is inadequate. The reasons are obvious: modern tolerance has a bad history. It was conceived in its present form by the merchants of the eighteenth century who, seeing that theological disputes hurt trade, suggested that men regard all religion as unimportant: it really made no difference what you believed. Thus tolerance became identified with indifference to truth; right and wrong were regarded as irrelevant points of view. The favorite slogan became: "There are two sides to every question," forgetful that religion, truth, and justice, if they had two sides, had them, exactly as flypaper does: the right and wrong. "There are many roads to Heaven, it makes no difference which one you take," was another expression of that broadminded era which gave error equal rights with truth, forgetful that the Divine Teacher said there were only two roads: the broad that led to destruction and the narrow that led to life everlasting.

The war has given a terrific jolt to this false tolerance, for if there is no objective difference between right and wrong, independent of our subjective point of view, why should we be fighting the Nazis and the Japs? How could Hitler be wrong and we be right, if it makes no difference what you believe?

Nothing has so much vitiated the wells of friendliness as that unspeakably stupid statement of Voltaire about tolerance which is so often quoted: "I disapprove of what you say, but I will defend to the death your right to say it." Now translate that into modern language: Voltaire would say to Hitler: "I disapprove of your saying that Nazism is human and democratic but I will defend to the death your right to say it." Or, "I disapprove of your saying that the president ought to be killed but I will defend to the death your right to say it."

And this same Voltaire who set himself up as the apostle of tolerance is the same Voltaire who spent most of his life writing: "Destroy Christianity, that infamy. It took only twelve men to found it; it will take only one to destroy it." Those who are most vehement in pleas for tolerance are often those most intolerant themselves. Shall we forget that in the early days of America the most vociferous propagandists of tolerance were also those who said it did not apply to "Jews and papists"?

In vain will we seek to crush anti-Semitism and anti-Christianity and class hatred and bigotry, if our appeals are based only on indifference to truth. Not until we recognize the dignity of human nature as such, created by a loving God and destined for an ineffable union of love with Him, will we find an adequate basis for loving one another. It is charity and not tolerance which must serve as the basis of unity.

There are two philosophies of life: The materialist says: "Man is descended from a monkey. Let us love one another." The Christian, in the words of the Son of God, says: "Love one another, as I have loved you" (John 13:34). If we came from the beast, then let us act like beasts. If we were made by love, then let us love one another. As the spokes of a wheel are united because they all are united in the hub, so we can be united only in our center who is God.

A good start toward this collaboration of men of goodwill would be to declare a moratorium on name-calling. Consider the present tendency among those who hate the Catholic Church to call the Church "Fascist"; or the tendency of many good Christians to call all men interested in forward social legislation "Communists"; or the more general tendency to call any one who opposes our pet ideas a "Nazi" and a "friend of Hitler." These "labels" are thrown about on the press and radio as commonly as ignorant boys write dirty words on back fences, and they mean nothing but hate. The Church, as a matter of fact, is no more Fascist than she is Buddhist, but the label "Fascism" is used because the Church is anti-Communist. The legislators, labor organizations, and schools which advocate the workers sharing in the profits of Capitalism, or a wise government control of monopolies for the common good, are no more "Communist" than they are Japanese, but the term is used solely to provoke hatred by confusing the issue. And because a fellow citizen cannot go into ecstasies about the honesty and integrity of certain foreign governments, but retains a judicial reserve, he is called a "Nazi" and accused of "impeding our war effort." We are indeed at a sorry impasse when a man's patriotism is challenged because he does not love an undemocratic government in a foreign land as much as he loves America.

Love of God and love for our neighbor applies to everyone, whomsoever he be, and regardless of his race, class, or color. Would that we would lay to heart the words of our president who wrote: "Against enemies who preach the principles of hate and practice them, we shall set our faith in human love and God's care for us and all men everywhere."[94]

There are millions who do not share the joys of a Catholic that come from and absolution or a visit to the Real Presence of Christ on the altar, but if any one of us shuts up the bowels of His mercy against a stranger in need, whomsoever he be, the blessing of God cannot be upon him. "And if I should distribute all my goods to feed the poor, and if I should deliver my body to be burned, and have not charity, it profiteth me nothing" (1 Cor. 13:3). Those who glory in the name of Christian forget! "A new commandment I give unto you: That you love one another, as I have loved you, that you also love one another" (John 13:34). Shall the Jew forget his Leviticus: "Seek not revenge, nor be mindful of the injury of thy citizens.

---

[94] Franklin D. Roosevelt, Christmas Address to the American People, December 24, 1941, as quoted in *The War Messages of Franklin D. Roosevelt: December 8, 1941, to April 13, 1945* (Washington, DC: United States of America, 1945), 24.

Thou shalt love thy friend as thyself. I am the Lord" (Lev. 19:18)? Shall the pagan forget that Aristotle said: "Nothing is more proper to friendship than to share each other's lives"?

Unity there must be, not because there is no divine religious voice in the world, for there is, but because society in abandoning the rule of conscience is on the verge of suicide. It is not a common political way of thinking we must create, for political relativity is the essence of democracy, but the recognition of a common ethos, a universal moral principle which binds all men of all nations of the earth.

There are deeper tensions than those of rival parties, capital and labor, systems of government, namely, the tension in history of the forces of good and evil, the seed of the Woman and the seed of the Beast, the City of God and the City of Satan, the Army of God and the Army of Anti-God.

Men of good will: unite! March separately according to the light of your consciences as presently given, but strike together for the moral betterment of the world.

Centuries ago the Star of Bethlehem became the beacon that led the truly wise men to the God whose love became incarnate and who preached love God and love your neighbor. On this day millions of stars are out again, shining in the crystal skies of millions of American homes, whence the flower of American manhood has gone out to right a world that forgot the meaning of that first star and the Love that lived at the end of its trail.

36

The Pillar of Morality

The air is full of plans, and of pacts and proposals. Every wind that blows through press and air carries patterns for new leagues, federal unions, spheres of influence, and hemisphere controls, each of which is spread out on the bargain counter of the world, and offered at a price so cheap as to require only a little manipulation of politics and economics—but never change of heart.

There is no quarreling with the necessity of post-war planning, but are we not still suffering from a mental "hangover" from the days of liberalism and the doctrine of the natural goodness of men? Does not the enthusiastic and fulsome praise we give to every three hundred word generalization prove that all we think the world needs is a few structural changes?

Truly, it looks as if our planners think that all we need for peace is to take some of the old rags from international guilt, such as a patch of the primacy of economics, a patch of hatred of *certain* forms of Totalitarianism, a patch of irrelevance of religion and morality here, and patch of the natural goodness of man there, and re-sew them all together in a new way. Thus could we keep ourselves warm in the bed of universal brotherhood while awaiting the sunrise of a brave new world.

What is more important than any plan is to understand what makes one plan right and another plan wrong. Why, for example, a plan to reduce armaments rather than to increase them? Why a plan to grant freedom to certain people rather than to enslave them? What we need to know is the basic standard by which all plans can be judged. *Quis custodiet custodes?* Who shall plan the planners? Upon what principle will they operate? Expediency, force, or morality?

Thus far we have pleaded for unity among Jews, Protestants, and Catholics. This unity, we said, must not be a union of churches which would do injustice to truth and history, but it must be a unity for a social purpose. Now, we ask: What is the one fundamental principle upon which we can unite? Now, we answer it: *the moral law.*

What is the moral law? The moral law is not to be identified with the physical laws of the universe which science studies, for, if science does not put laws into nature as an author, but merely discovers them, as does a proofreader, then who put the laws there? Whenever there is a law, there is a lawmaker, and whenever there is a lawmaker, there is reason.

Neither is the moral law to be identified with the customs of primitive people. The primitive people which anthropologists study are not necessarily the original people. But even among these primitive people, the moral law is recognized. Today we find these same people in the Pacific isles scratching their heads, wondering what civilization really means, when they see the so-called superior people butchering one another in mass suicide.

Neither is the moral law to be identified with instinct, because it sometimes contradicts instincts. All the marines at Tarawa had the instinct of self-preservation. What made them suppress that instinct, if there was not a higher moral force impelling them to do so?

What then is moral law? It is a participation or indwelling of the eternal reason of God in nature and in man. Everything in the world is governed by law. Falling stones are governed by the law of gravitation, animals by instinct, and man by conscience. God's reason is in each of these things directing them in different ways toward the perfection of their natures. But with man there is a difference. A stone *must* obey its law, but man merely *ought* to obey the law of reason which came from God. A falling star has no freedom; nature is determined. Man is free; therefore he can disobey. Every man, in other words, has a right to make a fool out of himself; and a Calvinist could think of a good adjective. A man is just as free to break the moral law of his conscience as he is free to defy the law of gravitation, but in both instances he hurts himself, because he does what is unreasonable, and it is unreasonable because opposed to the eternal reason of God. Immorality therefore is anti-reason.

Now this moral law is not written, except in the sense that St. Paul writes: it is the law written by the finger of the Creator Himself on the tablets of man's heart (see Rom. 2:15).

The moral law, men of good will take for granted; its premises are never mentioned; they are the foundation stones of the house in which we live and to which we but rarely advert. It is not in the front of the mind, but in the back of it; it does not see things, but rather through it we see things; it is the root that is not seen but without which the fruits of our civilization are impossible.

Almighty God, therefore, has given us an interior Sinai or monitor which speaks to us in His name, tells us before we perform an action whether it is right or wrong, and after we do it, approves, accuses, or excuses. Conscience, therefore, is reason passing judgments on the goodness or malice of our acts.

But how does our reason or conscience decide what is right or wrong? How do we know whether anything is good or bad? By reason inquiring whether it attains the purpose for which it was made. Everything has a purpose. Reason can discover purposes. A razor has a purpose, namely to shave. But if I pervert that purpose, discoverable by reason, by using the razor to hew a rock, not only do I not hew the rock; I even destroy the razor.

So likewise man's reason tells him he has a purpose: the attainment of truth for his intellect, goodness for his will, and life for his whole being. Whatever contributes to that purpose is good; whatever distorts it is *bad*. As a pencil is good when it writes, for that is its purpose, and as it is bad for opening a can, because that is not its purpose, so man is good when he fulfills the end for which God made him: the attainment of perfect life and truth and love. He is bad when he does not.

Right and wrong therefore are independent of the way people think, because the standard is not public opinion or self-satisfaction, but correspondence with the eternal reason of God. You cannot measure cloth except by something that is outside the cloth, and you cannot measure moral ideas and say, for example, that our moral ideas are better than those of the Nazis, except by law outside of both, namely, God.

If morality or decency meant only that we approve, then there could be no right and wrong. Hence, what is all the fighting about? What makes certain notes right on a keyboard and others wrong, if there is nothing but the keys on the piano? What makes one person right and another wrong, if each is a god and a law unto himself? The rightness and wrongness of keys is determined by their correspondence to the score. In like manner, what makes our actions right is the fact that they correspond to the eternal reason of God. And this is what we mean by the moral law.

Men of good will accept the moral law. They might not be able to define it, but they speak of it under disguise as "decency," "fair play," "the sporting thing," or that it is wrong to hit a man when he is down, or that stealing, cruelty, rage, treachery, deceit, the shooting of hostages, the deliberate bombing of hospitals and churches, the persecution of Jews, Protestants, and Catholics, the systematized starvation of vast populations, *are wrong*; and that the helping of one's neighbor in distress, the feeding of the hungry, the burying of the dead, the love of parents, the love of God, the hatred of evil, the defense of common basic liberties, are right.

Let it not be objected that the moral law is not universal, because the moral ideas of people differ. There are, of course, some instances of degeneration, but the fact that a few people distort the moral law proves nothing against it any more than a mistake in addition proves anything against arithmetic. Furthermore, the moral differences between people are not very big; they certainly are not conventions born of education. Some people drive on the right side of the road and some on the left—this is a convention, but no people believe that desertion from an army is honorable, or that society is an evil, or that the law is opposed to reason, or that a man ought not to do his duty.

The moral law did not originate with Judaism or Christianity. First Judaism and then Christianity brought it to perfection. It originated with man. The pagan Cicero said: "The foundation of law is not opinion, but nature ... and nothing is ever advantageous if it is not at the same time morally good; and it is only because it is morally good that it is advantageous." When our great and beloved country was founded, it took the moral law for granted; our rights to establish our own government were derived from "the laws of nature and nature's God." In fact, the Declaration of Independence declared that the political dictum of inalienable rights as a gift of God is "self-evident." The four freedoms are grounded on the moral law.

Why speak of the moral law? Does not every one accept it? Not any more! That is why we are at war to defend it. There are even some in our midst who do not accept it. One justice of the Supreme Court, for example, wrote: "The so-called immutable principles must accommodate themselves to facts of life, for facts are stubborn, and must not yield."

This justice of the Supreme Court should be confronted with one fact: the slaughter of the Jews in Germany. This is indeed a stubborn fact. Would this justice of our Supreme Court say that the moral right of the Jews to life and freedom should give way to stubborn facts, and if not, why not: If facts make right, then the persecution of the Jews is right. Must the immutable principles of right and wrong be changed to fit the way people live, or must our lives be changed to fit the immutable principles of right and wrong? That is the question!

From another well-known American jurist we hear: "Man must no longer search for God in law." But if there is no God in law, then there is no morality, and if no morality, then there is only force—the force of money, which is Capitalism; the force of steel, which is militarism; the force of the masses, which is Nazism, Fascism, and Communism.

Dr. Robert M. Hutchins, summarizing this growing repudiation of the moral law in American power politics, wrote during the past year: "In law school, I learned that law was not concerned with reason or justice. Law was what the courts would do. Hitler is what I would do. There is little to choose between the doctrines I learned in an American law school and that which Hitler proclaims."

Why is there darkness over the earth? For the simple reason that the moral law has been repudiated in a wholesale fashion by Totalitarian systems and in a retail fashion by some American jurists and intelligentsia—and by the intelligentsia I mean those who have been educated beyond their intelligence. With perfect accuracy did the Holy Father lay his finger on the source of all our woes and wars: "One leading mistake we may single out, and the fountain head, deeply hidden, from which the evils of the modern states derive their origin ... viz. the setting aside of one universal standard of morality: the Natural Law."

There are only two possible theories of law: law rooted in God and law rooted in force. The whole tradition of Western civilization from its beginning in ancient Greece down to the nineteenth century has been based upon the recognition of a common norm of moral law coming from outside man and outside the State, which men have always admitted in principle, even when its application went against them. It has remained for our generation to see the rebirth of another system of law which is grounded either in race, or class, or dictatorship, or State, or the individual, and which ends only in conflict, for if there is nothing but force, then violence alone can decide what is right. Everything that happens in the future depends on whether the world is to be run by blind irrational forces of power, or to be governed according to certain immutable moral principles with which man can cooperate as a free and rational being. This war is not being fought for political or economic issues; it is being fought to decide whether the moral law of God or the demonic lawlessness of force shall guide the world for the next hundred years.

This basic moral law of reason, which is a participation of each of us in the eternal reason of God, is the one principle upon which all can unite. It makes no difference if one be a Jew, a Protestant, or a Catholic, a Hottentot, a Mohammedan, Hindu, German, or Japanese. For as Blackstone wrote in the last century; "[The moral law is] coeval with mankind and dictated by God himself, [and] is of course superior in obligation to any other. It is binding all over the globe in all countries and at all times; no human laws are of any validity, if contrary to this."[95]

---

[95] William Blackstone, "On the Laws of Nature in General," in Vincent Wanostrocht, *Wanostroch's Epitome of Blackstone* (London: Longman, Hurst, Rees, Orme, and Brown, 1823), 5.

Why does not the moral law play a more important role in our lives today? Because we have so concentrated on the wickedness of our military enemies, that we have excused ourselves from asking if we ourselves obey the moral law. We lay the whole burden for the mess of the world on Hitler, and no one doubts that Hitler has contributed generously. But if Hitler died tomorrow, would peace and virtue automatically follow? Because disorder reigns we feel someone must be blamed. We blame Hitler. Hitler blames the Jews and the Bolsheviks; the pinks blame the Catholics, and on and on it goes. Hitler thus becomes the scapegoat who takes away the sins of the rest of the world.

Evil is thus always put outside ourselves. As a result, everywhere there is hate! Hate! Hate! Some well-known writers in this country have suggested exterminating all Germans. Others have asked that Hitler be put in a cage and paraded through the streets so on lookers could hiss at him! No wonder there is anti-Christianity! No wonder there is bigotry!

The war has taught us to despise and, in teaching us to despise, has given us a moral superiority which blinds us to our infractions of the moral law; to juvenile delinquency, increased divorces, selfishness among Capitalists, selfishness among certain labor leaders and the rejection of the moral law by so many jurists in high places. Our hate has turned this war into a negative, not a positive war, a war in which we know what we are fighting against, but not a war in which we know what we are fighting for! Only Germany and Japan have a positive goal, a definite purpose—and it is as wicked and as evil as Hell. Russia, too knows what it wants—but that is another matter.

But for too many this war has only a *negative* meaning: ask your fellow citizen what it is about and he will tell you, "To kill with Hitler and Tojo." If he uses a slogan such as "liberty" he will define it negatively in terms of freedom *from* these two dictators!

Do we think that peace will come because we put Hitler in a cage? Did peace come from exiling the kaiser to a woodpile? Shall it be said of us that we are united only because we have a common hate? Do we think that victory in arms alone will save civilization? Once we defeat those who would destroy freedom by force, do we automatically defeat those who would use freedom to destroy freedom?

Is not this war rather to preserve the moral law of God against the powers of darkness that challenge it? If that be so, why do we not humble ourselves before God? How many of us can go to the corpse of this tragic world and lay our hand upon its cold flesh and say: "I am innocent"? We all stand in need of God's mercy and pardon, and particularly our own country because to it has been given the high mission and vocation of defending man and therefore the rights of God.

America is not God! England is not God! Russia is not God! We are not the creators of law; we are only its trustees. We are not the womb of freedom; we are the feeble instruments God uses to break chains that men may be free on the outside as they are already free on the inside. We are not the saviors of the world; we too stand in need of salvation. May we be defenders, at home and in the world, of this moral law! May God in His mercy preserve us, bless us, and lead us to victory! It is not God that needs America. It is America that needs God!

37

The Pillar of Property

The basic moral principle in the economic order is: *the right to property is personal; the use of property is common.* Of the two: personal rights and common use—use is more fundamental than right, because God created the universe for all men, and not for the particular exploitation of any one group or class. Hence, if a man were starving, and had exhausted all other legitimate means of acquiring food, he might seize from his neighbor that which was necessary for his life. In this particular instance, the use is prior to the right. Among other reasons what justifies the personal *right* to property is that man will do most to develop it, administer it, when he has some control over it. No citizen picks up papers in the park. The park belongs to every one. But we do pick up papers in our own backyard.

Furthermore, *private property is the economic guarantee of human freedom.* Economic guarantee, for the spiritual guarantee of freedom is the fact that each man has a soul he can call his own. But there must be some *external* sign of the inner freedom, that is, something he can call his own on the outside, because he calls his soul his own on the inside. Freedom means responsibility for one's acts, but how can this interior mastery of one's acts be better guaranteed than by the ownership of something external over which he can exercise control?

Just as an artist is most free to express his spiritual idea when he owns the canvas, the brush, and the paints, so man knows he is responsible when he exercises responsibility. Because the owner of shares of stock admits no responsibility to his ownership, he ignores the rights of workers, and because the worker has no responsibility, he may stop work even when the nation needs it. Hence private property is the external guarantee of human freedom. That is why slaves were deemed not to be free because they had no property. They were property. Morality says: because I am, I may have: to have is the legitimate extension of my being. Property and freedom are one and the same problem.

This principle of personal right and social use avoids both the one extreme error of liberalism and Capitalism which makes the right to property absolute, and the extreme error of Communism which denies personal rights altogether by overstressing common use. We have become so accustomed to emphasizing property rights, that we completely ignore the fact that God made this world for all men. We forget that around each person there are various circles or zones, some very close to personality, others very distant. In the first zone are my rights to things which are absolutely necessary, food, clothing, habitation, and all the normal necessities of life, sufficient for self and family. In a second outer zone are things that are relatively necessary because of a peculiar position or state of life, or because one uses these superfluities for the good of others. In a still outer zone are things that are not necessary at all—luxuries, such as a yacht.

The repudiation of moral principles today has confused these zones or blurred them all into one, so that one uses the term *my* to cover them all without any distinction. For example, the modern man will speak of "my food," "my house," "my car," "my servant," "my gallery," "my stamp collection," "my private golf course," "my Paris residence," even "my God" with exactly the same stress on *my* as if the right to the outer zones was equal to the right of the inner zones, and as if the possessive pronoun was no different when I say "my bread" and "my bonds."

The moral law, on the contrary, affirms that the right to property varies in direct ratio to how close or how far away these zones of ownership are to personality. The nearer things are to our inner responsibility, the stronger the right to ownership; the nearer the "I," the stronger the "have," as the nearer we get to the fire, the greater the heat. That is why, incidentally, the right of a head of a corporation to his second million does not equal the right of a worker to share in the wealth which he has helped to create. The right to property, therefore, is not absolute and invariable.

The right to property and the use of property are therefore not bounded by the same limits. For example, a man may have a just right to the wine in his cellar. He may have acquired title to it honestly through his own labor. But he may not *use* that wine as he pleases. He may not call in his neighbor's children and put them all in a state of "amiable incandescence." And if he does, he violates the commandment against temperance and not the commandment about property rights. We have rights to things, but may not use them as we please.

Property has a double aspect: individual and social. The right is personal; the use is social. Hence, in a well-ordered society the two are inseparable, for whenever there is a right there is a responsibility. For example, I may have the right to a cow, but if I allow my cow to graze in your victory garden, I must remunerate you. And when the cow dies, I must bury it. My *right* to my cow is bound up with responsibility, or my use of the cow.

These principles are clear in relation to cows, houses, farms, pianos, and pigeons. But when one enters the field of modern industry, the application of the principles of right and responsibility is not so easy. This is because modern Capitalism has divorced right and use, or responsibility. Great industries are generally not owned by one man, but by millions. No one individual owns over 4 percent of the Bell Telephone Company. The right is diffused through stocks. But notice the difference between the ownership of a cow and the ownership of stock. Because I have a right to my cow, I am clearly responsible for the way I use it. But how many who own stocks feel any responsibility? How many who are stockholders in corporations are concerned as to whether the workers receive a living wage, or whether their rights of collective bargaining are recognized, or whether their hours are to long? The fact is that stockholders are concerned only with their *rights* to property, not with their *responsibilities* or use of property. There are instances of individuals who owned ten shares in a railroad, walking into a directors' meeting and insisting upon exercising some responsibility toward its operation, but the incidents were written up as humor in the newspaper.

The fact is that under finance-Capitalism there has been a divorce of right from responsibility, or use. Generally those who own the stocks do not manage or work or exercise any responsibility. And those who manage or exercise responsibility do not own. As family life has broken down because of the divorce of husband and wife, so the economic life has broken down because of the divorce of capital from responsibility and the divorce of labor from its tools and their fruits. The result is, we have Capitalists who do not labor, and labor leaders who are Capitalists, in the sense that they do not labor.

Thus, the two elements of private property which are clearly united in the ownership of a cow—responsibility and use—are divorced in the ownership of Capitalistic enterprises. The owner of the cow could claim all profits from the cow, because he owned the cow and was responsible for it. But the owner of stocks claims all the profits because he *owns* the stock, though he disowns responsibility. He has surrendered *half* of his title to profits, namely, responsibility, but lays claim to all the profits.

This does not mean that the moral principle concerning private property is wrong; it only means that the system is wrong. Now, how make it right? By granting to those who manage, use, work in, and are responsible for the production of profits some *share* in the social wealth which they have helped to create. If a farmer keeps his right to the cow, but surrenders its responsibility and care and use to a hired man, he at least ought to give that hired hand a glass of the milk.

"Property," we read in the papal encyclical, *Quadragesimo Anno,*

> that is, "capital," has undoubtedly long been able to appropriate too much to itself. Whatever was produced, whatever returns accrued, capital claimed for itself, hardly leaving to the worker enough to restore and renew his strength.... [This gave rise to] the equally fictitious moral principle that all products and profits, save only enough to repair and renew capital, belong by very right to the workers.[96]

---

[96] Pius XI, Encyclical Letter on the Reconstruction of the Social Order *Quadragesimo Anno* (May 15, 1931), nos. 54–55.

The moral law suggests that one class is forbidden to exclude the other from sharing in the benefits. Hence, the stockholding class violates this law when it thinks that it ought to get everything and the worker nothing. So does the non-owning working class when, angered deeply at outraged justice, it demands for itself everything as if produced by its own hands alone, and attacks and seeks to abolish, therefore, all property and returns or incomes.

> Therefore, with all our strength and effort we must strive that at least in the future the abundant fruits of production will accrue equitably to those who are rich and will be distributed in ample sufficiency among the workers—not that these may become remiss in work, for man is born to labor as the bird to fly—but that they may increase their property by thrift.... We consider it more advisable, however, in the present condition of human society that, so far as is possible, the work-contract be somewhat modified by a partnership-contract, as is already being done in various ways and with no small advantage to take workers and owners. Workers and other employees thus become shares in ownership or management or participate in some fashion in the profits received.[97]

The moral law suggests a partnership contract between capital and labor to such an extent that the worker share in some way in the ownership, management, or profits of industry.

This partnership may involve three things:

The right of employees to participate in the management of the industry by having one or more of their members represent them on the Board of Directors.

The right of employees to share in the ownership of industry, through special labor shares which ought not to be subject to market fluctuation of capital shares, and which should give them the right to vote on the distribution of dividends, even though it means changing the corporate structure.

The right of employees to share in the profits of industry over and above a just wage, since they did more to create those profits than the moneylender

---

[97] Pius XI, *Quadragesimo Anno*, nos. 61, 65.

with his stock certificate. The profits to be distributed must not be those profits left after a fat dividend has been declared to stockholders. They should be those over and above an amount agreed upon by capital and labor as a minimum, and not those set arbitrarily by capital alone. For example, in the Gospels, the wage principle of the laborers in the vineyard was not merely compensation for the work done, because all received the same wage, even those who worked only for an hour. There are therefore other factors governing just remuneration than wages for work done.

The advantages of this co-partnership are many: if capital wants labor to become interested in its work, it ought to give labor some capital to defend. A man is willing to sit down on someone else's tools, but he is not willing to sit down on his own. As regards labor, co-partnership will restore the vocation of work; it will transform a factory from a place where men find fault to a place where they find some joy. Having regained some self-respect, they will try to do as much as possible instead of trying to do as little as possible. Labor will feel that it is then working for itself as well as for the employer, and it will be to its advantage to increase output and reduce waste.

Finally as far as both capital and labor are concerned, it will mean they will cease seeing how much each can get out of the other but how much both can get out of common enterprise, thus creating a true industrial democracy. We will never have complete democracy in this country until we extend its blessings from politics to economics.

Thus, co-partnership has been opposed by capital and labor, and too often for selfish reasons. Capital refused to allow workers to share in the management of business and in the profits. And now it finds that management and profits are to a great extent being taken over by the government, with the result that neither capital nor labor get the profits.

Labor leaders too have often been shortsighted. They were against sharing this partnership, because they feared that the workers might become more attached to the employer than to them if they received the profits. It was a question of whether they should have dues or the worker profits, and the fear of alienation of affection drove them to make increasing demands for higher wages instead of co-partnership. If economics is to be reduced to a question of courtship, let the best man win.

Outside the wider diffusion of private property here suggested there are three solutions possible:

One is to keep the right to property in the hands of monopolistic Capitalism, cartels, and corporations, and thus create a servile State, even while satisfying the unions' demands every twelve months.

Another solution is Communism and Socialism which would remedy individual selfishness by collective selfishness, that is, by putting all the property in the hands of the State, and substituting for monopoly by Capitalism a monopoly by party. Communism is thus State Capitalism; it hates Capitalism because it wants to be Capitalistic itself. Every Communist is a Capitalist without any cash in his pockets; he is an involuntary Capitalist. And as for the worker, there is little to choose between living at the sufferance of a Capitalist or living at the sufferance of a party leader, for in either case, so long as he lives *by the will* of another he is not free.

A third solution is bureaucracy, or Capitalistic Fascism, which normally, instead of diffusing profits by giving some of it to the workers, collects profits in the form of taxes from industry, passes it through a thousand government offices, and the gives the residue as dole.

The worker who depends entirely and immediately upon the State for his security as is the tendency today, and not upon private ownership, eases his condition for a moment. But ultimately bureaucracy by a slow evolution ends in the abduction of personal dignity. Either we must diffuse ownership of private property or we will destroy *freedom*, for the abolition of private property is the beginning of slavery. Wherever property is, there is power. Put it into the hands of monopolistic Capitalism and it will dictate how to vote; put it in the hands of the State, and the State will dictate the vote, for as Alfred E. Smith once said: "No one wants to kill Santa Claus."

This moral solution of the economic problem is hardly ever discussed. It has been said that the American people must choose between individualism and collectivism: between a system in which the individual manages everything without government interference, and collectivism, in which the State manages everything without individual interference.

No! There is a golden mean in the economic problem: one in which the property rights are diffused through co-partnership, instead of being concentrated either in the hands of Capitalists or in the hands of the State. The State must guarantee the social security of its citizens, but it must not supply that security. Freedom from want must not be purchased by freedom from freedom, in which a bureaucratic State becomes the world's caterer. There is a world of difference between redistribution of income through the taxation chiefly of wage earners, as the Beveridge Plan suggests, and the redistribution of created wealth at the source, namely, *production*. There is an alternative to the reign of money in society, which is Capitalism, and the reign of the State which is Socialism; between a government of laws and a government of bureaucratic management; between a government in which the State is a policeman, and government in which the State is a nurse; between *laissez-faire* and dictatorship; between a system in which a few Capitalists get all the eggs and the workers the shells, and system in which the Socialistic State gets all the eggs and makes an omelet; and that alternation is, a system in which the hens are shared.

When you get down to rock bottom, what objection is there to the suggestion of the decentralization of property so that Capitalism and labor are made co-partners in industry? Basically, there is only one: selfishness. So long as there is no spiritual force to harness the wild acquisitive instincts, at what point will the Capitalist say: "Please, no more profits. I have already made 8 percent on my money." As a matter of fact, one Capitalist said: "If this war goes on two more years, I could make a million."

At what point will labor say: "Desist. Our wages are high enough! Our hours are short enough!" One of the largest labor journals wrote one week: "Let us prove to the boys at the front, that we can work harder and produce more for them." Three days later one hundred and twenty-five thousand of them were on strike for higher wages!

Given the unrestrained lust for money on the part of Capitalism and labor, there will be no stopping until both die of their own too much. Socialism is no answer to the problem, simply because Socialism is not social. Any State which concentrates property in its hands is the enemy of the people, and any theory which attempts to correct the irresponsibility of either Capitalism or labor by making them both irresponsible, has killed the free personality of man as much as an apple dumpling destroys the individuality of an apple. To cure this unbounded selfishness, the State has had to interfere with Capitalism, to preserve some semblance of the common good, and it will soon have to interfere with labor for the same reason. So long as Capitalism and labor regard the other as so much carrion upon which as vultures they may devour their fill, the common good of a free and decent America will be only a cemetery wherein ghouls may feed on buried treasure.

This is basic: the selfish, acquisitive spirit of capital and labor must be crushed if we are ever to have economic peace and security.

There are two ways to kill it. Neither of these methods lies in the economic order; one is in the political, the other in the spiritual. The first kills selfishness from the outside; the other from the inside. The first is the way of the Nazi, Fascist, and Communist which destroys freedom. It works for a time. For example, Germany was at the top of the exporting countries of the world; Fascism even had the trains running on time; and Communism had no more unemployment than Sing Sing—and for the same reason. But in killing selfishness the Socialistic way, these systems killed free enterprise and free men.

There is one other way open to us, and that is to crush selfishness from the inside by a spiritual rebirth, for not until we begin living for the moral law of God will we ever live for one another.

Something radical must be done! We cannot go on as we have. It is positively a disgrace for any country to have plenty of work and plenty of money only when it is engaged in the dirty business of war. Shall our selfish interests be killed only while we are killing? Shall we work as a united nation for the good of all only when Mars sits on our altars? This much is certain: any nation that can provide work in war can provide work in peace. Work for all, and security for all.

To suggest that the solution of our economic problem is not in the economic order, but in the moral, is to bring down upon one's offending head the charge: the suggestion is impractical. Certainly it is impractical! That is why it will work. When things are half out of order any tinker or bureaucratic planner can fix them, but when the world is in a mess, it takes more than a practical solution.

It is just as impracticable as saying; "Seek ye therefore first the kingdom of God, and his justice; and all these things shall be added unto you" (Matt. 6:33).

Our choice is not between individualism and collectivism; it is between a mechanistic Socialistic collectivism and a moral spiritual collectivism.

Capitalists will not like this suggestion of co-partnership because it means reduced profits. Labor leaders will not like it because it will mean less dues, but men of goodwill will like it because it will create a new America where no man will claim a right without acknowledging a duty. An America where capital will do some labor, and labor will have some capital; where the right to property will be personal and where the use of property will be common; where no one will recognize he is free until all are free; and where none can be free until he submits to that Truth of God which makes all men free, and in making all men free, makes them Americans!

38

The Pillar of Personality

The basic moral principle of the political order is: *the State exists for the person; not the person for the State.*

Democracy is founded on this moral principle. Totalitarianism in all its forms, on the contrary, believes the person exists for the State.

Why in the United States does the State exist for the person?

Because the person is prior *in origin* to the State, that is, he existed before the State. God made man according to His image and likeness; and man made the State according to his image and likeness. The government, therefore, derives its just powers from the consent of the governed, and the governed get theirs from God.

The State exists for the person because the person is nobler *in nature* than the State; the person has an eternal destiny, whereas the State has only a temporal destiny. The State is not a distinct entity from the person who comprise it. A citizen is a person who works out his salvation in time, while living in a State.

The State exists for the person because the person, having an immortal soul, is the subject of rights. Centipedes have no rights, nor have cabbages, and they have no rights because they have no souls.

This moral truth of the supremacy of the person is enshrined in our Constitution and in our American traditions.

Our Declaration of Independence declares, "It is a self-evident principle that the Creator has endowed man with certain inalienable rights, among which are the right to life, liberty and the pursuit of happiness." To our Founding Fathers, it was clear to every one that these rights and freedom flowed from a divinely created personality. To safeguard further this self-evident principle the ninth amendment to the Constitution stated that it must not be assumed that the people have no rights other than those given to them by the Constitution. In other words, since rights and liberties were not State-given, but God-given, they existed before any State. The only reason a government was instituted was, in the language of the Declaration of Independence, "to secure those rights," that is, to protect and safeguard rights already existing in virtue of the value of the human person created by God.

In establishing our government on the principle that the State exists for the person, our political forebears were merely reiterating the great Christian tradition that the supreme value on this earth is the human person because God made him, because Christ died for his sins, and the Holy Spirit sanctified him. Not upon any psychological or anthropological or biological theories concerning man was this democratic doctrine grounded, but upon the Christian tradition that a single man is precious because he has an immortal soul. What, therefore, our ancestors in the Declaration of Independence called "self-evident" was, in reality, a matter of faith and tradition. No chemical analysis or biological proddings, or psychological soundings, will show that the slaves, the refugees, the Jews, the so-called "papists," John Jones and Baron Rothschild, Mary Smith, and Queen Elizabeth were "all created free and equal" and all entitled to "life, liberty, and the pursuit of happiness." This idea comes from theology and not from anthropology. It comes from the natural law and faith, not from human law and sentimentalism.

It was part and parcel of a large synthesis: as God is in the universe, but transcendent and superior to it; as the Kingdom of God is in the world, but not of it; as the soul is in the body but not immersed and identical with it, so the human person is in the State but does not exist solely for the State. What was latent in the minds of our Founding Fathers was explicitly stated five centuries before by St. Thomas in a phrase that needs to be remembered by every statesman today: "Man is not subordinated to the body politic to the whole extent of all he is and all that he has. For a man's whole being and powers and possessions must be referred to God."

Our Constitution puts politics under theology, democracy under God. But today, politics denies its divine foundation. Politics is today the supreme and absolute science. We once lived in the age of the theological man; then came the age of the economic man; now we are in the age of political man. The theological man lived for God; the economic man lived for profit; the political man lives for the State.

The theological man believed he came from God into this earth as a kind of novitiate, and that some day he would go back to God to render an account of his stewardship. There are still theological creatures in the world, but there are not enough of them to give a tone and temper to the society in which we live. They are the exception; once they were the rule.

About one hundred years ago the economic man came into being. He was not concerned with saving his soul, but with making money. For if this life is all, why not get all we can out of it? He insisted that freedom be understood as the absence of law and restraint, in order that he could accumulate as much wealth as he wished.

Into that age of the economic man, there came Karl Marx, the founder of Communism, and also the spiritual father of the political man. He had one good thought, and one very bad one. His good idea was that, if men were allowed freedom to make as much money as they pleased, we should soon reach a condition where wealth would be concentrated in the hands of the few, while the masses would become impoverished. His bad idea was the plan to prevent this: namely, put all property into the hands of the State, thus making the State supply the needs of the citizens.

Now once you put property into the hands of the State you concentrate power, for property is power. And once power is in the hands of the State, men want to be where that power is in order that they might distribute it. Thus was begotten the political man who as the new Capitalist seeks the new wealth, which is not money but privilege.

What economics was to the days of liberalism, politics is to the modern man. So important has politics become, that now men judge religion by its attitude toward politics, rather than politics by its attitude toward religion. It is like judging health by the kind of a plate from which one eats.

How did politics become so important? Through a loss of the moral law. In the days when Christianity was the soul of civilization, when all men recognized they had a common end, both eternal and temporal, politics and economics held a secondary place. No one system of politics was absolutely right; they were all means to an end, purely relative in character, and varied with the background, and traditions, and nature of a given society. This is why St. Thomas, in discussing three possible forms of politics, is not absolutely certain which he preferred. The Church has always taught that one form of government is not absolutely better than any other form of government, so long as the person is recognized as superior to the State.

But today, when men abandon a common philosophy of life, that is, when they disagree about ends, namely, why we are living, where we are going, whether God exists, whether the moral law should be obeyed, they begin to concentrate their attention upon *means*, and principally upon systems of politics. Politics thus becomes an absolute. Once men agreed that to enjoy shooting, men should have a common target—the kind of arrows they used being of little importance. Today, they disagree about the target and insist every one should use the same arrow. Once when men sat down at table, they were agreed on the necessity of eating; now they disagree on eating, and quarrel about the knives and forks. When men agreed on the purpose of life, they admitted political relativities. But now they differ on the purpose of life, they make politics a theology and erect the means of life, about which there should be legitimate disagreement, into an end of life about which no man may disagree.

That is why in all the Totalitarian countries, for example, Russia, Germany, and Italy up until the political demise, there is only *one party*. Every one must think alike, and where every one thinks alike, there is no thinking.

The result is that politics enjoys the same status that theology enjoyed in a Christian society, and appropriates even the same emotions which once surrounded religion. The heretics today are enemies of a party, not enemies of God's Truth. Fascism, Nazism, and Communism have their inquisitorial sanction which makes the religious persecutions of the past pale into insignificance. The modern man would only smile if you told him his attitude was not Christian, but he would knock you down if you told him he was a Fascist.

The word *Fascism* is never defined. It often means every one who is anti-Communistic; sometimes it means one who believes in God, or authority, or religion. As matter of fact, we do not know what Fascism is; it is the subjection of the person to the State, as Nazism is the subjection of the person to the race, and as Communism is the subjection of the person to the class. But that is too clear-cut to satisfy the muddle-minded. They want to keep it undefined, so as to beat down with a sneer any one who refuses to accept their political outlook. Every one is so touchy about politics. To say a world against Russia today would be regarded by many as more serious than to blaspheme the Holy Spirit of God. In fact, if one says it is cold in Moscow, he is called a Fascist. Well! It is cold in Russia. All the intolerance which once surrounded absolute truth and the multiplication table is now bestowed to the relativity of politics. The relative of a Christian society thus becomes the absolute of a pagan society.

One could go through history and find a dozen historical instances to prove that, as men lose their belief in God, the State becomes an absolute. Men must have a God, and if it will not be the God of hearts, it will be the State god. About the time of the birth of Christ, religion had reached its lowest ebb in Rome and it was the moment when the State became absolute and the Caesars deified. Virgil spoke of Caesar Augustus as of "Divine Origin"; Pompey called himself "god"; Cicero said, "Augustus came from Heaven"; Herod paraded before the people in silvered costume, letting his subjects burn incense before him with the flattery: "It is the voice of god, and not the voice of man."

Fifteen centuries later when religion ceased to be a unifying power of men, the State began to assert itself and the divine right of kings became the secular substitute of the divine right of the vicar of the King of Kings. Finally, in our day, Stalin has permitted himself to be called "Creator of World Order," while Hitler has declared himself greater than Christ.

What are the effects of the absoluteness of politics? The most general effect is the dehumanization of man. Once man became loosened from his divine moorings, he became "autonomous," or an independent god. But no State could survive if every man was a god and a law unto himself, any more than a machine would work if every little wheel in it turned according to its own selfish ends.

To change the figure, men became as so many independent atoms without reference to any other universe than themselves. It was natural, therefore, for some powerful dictator to arise and say, "Well, we must now organize you into a unity." This unity became the collectivity of the race which was Nazism, of the State which was Fascism, and of the class which was Communism. From that point on, freedom and rights took on a new meaning. Freedom was no longer in man; it was in the race, the nation, the class. A man was free only when he thought, acted, and willed as the dictator bade. Rights, in like manner, were no longer in man for if God did not give him rights, how could he have rights? Rights were only in the totality or the herd; man was given rights; but he possessed none.

In democracies, the dehumanization of man has taken an academic or quasi-scientific background. The whole tendency of our thinking for the last seventy years has been to destroy man's dignity by identifying him with nature, that is, with the stones and the beasts. Evolution, for example, made him one with the animal in his *origin*; behaviorism identified him with the animal in his *actions*, and his *nature*; Freudianism identified him with the animal in his mental processes; Pragmatism identified him with the animal in his *goals* and *purposes*. What follows? If man is one with nature, then why should he not be treated as nature, that is, as a *thing*, or a *means* to an *end*. Human rights and freedom lost their outside purchase in God, where the Declaration of Independence put them. In fact, all rights and liberties disappeared, for nature has no rights. The result is that a new system of law, or political theory, has arisen which makes law merely a positive fact like a poker or a broom.

Democracy with God	Democracy without God
Rights come to us from God.	Our rights come to us from the State.
Because rights are God-given they are inalienable.	Since the State gives rights, the State can take them away.

Democracy with God	Democracy without God
Law is the reflection of the eternal reason of God and therefore any law which contradicts it is unjust.	Man is the creator of law, and whatever the courts decide is just.
All men are equal because all are made to the image of God, and all are destined for the same end.	All men are equal, because all men, since they are creators of their own law, are all gods.

If the moral basis of politics is rejected, the nation falls, for unless the electorate votes from an informed conscience rather than on the basis of propaganda, a democracy can vote itself right out of a democracy—as Germany did.

A triple obligation is incumbent upon us:

(1) Preserve the moral law in domestic politics. One of the grave dangers to the world is Fascism, either black, brown, or red. Here I speak of Red Fascism or Communism, because the black and brown Fascism arose only in reaction to the Red. In this connection, it might be well to realize that the so-called "dissolution" of the Third International was only a change of coat, not a change of heart. Communism today is dressing up. It tells us that it will no longer function as a political party in the United States. And why? Because it has discovered that by supporting either one or the other of the two major political parties, as circumstances demand, it can place more Communists in key positions of government than if it depended on the ballot and the common sense of the American people.

Communist agents will no longer talk revolution against our government; rather they will seek to make it conform itself to the foreign policy of Communism. America can be destroyed in one of two ways: by a revolt against it, or by selling its soul. Communism now chooses to corrupt its soul. From now on the Communist agent is no longer a domestic revolutionist; he is a foreign diplomat. He is no longer a Bolshevik; he is an educator. America is the sea in which he fishes; the bait is in "international unity" and the poor fish who bite best are the pinks and the intellectuals. Please God, not too many have scales on their backs!

(2) Keep America on the single standard, by conforming to the moral law of God. Once human law loses its objective standard, it becomes absurd to speak of any policy or law as being right or wrong. Right becomes "legality," or whatever happens is right. The result would be a double standard of morality. We must not have one code for certain nations, and another code for other nations. It would be wrong when one country absorbs another into itself to say: "Go to war," but when a third country absorbs still another into itself to say: "It will make for a world peace." It would be wrong, when one form of Totalitarianism extinguishes all other parties and allows no freedom of press, to call it *Fascism*, and when another country does exactly the same thing to call it *democracy*. It would be wrong, when one country breaks a treaty with another to defend its selfish interests, to call it "international banditry," and when another country does it to call it "self-defense." It would be wrong to have one standard for soldiers and another for civilians in defense plants, calling it a "crime" for the soldier to desert his post of duty and calling it "progress" when a defense worker deserts his duty. There must be no choosing between barbarities. Right is right if nobody is right, and wrong is wrong if everybody is wrong.

(3) Love America as a duty. Patriotism is a form of piety. And there are three principal forms of piety: love of God, love of neighbor, and love of country. All three are grounded in justice.

It is an historical fact that a country begins to decline at that moment when its citizens begin to love a foreign power more than its own. This happens the very moment justice and morality cease to be the root of patriotism. It happened, for example, when Frederick the Great refused to learn German and became so enamored of the godlessness of France that he loved it more than decent traditions of his own land. The spiritual zero of morality was reached when Frederick invited Voltaire to Germany to absorb some of his atheistic irresponsibility. When these two individuals looked into one another's empty souls, they made a sneer that was as eternal as the smile of a skull. What Fredrick did to the moral heritage to his people, we must not do with ours.

In a time of crisis, the difference between those who believe in and live by the moral law, and those who do not, becomes intensified. The less moral we are, the less Christian, the less God-fearing, the less we protest against the disruption of family life by divorces and the like, the more we will be accepted by this world, as our Lord was accepted on Palm Sunday when it was thought that His ideas coincided with those of the mob. But the more Christian we become, the more God-fearing we are, the more we insist on morality in education, family life, and politics, the more we will be regarded with suspicion and with hate. Our very existence will be regarded as a danger. We need do nothing to bring a reaction against us, any more than the early Christians of Rome, who were good citizens, were guilty of any other crime than that of refusing to call Nero *führer* or god.

We will be hated because our moral code is a reproach to the world. The word of our Lord will be verified: "If you had been of the world, the world would love its own: but because you are not of the world, but I have chosen you out of the world, therefore the world hateth you" (John 15:19).

So strong is this spirit growing in the world today, that one can predict with infallible accuracy which of two contending groups in any State in Europe will be favored by most of those journalists, commentators, and publicists who are making world opinion; it will invariably be that party, that group, that underground whose background is irreligious, or atheistic, or even anti-Christian.

As the world grows into an ideological uniformity in which all men are supposed to think alike, the believer in the moral law and particularly the Church will come in increasing conflict with it, and for no other reason than that they assert and believe in God and the moral law! The great scene in the courtroom of the Roman Governor may be repeated, when Pilate said to our Lord: "Knowest thou not that I have power to crucify thee, and I have power to release thee?" (John 19:10). To him the Savior answered: "Thou shouldst not have any power against me, unless it were given thee from above" (John 19:11).

This is at the heart of the present world conflict—that of State-given rights and of God-given rights. Because that conflict was destined to come to the surface, it was kept in the Creed and we still repeat it daily. In the truest sense of the word, the Church and men of good will are now "suffering under Pontius Pilate."

One thing we must never do is to purchase a transitory freedom by the sacrifice of God's truth! If the choice is to stultify ourselves by sacrificing our moral being for a false peace, or to endure persecution, let us in God's name choose the ennoblement of a persecution. "And fear ye not them that kill the body, and are not able to kill the soul: but rather fear him that can destroy both soul and body in hell" (Matt. 10:28).

That brings us back to the beginning. What is an American? An American is one who believes that his rights and liberties come to him from God, and that they are therefore inalienable, and that no State on the face of God's earth can take them away. On April 30, 1777, George Washington, fearful that some of his men were more loyal to foreign powers than to their own country, posted up an order that was to be obeyed absolutely at night. And now as men forget God and darkness settles over the earth we needs must repost that order of Washington. "Put none but Americans on guard tonight." How true! It is night! Put none but Americans on guard!

39

The Pillar of the Family

The basic moral principle of Domestic Society is: *the family is the natural unit of society and the right of education belongs primarily to the parents, not to the State.*

The family in the *natural order* is the only divine instruction in the world. God did not found the American Chamber of Commerce, the CIO, the National League, or the USSR, but in making man and woman, who find the natural complement in one another, and whose children are the incarnation of their mutual love, God did found the family.

As the family is the divinely organized society of the natural order, so the Church is the divinely organized society of the supernatural order. Since grace is built upon nature, the Church cannot destroy the natural rights of society. The family, therefore, as a society, precedes both the State and the Church.

Since the family is the natural unit of society and precedes both the State and the Church in nature and in time it follows that the parents, and not the State, have the primary and normal right of education. The family holds directly from the Creator the inalienable right to educate. This right is inviolable by any power on earth, as is evident from the fact that the education of the children is the concern of the parents long before it is the concern of anyone else. The State exists for the family, the family does not exist for the State.

The parents may, if they wish, delegate the exercise of this right to the State, but even then the primary responsibility for the education of the child remains with the parents, not with the teacher. The teacher only *supplements*, but never *supplants* either the right or duty of parents. The function of the State, when it receives this delegation, is merely to protect and foster but never to absorb either the individual or the family, or to substitute itself for them.

The teacher always acts in the name of the parents, not in the name of the State; though the State, to safeguard its citizenship, may guarantee the efficiency of the teachers. A teacher receives his mission from humanity, not from the government. Whatever authority he exercises over the children to teach, control, and discipline them comes from God, through the parents, and not from the State, except insofar as the State acts on behalf of the parents. To make the teacher the representative of the State, as in Nazi Germany, is to make him the guardian of a party, its fleeting policies, its ideologies, its theories, and thus an enemy of culture, of tradition, and of humanity.

This basic principle of domestic society, that the primary and normal right of education belongs to the parents and not to the State, is a conclusion of the moral law. It is not Catholic doctrine exclusively, though it has wrongly become identified as Catholic teaching. As a matter of fact, it is part of the legal tradition of the United States enthroned in both the fourteenth amendment and the decisions of the Supreme Court. For example, the Supreme Court of the United States handed down this decision:

> The fundamental theory of liberty upon which all governments
> in the Union repose, excludes any general power of the state to
> standardize its children by forcing them to accept instruction from
> public teachers only. The child is not the mere creature of the
> state; those who nurture him and direct his destiny have the right,
> coupled with the high duty, to recognize and prepare him for additional obligations.[98]

---

[98] As quoted in *Federal Aid to Education: Hearings before a Subcommittee of the Committee on Labor and Public Welfare* (Washington, DC: Government Printing Office,1947), 239.

The principle is denied by all Totalitarian ideologies which affirm that the total man, body and soul, belongs to the State. It is also denied by some of those intelligentsia and so-called "expert" educators at home. In a survey made by Dr. A. P. Raup of two thousand students seeking teaching certificates in seventy institutions, it was discovered that 50 percent of them had been indoctrinated by naturalist teachers who denied both the moral law and the existence of any rights except State-given rights, and whose basic assumption was that man is an animal.

Too many parents today shift their responsibility to the school and assume that by doing so they have fulfilled their parental obligations. Have they forgotten that the education of their children is their concern seven years before it is the concern of the school? A rough calculation will show too that, when schooling starts, the child still spends about 85 percent of his time at home. The child has been given by God to the parents as so much putty in their hands; and how the little ones will be moulded and formed is the primary responsibility of the home. There is such a thing in the Providence of God as "mother-craft" and "father-craft," but there never was a time when these noble professions were in such danger of being lost. Sending a child to school no more acquits the parents of responsibility than sending a child to a swimming pool acquits the parents of responsibility for that child's cleanliness.

What has complicated and intensified parental irresponsibility is the fact that most schools today assume that education consists only of the *imparting of knowledge*. This is an egregious error, because knowledge is only a part of education. The whole man must be educated, and this means the will must be trained as well as the intellect. More important than knowledge is the formation of character, the right ordering of conscience, and the formation of personality, none of which can be taught in a school which deliberately rejects the teaching of morality and religion. Plato was right when he taught that the primary purpose of education is the inculcation of the distinction of right and wrong.

Parents have, perhaps unconsciously, fallen prey to the fallacy propounded by those intelligentsia who, to cover up their own reactionary theories, call themselves "progressives." This group has led parents to believe that evil, sin, and crime are due to ignorance, and that if we educate by imparting knowledge we will abolish crime. Typical of this was Guizot, who when nonreligious education began said: "He, who opens a school, closes a prison." Today the facts retort to Guizot: "Well, we opened thousands of schools, but we closed no prisons."

Our crime bill today is forty million dollars a day. Our prison population has nearly doubled since 1927. We have the largest homicide rate in the world. This rate has doubled in the last thirty years. Our murder rate is from six to forty times higher than European countries in normal times. A major crime is committed every twenty-four seconds. We have a murder every forty minutes.

Never before in the history of the world was there so much knowledge; and never before so little coming to the knowledge of the Truth. Never before so much straining for life; never before so many unhappy lives. Never before so much science; never before was it used so for the destruction of human life.

In the face of this, then, shall parents not see that it is not the intellects of the world that have gone wrong; it is consciences. Reason, without moral purpose, can be reason at the service of evil as well as good. It is not the schools that are to blame; it is the parents. The right to educate belongs to them.

A final indication of the breakdown of parental authority is the present tendency of mothers who, outside o cases of necessity, work in war plants to the utter neglect and detriment of their children. In Los Angeles a social worker counted forty-five infants locked in cars at a single parking lot while their mothers were at work in war plants. In jam-packed Warren Township, outside of Detroit, children who go to school on an afternoon shift have actually been sent out to wander the streets at night so they will sleep later and not wake up their working parents early in the morning. One thirteen-year-old girl in a beer hall told the California State Department of Health officer, "I'm just waiting until twelve. My bed is not empty until then."

The root of this trouble is in the *home*; and those who talk about more nurseries, better playgrounds, curfews, better milk, and more dance halls, are perhaps diminishing the effect but not removing the cause. Behind every delinquent child is a delinquent parent. Behind every broken young life is a broken home. There are problem children only because there are problem parents.

It, therefore, behooves those mothers who are doing defense work, to the utter neglect of their children, not to flatter themselves that they are aiding the war effort. The price for working in a war plant is too high, when a little less time spent in welding pipe to pipe, and a little more time spent in welding child to virtue would profit America a thousand times more. In many cases, it is not a desire to hasten victory and peace that spurs such a mother on to work, but a desire to make money. And what kind of peace will we have if, during the war, these mothers turn out future mothers with a sordid background of disease and crime? Our soldiers at the front are entitled to better wives when they return, or else the fighting is all in vain. This war's greatest casualty so far is — *the American home.*

Does this mean the American home is doomed? No! There are high hopes for better home life in the new America arising in the hearts of the soldiers. This war has brought home to the American soldier a glaring contradiction between his education and the ideas for which he is fighting. He has thus come to see some of his peace education was wrong, and his war ideas are right.

Such statements as the following are commonly heard today:

In college I was taught that I was only an animal, but in the army I am taught to act like a man; or my professor told me that there was no difference between right and wrong, good and evil; but now my buddies die, and I prepare to die to prove that Hitler was wrong and we are right. My textbooks ridiculed sin and evil, but I find that war is caused because some men are evil. In school I was taught to be self-expressive; I was told that inhibitions and restraints were wrong, and that liberty meant to do whatever I pleased. In war I learned obedience, discipline, restraint, and, above all, that anyone who died to preserve that kind of eviscerated liberty was a fool. In law school I was taught that there were no inalienable rights, but on last July 4th I recalled the Declaration of Independence and realized that I was fighting to preserve those inalienable rights which my law school denied. My teachers told me that I must try to get all I can out of life, but on the battlefield I learned to give even my life.

Thus has our youth aroused himself to the tremendous disproportion between what his head was taught in school and what his heart learned amid death and shell and sweat and blood; *theoretical* repudiation of the moral law in education, and the *practical* necessity of it to win a war and establish peace.

This war has knocked into a cocked hat all those vaporous theorizings of naturalist education which separated education from morality, which understood freedom of speech as freedom from morality; freedom of religion as freedom from worship; freedom from Fascism as freedom from Communism; freedom from fear as freedom from law; and freedom of thought as freedom from truth.

The future of America is in the homes. This sounds like a platitude, but it is not, for unless the home is sound, America will not be sound. The rebirth of the home is conditioned upon three factors, all of which are grounded in the moral law:

First, marriage is a permanent bond until death. There are only two words in the vocabulary of love: *you* and *always*. *You* because love is unique; *always* because love is timeless. No one ever said, "I will love you for two years and six months." The modern rubbish about sex confuses feeling with love, an organic reaction with an act of will, and falsely believes that when the "thrill" is gone, marriage is ended, forgetful that in marriage, as in running a race, there is a second wind. What the moderns call the "thrill" is only the choke that starts the motor; moderns never stay together long enough to enjoy the thrill of driving. The frosting is not the cake, but the moral law says you may not take the frosting unless you eat the cake. One of the great values of a vow is that it keeps couples together during the shock of the first cold plunge, that later on they may enjoy the swim. Love is life's courier and must not linger only in the rivers of rapture, but must launch out into the deeper and more authentic waters where the single happiness of "being together" mirrors the mystery of God's eternity and reflects the harmonies of the triune God.

Second, marriage by its very nature is destined to bear fruit, for love is mutual self-giving which ends in self-recovery. All love is creative—even God's. All love tends to an incarnation—even God's. The spark of love, caught from the flames of Heaven's altars, was not given to scorch the flesh, but to solder life. The only reason life ever surrenders itself to life is to meet the challenge of death and conquer individual weakness by filling up the other's lacking measure in the birth of their mutual love. As the marriage of earth and tree is messianic to new life, so man and woman must not make a covenant with death but, in obedience to nature's law, pay back life's loan of life with life and not with death. In vain will they who break the lute of God's designs ever hope to snare the music. Humanity is the quarry, husband and wife the sculptors, and every child they beget a living stone to be fitted and compacted into the temple, the cornerstone of which is God.

Third, marriage can prosper only on condition of sacrifice. All love craves a cross—even God's. True love is sacrificial. That is why courtship is characterized by gift-giving—a surrender of what one *has*. In marriage this sacrificial love should deepen by a surrender of what one *is*. Because too many measure their love for another by the pleasure which the other gives, they are in reality not in love, but in the swamps of selfishness. Hence to preserve the family, the greatest sorrow of each member should be to be outdone by the cherished rival in the least advantage of self-giving. Our poor, frail human souls at best are like jangled strings, made toneless by self-love; and not until we tighten them with self-discipline can we attune them to those harmonies that come from God, wherein each, having given to the other hostage of its heart, finds himself free in the glorious liberty of the children of God.

Peace first came to the world when the wise men discovered a family. And the dawn of peace will come again when other wise men return to homes where, in the new vision of domesticity, they see the human family of father, mother, and children, as the reverse order of the Holy Family: a Child, a Mother, and a Father.

40

The Pillar of Freedom

The basic moral principle of the social order is: *freedom is a moral power, not a physical power.*

The most often used word in this world war is *freedom*, as the word most often used in the last world war was *democracy*. What the slogan "make the world safe for democracy" was to the last world war, the phrase *the four freedoms* is to this. We do hope that this war does not do to the freedom of the world what the last world war did to democracy.

It could happen that as democracy ended in Totalitarianism in Germany, Italy, and Russia, so freedom could end in slavery—unless we understand aright the nature of freedom, and how to keep it.

Freedom may be understood in either of two ways, one of which is wrong, and the other right; that is: physical freedom and moral freedom. Physical freedom is the power to do whatever you *please*; moral freedom is the right to do whatever you *ought*. I can do many things if I please; for example, stuff your mattress with old razor blades or turn a machine gun on your chickens; but *ought* I?

Physical freedom is based on power, either the power of the individual, as in the doctrine of liberalism, or the power of race, nation, or class, as with the systems of Fascism, Nazism, and Communism.

Moral freedom, on the contrary, is based not on power but on the moral law of God. It envisages freedom as perfected within the law, rather than outside it, for the best self-expression is self-perfection.

Physical freedom means license, the power to draw triangles with four sides, giraffes with short necks, the power to plot against one's country and to break the commandments of God and of men, on the theory that he who restrains individual egotism restrains freedom.

Moral freedom means purchasing the right to fly by obeying the laws of gravitation, the right to drive a car by obeying the traffic laws, the right to be an American by obeying the laws of America, the right to be a child of God by obeying the moral law.

Moral freedom is upheld by men of good will, who, whether they have analyzed the concept thoroughly or not, believe in the words of the Savior: "And the truth shall make you free" (John 8:32), and "Where the Spirit of the Lord is, there is liberty" (2 Cor. 3:17).

It was this moral kind of freedom in a *political* form that the Greeks fought to preserve from the despotism of the Persians; it was the kind of freedom in a *spiritual* form which the Christians suffered martyrdom to preserve from the absolutism of Caesar. And it is this kind of freedom in an *international* form that we are seeking to preserve against the brutality of dictatorships.

The point we are making is that freedom is meaningless apart from the moral law. To prove it, let us glance at the four freedoms for which we are fighting: freedom of religion, freedom of speech, freedom from want, freedom from fear.

Not a single one of these four freedoms is an end in itself; they have meaning only in the context of the moral law of God.

(1) Why, for example, should there be freedom of religion? Because of the sacredness and inviolability of the human person, and his right to adore God according to the light of his conscience. Freedom of religion does not mean therefore the right to impose irreligion on people any more than freedom to live means the right to murder.

(2) Why should there be freedom of speech? Because speech, being an instrument, is to be used for the proper purpose of speech; that is, the communication of truth, goodness, knowledge, and information; and not for the diffusion of scandals, lies, treason, or immorality. Freedom of speech does not give one the right to destroy freedom of speech, any more

than the freedom to light a match gives one the right to burn down one's neighbor's house.

(3) Why should there be freedom from want? Because the necessities and the decent comforts of life are the material conditions for the development of personality, and therefore for the salvation of the soul. Freedom from want no more gives one the right to abundance purchased by making others want than freedom to possess means freedom to dispossess.

(4) Why should there be freedom from fear? Because peace of mind is the condition of culture, and culture is impossible when a man fears either the consequences of his own sins or the consequences of the sins of others. The right to freedom from fear never means the right to terrorize others, any more than the murderer's fear of jail gives him a right to kill the judge.

Thus we are brought back to the beginning: if we destroy the moral roots of freedom we cannot expect to keep the fruits of freedom. Freedom is responsibility, not license. Freedom divorced from moral responsibility—that is, freedom divorced from God—is anarchy.

Freedom of religion will die if we shirk our responsibilities or duties to God.

Freedom of speech will die if we shirk our responsibility to truth.

Freedom from want will vanish if we shirk our responsibility to our fellow man.

Freedom from fear will vanish if we shirk our responsibility to love those who are in distress.

Four freedoms set in the moral law are therefore quite different from four freedoms isolated from it. As a matter of fact, in the latter case, they would be absolutely wicked and should be spurned, as they were by our Blessed Lord on four occasions.

(1) Our Lord rejected a false freedom of religion. Satan appeared to Him on the mountaintop, and unrolled before His mind's eye all the nations, kingdoms, and empires of the world in an increasing panorama of pomp and power, and in one of the most frightening and terrifying statements in all Scripture, Satan said: "All these will I give thee, if falling down thou wilt adore me" (Matt. 4:9). Here was a freedom of religion in the false sense of the term; that is, the freedom to adore either God or Satan. And our

Blessed Lord rejected it, for He would not have a freedom of religion that meant the freedom to be diabolical, anti-God, and anti-moral.

(2) Our Lord rejected a false freedom of speech. Led before one of the judges, false charges, lies, and accusations were hurled in His face. The judge offered the Divine Master a false freedom of speech: "Answerest thou nothing to the things that are laid to thy charge by these men?" (Mark 14:60). But He held His peace, and would not speak, for freedom of speech ceases to be freedom of speech when speech may be used only to confirm a lie. It is the truth that makes you free—not a lie.

(3) Our Lord rejected a false freedom from want. After our Lord fasted for forty days, Satan appeared before him and pointed to little stones that resembled in appearance Jewish bread, and suggested, "If thou be the Son of God, command that these stones be made bread" (Matt. 4:3). Satan, too, it seems, believes in freedom from want—but our Lord refused to accept Satan's abundance, for it would have been purchased at the cost of disobedience to His Father's Will.

(4) Our Lord rejected a false freedom from fear. On Holy Thursday night, when Judas led a band of soldiers down to the Brook of Cedron and into the Garden to apprehend our Divine Lord, Peter in one of his frequent impetuous moments drew a sword, and hacked off the ear of the servant of the high priest. Peter apparently believed in security or freedom from fear; but it was the wrong kind. In reprimand, our Lord said to Peter; "Put up again thy sword into its place: for all that take the sword shall perish with the sword" (Matt. 26:52). No freedom from fear would the Savior of the world have if it were purchased at the cost of injury to our fellow man.

Hence not a single one of the four freedoms is an end in itself. Either they are means to the attainment of moral purposes or they are evil and wicked. Freedom *from* something is meaningful only when we are free *for* something, and until we know what we want to be free for, there is not much use in struggling or risking our lives.

What use is freedom of religion, if there is no God to worship?

What use is freedom of speech, if there is no truth to defend?

What use is freedom from want, if such security is purchased at the cost of another's privation?

What use is freedom from fear, if such security is purchased at the cost of one's soul?

Once you divorce freedom of religion from God, freedom of speech from truth, freedom from want and freedom from fear from justice, and the four freedoms will become the Four Horsemen of the Apocalypse riding roughshod over the world in satanic fury, trampling out every freedom on earth except the glorious freedom to be a martyr for the glory of God who made us free.

This being true, these corollaries of freedom follow from the moral law:

First: When we affirm the four freedoms, we must not assume that we can give freedom to the enslaved peoples of Europe. All we can do is to remove external hindrance to freedom.

Freedom is from the spirit, not from power. We can no more give Europe freedom than we can give a European a soul. All we can do is to say that the European's moral freedom shall not be inhibited by external compulsions. You can lead a horse to water, but you cannot make him drink. You can lead the enslaved masses of Europe to the fountains of the four liberties, but they will not drink unless in their souls they choose to be free with the glorious liberty of the children of God. Freedom is in the inner will, not in external power. That is why no power on earth can make men free.

In order to be free, each man must make a pact with his soul. Let us not then promise to the enslaved peoples of Europe something we cannot deliver. They have already been deceived too much. Communism promised freedom through economic abundance, and gave them spiritual starvation; Nazism promised them freedom through *lebensraum* and gave them *totesraum*; Fascism promised them freedom through law, but gave them law without freedom. Democracy must not add to this tragic litany by promising a freedom which only God can give. We enjoy God's liberty, but we do not create it, All that we can promise is this: "We will take the shackles off your legs so you can walk out of prison and get down on your knees and remake your soul! We will make you *freed* men, but only God can make you *free* men." More than that we cannot say without blasphemy.

We are born free!

And the tribune coming, said to him: Tell me, art thou a Roman? But he said: Yea. And the tribune answered: I obtained the being free of this city with a great sum. And Paul said: But I was born so. Immediately therefore they departed from him that were about to torture him. The tribune also was afraid after he understood that he was a Roman citizen, and because he had bound him. (Acts 22:27–29)

Second: freedom is not an heirloom which originally belonged to the Founding Fathers of our country and which has been passed down to us from generation to generation ever since. Freedom is rather an endowment like life, which is preserved by resisting from time to time the challenge of disease and death.

The freedom that Washington won for us has not come down to us as an antique. Freedom for those days is not necessarily freedom for ours, unless we win it too, as they did—by sacrifice, fire, and tears.

A freedom that costs nothing is worth nothing. Freedom, like a tree, needs to be quickened and refreshed now and then by the blood of patriots and the dew of self-sacrificing citizens. It is not only the original cost of freedom that is high; it is the upkeep.

Freedom therefore is not foolproof; it demands restraint, law, and discipline. Therefore it will never mean the right to abuse justice, to spurn mercy, and to ignore truth. Set within the moral law, freedom must always be strong enough to preserve freedom.

Finally, freedom is ours only to give away. Every man may give his freedom away, either to creatures, to public opinion, or to God. The creature to which he surrenders his freedom may be money, or power, or a human being—for all love is slavery, seeking to unburden itself for the object of its affection.

Others give up their freedom to the moods and opinions of the moment, and they are legion. Swayed by the winds of every commentator and propagandist, they have no judgments of their own, no standards of their own; and thus, while mounting slogans of liberty, they surrender the last vestige of it to a slavery worse than chains, for here the mind is bound.

Finally, others give up freedom to God, wanting nothing, seeking nothing, desiring nothing except to do His Will in all things, in a slavery to Perfect Life, Perfect Truth, Perfect Love, which ends in the highest kind of freedom; for to "serve Him is to rule."

There is not a man alive who does not make one of these three surrenders! And of the three, only the last makes freedom eternal, for "If therefore the son shall make you free, you shall be free indeed" (John 8:36).

41

The Pillar of World Unity

The basic principle of the international order is: *the world is one because it was made by one Lord and is governed by His moral law.*

All men are one because God made man. Paul, a Jew, standing on the hill of the Areopagus, declared this great truth to the Senators of Greece: "God.... hath made of one, all mankind, to dwell upon the whole face of the earth" (Acts 17:24, 26). And then, as if to remind them that this was not the teaching of his people alone, he quoted for them Aratus and Clianthus, saying; "As some also of your own poets said: For we are also his offspring" (Acts 17:28).

The world became united only in those periods of history in which men recognized the overlordship of God. It was because the pagan, Cyrus, recognized that he was but an instrument in the hands of the God of Israel that he could bring himself to respect the rights of a conquered people and order rebuilt for them their Temple at Jerusalem. Alexander the Great is quoted by Plutarch as saying; "God is the common father of all men."[99] No wonder then that he ordered that every city and every state should open its gates to the exiled opponents of the party and that his own offers should take brides from among the conquered people. And

---

[99] Plutarch, *Plutarch's Lives*, vol. 3, trans. Aubrey Stewart and George Long (London: George Bell, 1906), 329.

who shall forget Cicero's words that "the universe is to be regarded as a single commonwealth, since all are subject to the Heavenly law and divine intelligence of Almighty God"?

These dim aspirations of pre-Christian times were but feeble echoes of the Hebrew truth that God "Shall be called the God of all the earth" (Isa. 54:5). All of them were but dim foreshadowings of the day when the whole world would be enrolled, when the King of Kings and the Lord of Lords should be born—Creator of all men, Redeemer who made all men one because of all men. How much wiser the pre-Christian pagan was than our post-Christian pagan! Shall those of us who have forgotten the wisdom of the ancient pagans, the revelation of the Jews, and the sublime truths of Christianity, think that we can build one world on any other foundation? To unite men there must be something outside men, just as to tie up a bundle of sticks there must be someone outside the sticks. A moral law outside of nations to which all nations can appeal, and to which they must submit even when the decision goes against them, is the only condition of world peace. That is why we say there will never be one world until we all learn to pray, "Our Father, who art in Heaven."

The only alternative to one world based on one Lord and one moral law is to have many worlds and many lords, where each nation is its own law, its own god. Like the workers on the Tower of Babel, each of us will then speak a different language and live by a different code: Having naught in common, the project of world peace must, like the Tower, be abandoned. In that case, there would be no way to decide whether Japanese atrocities were wrong and American humanitarianism right, except by a war between these gods in which might decides what is right. To all who have eyes it should be as clear as the stones in the road that the day we make a godless world we make also a loveless world.

There were 4,568 treaties of peace signed before the League of Nations between the two world wars, and 211 in the nine months before this war broke out. Only the smaller fraction of them were kept. What great change in the heart of man has taken place since 1939 to make us believe that from now on treaties and pledges will be kept? Have our souls been reborn? Let us be realistic about it! Why should any treaty be kept under the present setup of the world? What is the source of their obligation? Is the obligation rooted in God and conscience, or in convenience, strategy, or force? It is either right or might. It is just as simple as that, for *no treaty creates its own obligation.* Obligation is outside the treaty or else there is no obligation. In such a case, *either an obligation does not exist or its basis is force.*

This moral principle that we can have one world only on condition of one law breaks immediately with the commonly accepted principle that (because no city in the world is more than sixty hours from an airport) the world is one. It should be obvious to anyone who had lived through two world wars in twenty-one years that rapid communications have the same potentialities for destruction as they have for unity. An airplane in itself is indifferent as to whether it scatters flowers or bombs. Unity depends therefore not on communication but on the singleness of purpose for which communications are used.

This brings us back to the antiphon that has been ringing through these chapters. "We must gather together the hearts of all those who are magnanimous and upright in a solemn vow not to rest until in all peoples and all the nations of the earth a vast legion shall be formed, bent on bringing society back to its center of gravity which is the law of God."[100]

What are some corollaries of the moral law as applied the international order? The moral law in its application to the world must provide a new international order with five characteristics: it must be positive, juridical, realistic, single in purpose, and uncompromising.

The unity of nations for the defeat of barbarism must not be negative, but positive; that is, it must not be grounded on the common hatred of an aggressor but on the acceptance of common moral principles. Military unity does not necessarily mean political unity. The two are commonly confused. Gratitude for military cooperation does not oblige us to go into ecstasies about the political ideology of any foreign power. The firemen who put out the fire in your home render a negative help, but they never help rebuild your home. In like manner, it is not the defeat of a particular barbarism which makes us true allies, but rather the agreement that a

---

[100] Pius XII, Christmas Message on the Internal Order of States and People.

temple of peace can be built only on the foundation of the moral order and with the stone of justice and the cement of love.

The new international order must be juridical. The moral law forbids any nation to satisfy its selfish ambitions or imperialistic aims by violating the sovereignty of other nations, independently of a judicial process and before the court convenes. Therefore, no signatory of a declaration of united peace may settle international questions unilaterally, by force, independently of the moral judgment of other nations. Justice becomes a farce of a thief is permitted to say to the court: "I will permit you to hear my case only on condition that I keep my loot."

The new international order must be realistic. The moral law realistically affirms that no one can give that which he has not. Therefore any nation which does not give freedom of religion, freedom of speech, and freedom of press to its own citizens, can hardly be counted on, in a society of nations, to give to other peoples those rights which its own citizens do not enjoy.

In the new international order there must be singleness of purpose. The moral law admits of no double standard. Non-belligerency is right in certain circumstances, but it is wrong when purchased at the cost of morality. No one more strongly condemned appeasement of the strong powers who were violating the sovereignty of other nations than Marshal Stalin who, speaking to England and America in 1939, said:

> [England and America let Germany] have Austria, despite the undertaking to defend her independence; they let her have the Sudeten region; they abandoned Czechoslovakia to her fate, thereby violating all their obligations.... Far be it from me to moralize on the policy of non-intervention, to talk of treason, treachery, and so on. It would be naive to preach morals to people who recognize no human morality.[101]

Stalin here hailed America and England before the bar of justice and condemned them for appeasing Germany when it violated the sovereignty

---

[101] Joseph Stalin, *Stalin's Kampf: Joseph Stalinm's Credo*, ed. Morris Robert Werner (New York: Howell and Soskin, 1940), 334-335.

of the Sudeten, Austria, and Czechoslovakia. Would it not then be equally wrong for us to appease another foreign power if it violated the sovereignty of other lands in the same manner? The morality of an action is not decided by who violates, bet by what is violated. Would it not be wrong of America to invade Canada on the basis of mutual assistance pacts and incorporate it into our republic? Was it not wrong for Germany to do that with Czechoslovakia? Then what makes it right when another foreign power does it? Unless we defend moral rights when the needs must be defended, we may get into that state described by Shakespeare:

> Now, as fond fathers,
> Having bound up the threatening twigs of birch,
> Only to stick it in their children's sight
> For terror, not to use, in time the rod
> Becomes more mock'd than fear'd; so our decrees
> Dead to infliction, to themselves are dead,
> And liberty plucks justice by the nose.[102]

The new international order, finally, must be uncompromising. The moral integrity of a nation depends on fidelity to its pledges. In the Atlantic Charter we pledged (1) "No aggrandizement, territorial or other"; (2) "No territorial changes that do not accord with the freely expressed wishes of the people concerned"; (3) "All nations of the world must come to the abandonment of the use of force."

No other joint declaration was ever as specific as this, nor did any other so unify men of good will behind the war effort. If America ever sacrifices that charter for any temporary benefit or appeasement, it will not regain the good will of the people within a generation. It is therefore a shock to read this editorial in a metropolitan newspaper:

> We must find out what Russia wants in payment for her fight, and we must be realistic about it. If Russia wants, as is now supposed, something like the old Czarist boundaries—including Finland,

---

[102] Shakespeare, *Measure for Measure*, act 1, scene 3.

Latvia, Lithuania, Estonia, and a large chunk of Poland—we had better concede to her wishes, rather than stick to the Atlantic Charter.

Another metropolitan newspaper states that "if Russia wants Poland, it is far better to give up Poland than to offend Russia." By the same logic, why not give up the Philippines rather than offend Japan? Why, in other words, is Russia right in doing the very same thing which Stalin said was wrong when Hitler invaded Austria, the Sudeten region, and Czechoslovakia?

Herein lies America's greatest danger—paralysis of spirit, refusal to stand up for the right regardless of consequences. We will never be conquered from without; no one can conquer us but ourselves. Never will we be murdered! But America can commit suicide! Other nations may sentence her to die, but America alone can be the executioner. It will never be invaded by armies; but it can be pervaded by a supine submission to evil! Our frontiers are safe; our inner defense can be betrayed only by what is false within! As Lincoln said:

> At what point then is the approach of danger to be expected? I answer, If it ever reach us it must spring up amongst us; it cannot come from abroad. If destruction be our lot we must ourselves be its author and finisher. As a nation of freemen we must live through all time, or die by suicide.... Many free countries have lost their liberty, and ours may lose hers; but if she shall, be it my proudest plume, not that I was the last to desert, but that I never deserted her.[103]

We have had political expressions of the moral law in the Atlantic Charter, in the four freedoms, and in the following magnificent words of the State Department, which makes one feel proud of being American. They were written in defense of Latvia, Estonia, and Lithuania:

> The United States will continue to stand by these principles [of sovereignty], because of the conviction of the American people that unless the doctrine in which these principles are inherent once

---

[103] Abraham Lincoln, *Abraham Lincoln: Complete Works*, vol. 1, ed. John G. Nicolay and John Hay (New York: Century, 1907), 9, 36.

again governs the relations between nations, the rule of reason, of justice, and of law—in other words, the basis of modern civilization itself—cannot be preserved.[104]

These declarations are in the great tradition of Washington, who reminds us that religion and morality are the indispensable pillars of good government. Because Americans generally accept the moral and religious basis of an international order, they are embarrassed by attacks on religion, whether official or unofficial. Some, inspired by the best of sentiments, protest against such attacks on the ground that those who make them forget that politics is separate from religion, and that it hurts international relations to confuse them. This criticism is based on a nineteenth-century attitude which no longer fits the twentieth-century facts. During the nineteenth century religion and politics established a kind of *modus vivendi*, or tacit agreement not to interfere in the other's domain. It was an arrangement like unto a husband and wife who lived peaceably so long as the husband stayed out of the kitchen.

But what actually happened was that while religion was staying in the parlor, irreligion, the next door neighbor, came in and stole the political wife. In other words, while politics asked religion not to interfere, politics became irreligious, first with the Communists, then with the Fascists, and finally with the Nazis. That is why the Church condemned all three. And the Church condemned these three ideologies not because they were bad political systems, but because they were bad religions. In other words, the new politics is a religion. Nothing today is secular. The temporal smothers the spiritual.

This war is therefore more a religious war than it is a nationalistic war. It is a conflict between two totally different philosophies of life. Never before in the history of Christianity has the cause of God and man, of religion and freedom, been as nearly identical as it is at this very hour. As Joan of Arc fought simultaneously for the Kingdom of God and for France, so America is fighting, in an analogical sense, for a political idea which is essentially a *moral* ideal.

---

[104] United States Department of State, Statement concerning the Baltic Republics, July 23, 1940, as quoted in *Digest of International Law*, vol. 5, ed. Marjorie M. Whiteman (Washington, DC: government Printing Office, 1965), 942.

The tragedy of attacks on religion within our own camp is not that they may endanger our military success, but that they reveal a disparity of ideals—as different as night and day. There is therefore not much point in reminding the enemies of religion that religion and politics are separate, because to them politics is religion in the sense that politics is anti-religious, and admits of no other law or code or morality than itself.

From quite another point of view there is such a thing as looking at such disturbances of the international moral order through the eyes of faith.

There is nothing new in this world. There are only the same old things happening to new people. The gospel is the pre-history of the Church. No sword is lifted against Christ's Church but that Christ feels the wound. Of each new agony and woe, He can say: "My pain, my grief, my death." Hence, when I read of attacks launched against religion, I remember that they happened before. I go back to the Gospels, and as if it were an eternal newspaper I read the old news that is eternally new.

If I hear it said that the Church is opposed to the freedom-loving peoples of the world, and that there can be no peace in Europe until religion is crushed, somehow or other my mind immediately begins to think of the day that the Son of the Most High was standing in the sunlit balustrade of the Fortress Antonia, and the same charges were hurled against Him. "We have found this man perverting our nation, and forbidding to give tribute to Caesar, and saying that he is Christ the king" (Luke 23:2). That was a roundabout way, in those less clever days of name-calling, of saying that He was a Fascist. They were all lies! But what difference does it make? Did not Hitler say, "You can never get people to believe little lies, but you can get them to believe big ones"? But though the dictator boasts of his power, the words of the Savior still ring above him in a message of hope: "Thou shouldst not have any power against me, unless it were given thee from above" (John 19:11).

Then when I hear the enemies of religion say the Church is hated—hated in Belgium, in France, in Italy, in Holland, in Great Britain, and the United States—I remember how well our Lord foretold that this day would come to pass. "If the world hate you, know ye, that it hath hated me before you. If you had been of the world, the world would love its own; but because you are not of the world, but I have chosen you out of the world, therefore the world hateth you.... If they have persecuted me, they will also persecute you" (John 15:18-20).

He was hated too! Once there echoed in His ears the final shout of those who said, "Crucify him, crucify him" (Luke 23:21). Who cried for His death? The masses! Every one! But who moved the masses to hate? The leaders, the ancients, the makers of public opinion. In the simple language of the Gospel: "[They] persuaded the people" (Matt. 27:20). St. Matthew here reads like today's newspaper—the people are still being persuaded!

Now as then, like its Master, the Church is caught between two political fires which are themselves at war. Just as the Christ was buffeted between Pilate and Herod, who hated one another, so the Church is attacked by those who hate one another, by its Pilates who regard the Church as a political menace, and by the Herods who regard the Church as a political fool.

Conscience has always been defenseless before power, and justice made ridiculous before the imperial impulses!

But what a terrible ending to the story: so simply stated—"And Herod and Pilate were made friends, that same day" (Luke 23:12).

It was the one thing on which they could agree—a common dictational hatred of Divine Love!

How shall we know whether the world will make a peace grounded on the moral law? By what test shall we recognize fidelity to the Atlantic Charter? The test is Poland. Poland is a cameo, not a piece in the mosaic of nations. Poland is not an aspect of the international problem; it is the international problem in miniature. Whatever happens to Poland will happen to the world. If we fail to sustain the moral law in this test, then, since there is a God in the Heavens, we may expect this war to be followed by an interregnum of barbarism, and that in turn by World War III.

The disintegration of any civilization, or a crisis in history, bears within it the threat of an interregnum of barbarism. As in the physical order the putrid remains of the unburied dead create a pestilence, so the disintegration of the liberal civilization through which we have just lived, and which was strong only because it was a parasite on Christianity, creates the possibility of chaos. Liberalism left to itself is really only a transition between a culture which was Christian and one which will be anti-Christian.

By barbarism we mean the destruction of moral values, or the repudiation of the funded heritage of culture. The barbarism of the new era will not be like that of the Huns of old; it will be technical, scientific, secular, and propagandized. It will come not from without, but from within, for barbarism is not *outside* us; it is *underneath* us. Older civilizations were destroyed by imported barbarism; modern civilization breeds its own.

A high government official has told us to expect the loss of five hundred thousand men. That is not too high a price to pay for justice, honor, and peace. But if these deaths, like that of Simeon, do not point to the salvation of the world, then their souls, like ghosts, will arise to haunt us in the night. No material profit, no conquest of any land, no crushing of any particular barbarities, can justify such crimson rivers, unless they purchase for us the greatest intangibles and imponderables of all: justice, peace, and freedom.

Our hope for the reign of the moral law must be in prayer. Pray for the world, for the Church, for the enemies of the Church. What happens between you and God when you are on your knees is of vital significance for the world. Pray for Russia! Ever since 1929 all the priests all over the world and all the Catholics who attend daily Mass say the prayers at the end of Low Mass for the intention of Russia. Dostoevsky foretold of his own country that after it had passed through a diabolical anti-God stage it would sit at the feet of Christ and learn His gospel. To the dawn of that day our eyes expectantly look wherein nations can live in one world because there is one moral law and one Lord.

These are hard days for the Church. All that she is trying to do today is to preserve the negatives of a moral order as warring nations tear up the photograph. She is no more interested in political regimes than was her Divine Master.

Christ in His Church rides through the world not on a war horse conquering all things, but on an animal which is the symbol of docility and peace and He rides it into the jaws of death.

Hold fast to your God, your Faith, your Church. The time is now five minutes to twelve. We are in the valley of decision. Either the bloom—or the blight.

A new crime is arising in the world today; be prepared for it. The crime of being a Christian. The crime of believing in God.

Acknowledgements

I want to thank Almighty God for the health of mind, body, and spirit to put together these reflections.

To my good wife, Isabel, my children, and my grandchildren, who keep me young at heart and are truly a blessing from God. Thank you for sharing in my joy.

I wish to express my gratitude to members of the Archbishop Fulton John Sheen Foundation in Peoria, Illinois—in particular, to the Most Rev. Daniel R. Jenky, C.S.C., Bishop of Peoria, for your leadership and fidelity to the cause of Sheen's canonization and the creation of this book.

To Julie Enzenberger, O.C.V., who repeated to me time and time again Sheen's words: "Believe the incredible, and you can do the impossible."

To the staff and volunteers at Sophia Institute Press for their invaluable assistance in helping to publish the writings of Archbishop Fulton J. Sheen. I am indebted to them for this great work.

To the many seminarians, priests, religious, bishops, and cardinals I have met during this journey. Always remember the words of Archbishop Sheen that "The priest is not his own."

To the tens of thousands of people I have met in my travels, giving presentations about Archbishop Fulton J. Sheen at parishes, conferences, universities, high schools, church groups, and even pubs: thank you for sharing with me your many "Sheen Stories." I truly cherish each one of them.

And lastly, to Archbishop Fulton J. Sheen, whose teachings on prayer, the sacraments, our Lord's Passion, and *The Seven Last Words* continue to inspire me to love God more and to appreciate the gift of the Church. His teachings and his encouragement to make a holy hour each day have been a true gift in my life. May I be so blessed as to imitate Archbishop Sheen's love for the saints, the sacraments, the Eucharist, and the Mother of God. May the Good Lord grant him a very high place in Heaven!

—Al Smith

About the Author
Fulton J. Sheen
(1895–1979)

Fulton John Sheen was born in El Paso, Illinois, in 1895. In high school, he won a three-year university scholarship, but he turned it down to pursue a vocation to the priesthood. He attended St. Viator College Seminary in Illinois and St. Paul Seminary in Minnesota. In 1919, he was ordained a priest for the Diocese of Peoria, Illinois. He earned a licentiate in sacred theology, a bachelor of canon law at the Catholic University of America, and a doctorate at the Catholic University of Louvain, Belgium.

Sheen received numerous teaching offers but declined them in obedience to his bishop and became an assistant pastor in a rural parish. Having thus tested his obedience, the bishop later permitted him to teach at the Catholic University of America and at St. Edmund's College in Ware, England, where he met G. K. Chesterton, whose weekly BBC radio broadcast inspired Sheen's later NBC broadcast, *The Catholic Hour* (1930–1952).

In 1952, Sheen began appearing on ABC in his own series, *Life Is Worth Living*. Despite being given a time slot that forced him to compete with Milton Berle and Frank Sinatra, the dynamic Sheen enjoyed enormous success and in 1954 reached tens of millions of viewers, non-Catholics as well as Catholics.

When asked by Pope Pius XII how many converts he had made, Sheen responded, "Your Holiness, I have never counted them. I am always afraid if I did count them, I might think I made them, instead of the Lord."

Sheen gave annual Good Friday homilies at New York's St. Patrick's Cathedral, led numerous retreats for priests and religious, and preached at summer conferences in England.

"If you want people to stay as they are," he said, "tell them what they want to hear. If you want to improve them, tell them what they should know." This he did, not only in his preaching but also in the more than ninety books he wrote. His *Peace of Soul* was sixth on the New York Times best-seller list.

Sheen served as auxiliary bishop of New York (1951–1966) and as bishop of Rochester (1966–1969).

Two of his great loves were for the Blessed Mother and the Eucharist. He made a daily holy hour before the Blessed Sacrament, from which he drew strength and inspiration to preach the gospel and in the presence of which he prepared his homilies. "I beg [Christ] every day to keep me strong physically and alert mentally in order to preach His gospel and proclaim His Cross and Resurrection," he said. "I am so happy doing this that I sometimes feel that when I come to the Good Lord in Heaven, I will take a few days' rest and then ask Him to allow me to come back again to this earth to do some more work."

Sheen also said that "the greatest love story of all time is contained in a tiny white host." This was the love that transformed him. His daily eucharistic holy hour was legendary. From his office desk, through an open door, he could gaze upon the tabernacle at all times. His union with Christ enabled him to more fully, more accurately, and more convincingly lead others to Christ in all he said and did. Sheen was a man of many talents and accomplishments, but it was Christ who enabled him to use them in the best ways.

The Good Lord called Fulton Sheen home in 1979. His television broadcasts, now on tape, and his books continue his earthly work of winning souls for Christ. Sheen's cause for canonization was opened in 2002. In 2012, Pope Benedict XVI declared him "Venerable." In 2019, Pope Francis approved a miracle attributed to the intercession of the Venerable Fulton Sheen, clearing the way for his beatification.

Fulton J. Sheen Works Used in This Book

1. *For God and Country* (New York: P. J. Kenedy, 1941)

2. *God and War* (New York: P. J. Kenedy, 1942)

3. *The Divine Verdict* (New York: P. J. Kenedy, 1943)

4. *Philosophies of War* (New York: Charles Scribner, 1943)

5. *Seven Pillars of Peace* (New York: Charles Scribner, 1944)

Sophia Institute

Sophia Institute is a nonprofit institution that seeks to nurture the spiritual, moral, and cultural life of souls and to spread the Gospel of Christ in conformity with the authentic teachings of the Roman Catholic Church.

Sophia Institute Press fulfills this mission by offering translations, reprints, and new publications that afford readers a rich source of the enduring wisdom of mankind.

Sophia Institute also operates the popular online resource CatholicExchange.com. *Catholic Exchange* provides world news from a Catholic perspective as well as daily devotionals and articles that will help readers to grow in holiness and live a life consistent with the teachings of the Church.

In 2013, Sophia Institute launched Sophia Institute for Teachers to renew and rebuild Catholic culture through service to Catholic education. With the goal of nurturing the spiritual, moral, and cultural life of souls, and an abiding respect for the role and work of teachers, we strive to provide materials and programs that are at once enlightening to the mind and ennobling to the heart; faithful and complete, as well as useful and practical.

Sophia Institute gratefully recognizes the Solidarity Association for preserving and encouraging the growth of our apostolate over the course of many years. Without their generous and timely support, this book would not be in your hands.

www.SophiaInstitute.com
www.CatholicExchange.com
www.SophiaInstituteforTeachers.org

Sophia Institute Press® is a registered trademark of Sophia Institute.
Sophia Institute is a tax-exempt institution as defined by the
Internal Revenue Code, Section 501(c)(3). Tax ID 22-2548708.